ALICHINO
アリキーノ

DISCARD 2

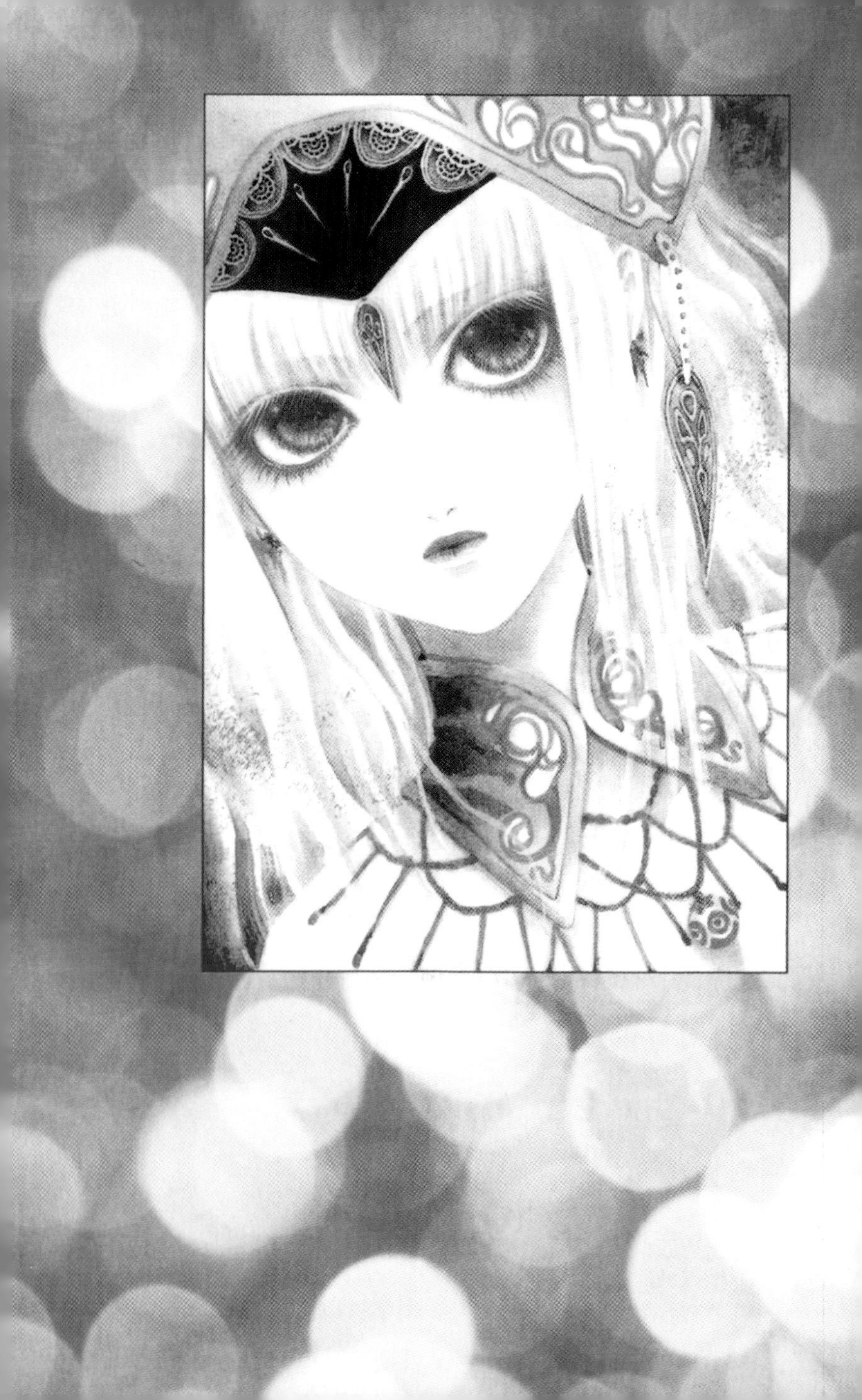

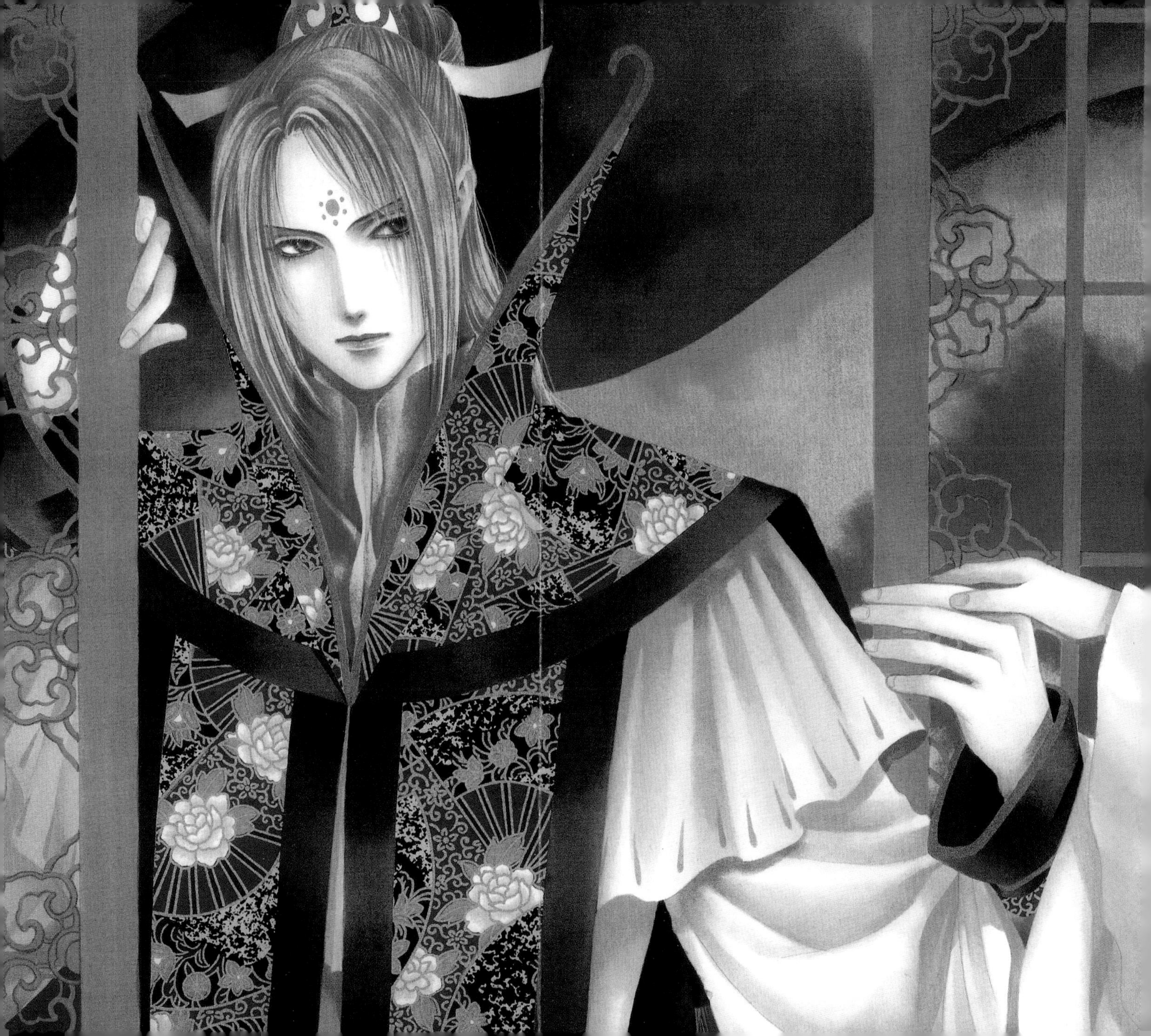

Alichino

Alichino Vol. 2
Created by Kouyu Shurei

Translation - Amy Forsyth
English Adaptation - Paul Morrissey
Copy Editor - Suzanne Waldman
Retouch and Lettering - Bowen Park
Production Artist - Gloria Wu
Cover Design - Anna Kernbaum and Seth Cable

Editor - Tim Beedle
Digital Imaging Manager - Chris Buford
Pre-Press Manager - Antonio DePietro
Production Managers - Jennifer Miller and Mutsumi Miyazaki
Art Director - Matt Alford
Managing Editor - Jill Freshney
VP of Production - Ron Klamert
Editor-in-Chief - Mike Kiley
President and C.O.O. - John Parker
Publisher and C.E.O. - Stuart Levy

A  Manga

TOKYOPOP Inc.
5900 Wilshire Blvd. Suite 2000
Los Angeles, CA 90036

E-mail: info@TOKYOPOP.com
Come visit us online at www.TOKYOPOP.com

ISBN: 1-59532-479-8

First TOKYOPOP printing: June 2005
10 9 8 7 6 5 4 3 2 1
Printed in the USA

Volume 2

by
Kouyu Shurei

HAMBURG // LONDON // LOS ANGELES // TOKYO

TABLE OF CONTENTS

The power to
influence and
dominate...

Beckoning me...

Embracing me...

Deserting me...

Chapter 6
Determination

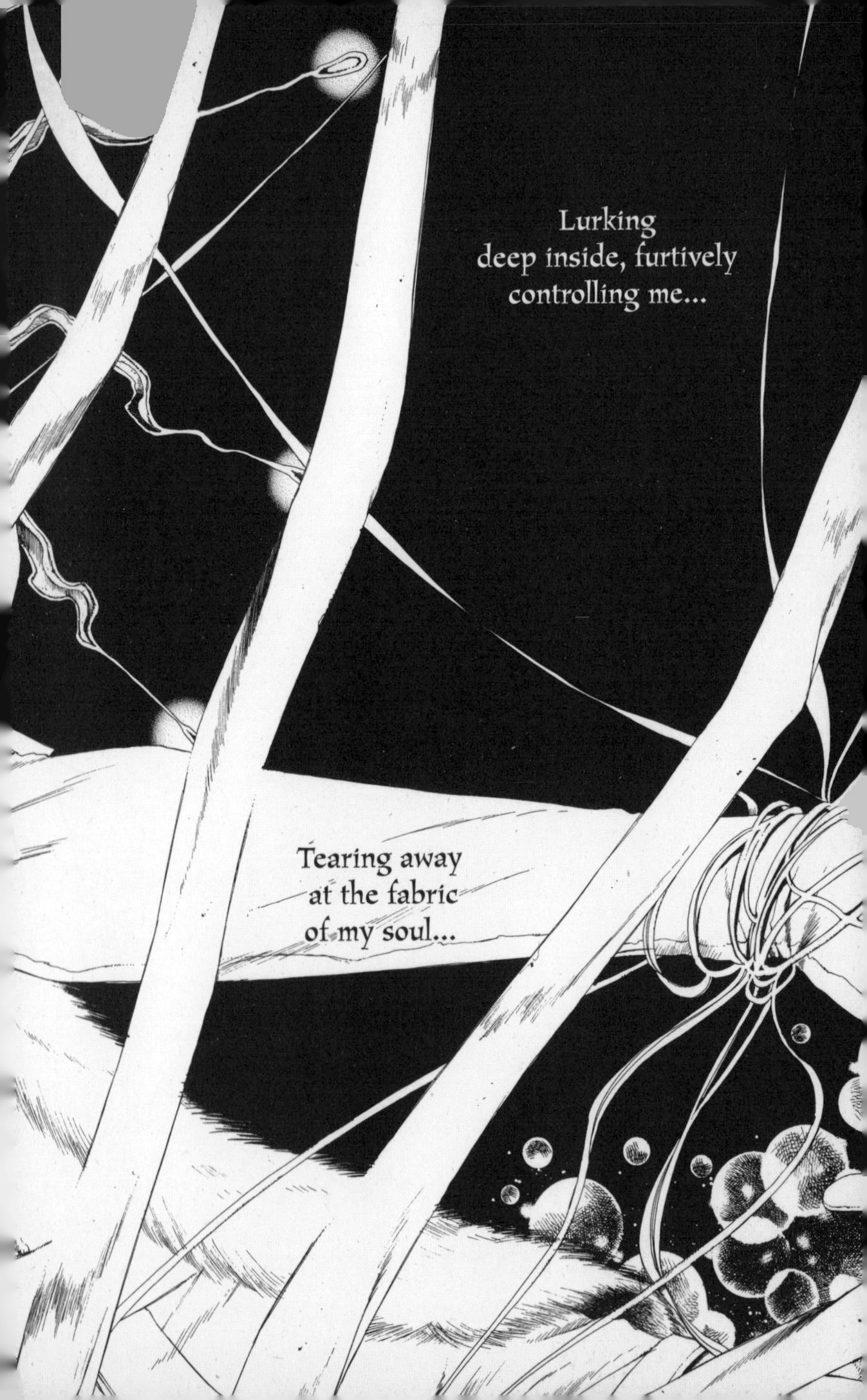
Lurking deep inside, furtively controlling me...
Tearing away at the fabric of my soul...

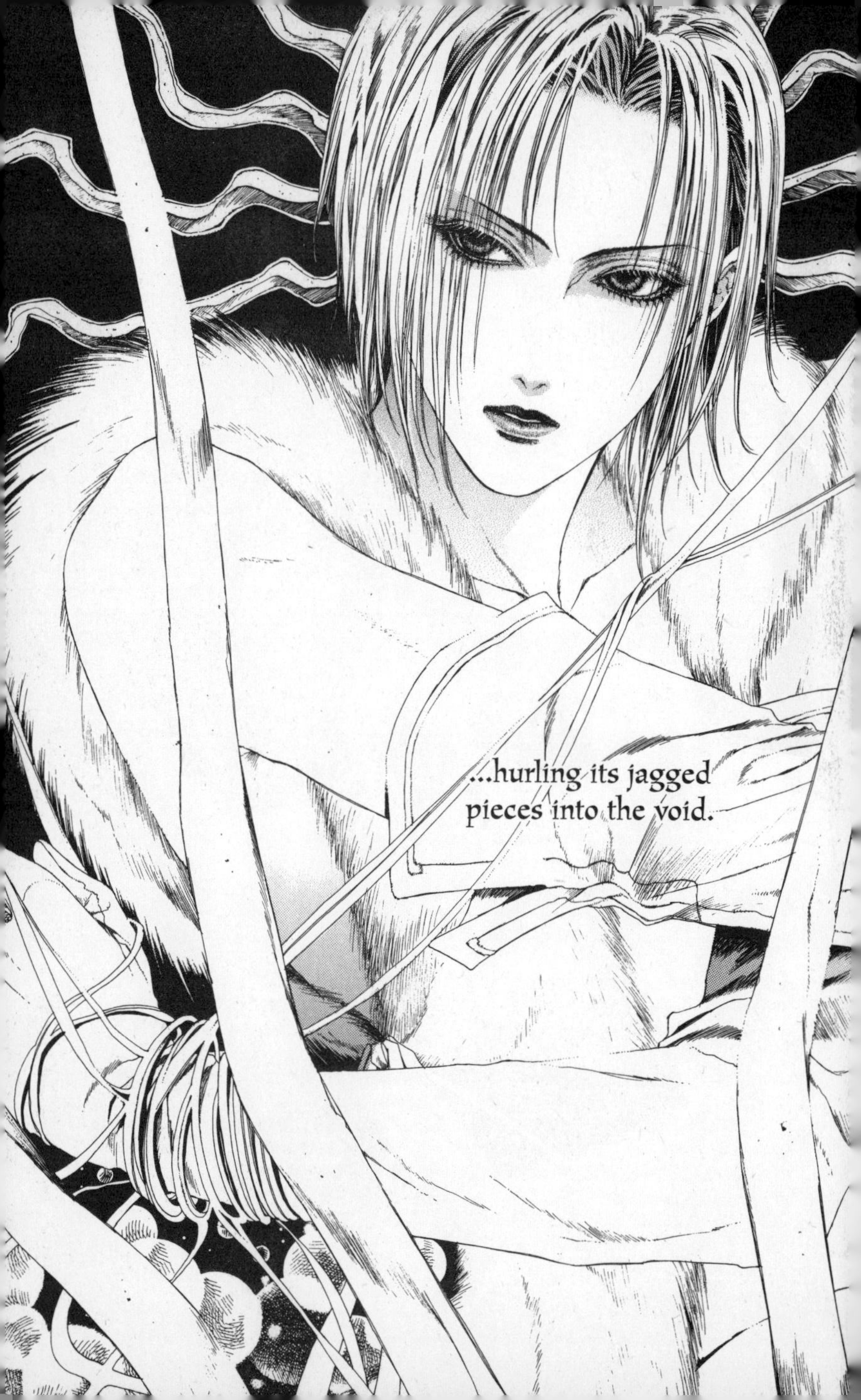
...hurling its jagged pieces into the void.

Introduction to the Characters

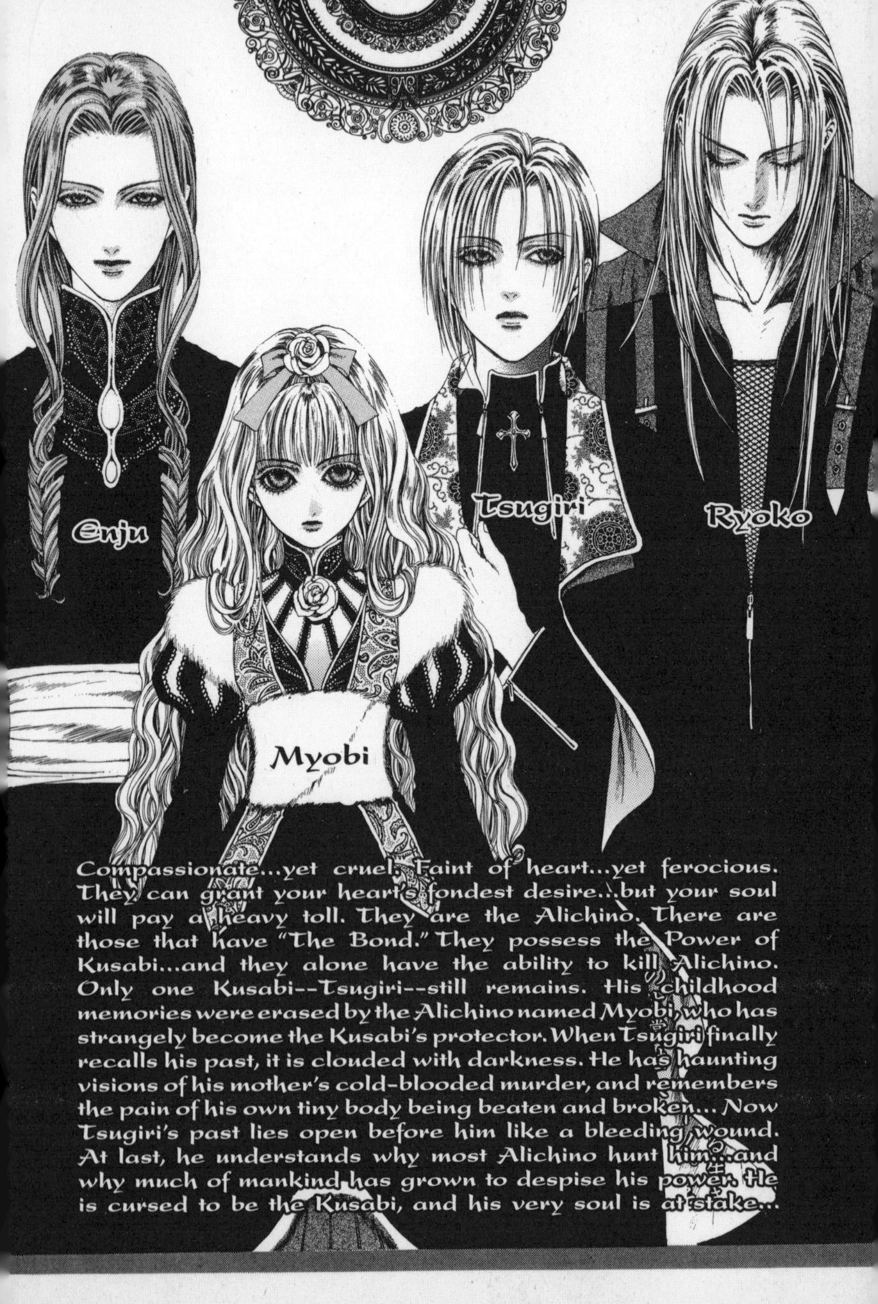
Ryoko
Tsugiri
Enju
Myobi

Compassionate...yet cruel. Faint of heart...yet ferocious. They can grant your heart's fondest desire...but your soul will pay a heavy toll. They are the Alichino. There are those that have "The Bond." They possess the Power of Kusabi...and they alone have the ability to kill Alichino. Only one Kusabi--Tsugiri--still remains. His childhood memories were erased by the Alichino named Myobi, who has strangely become the Kusabi's protector. When Tsugiri finally recalls his past, it is clouded with darkness. He has haunting visions of his mother's cold-blooded murder, and remembers the pain of his own tiny body being beaten and broken... Now Tsugiri's past lies open before him like a bleeding wound. At last, he understands why most Alichino hunt him...and why much of mankind has grown to despise his power. He is cursed to be the Kusabi, and his very soul is at stake...

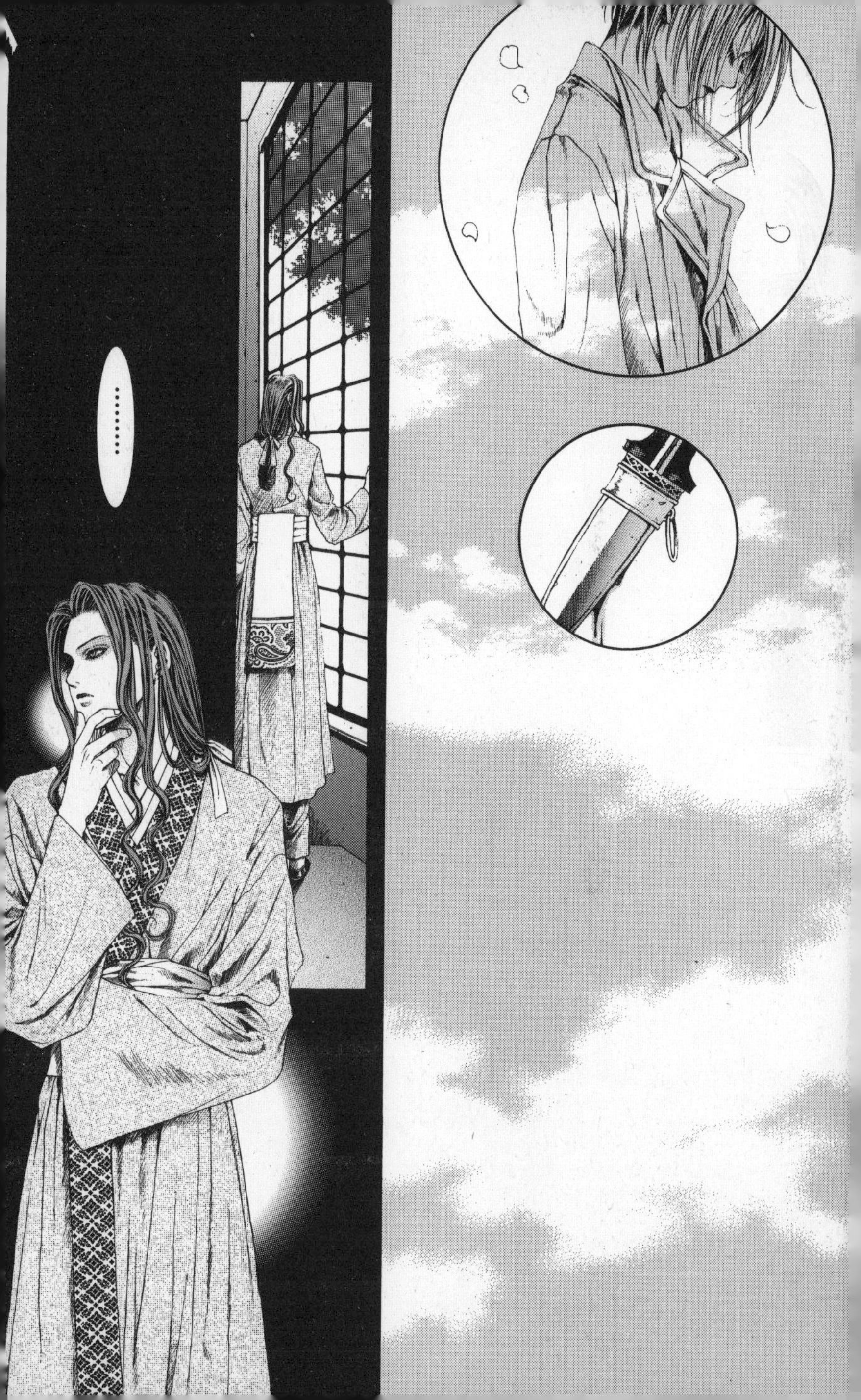
……

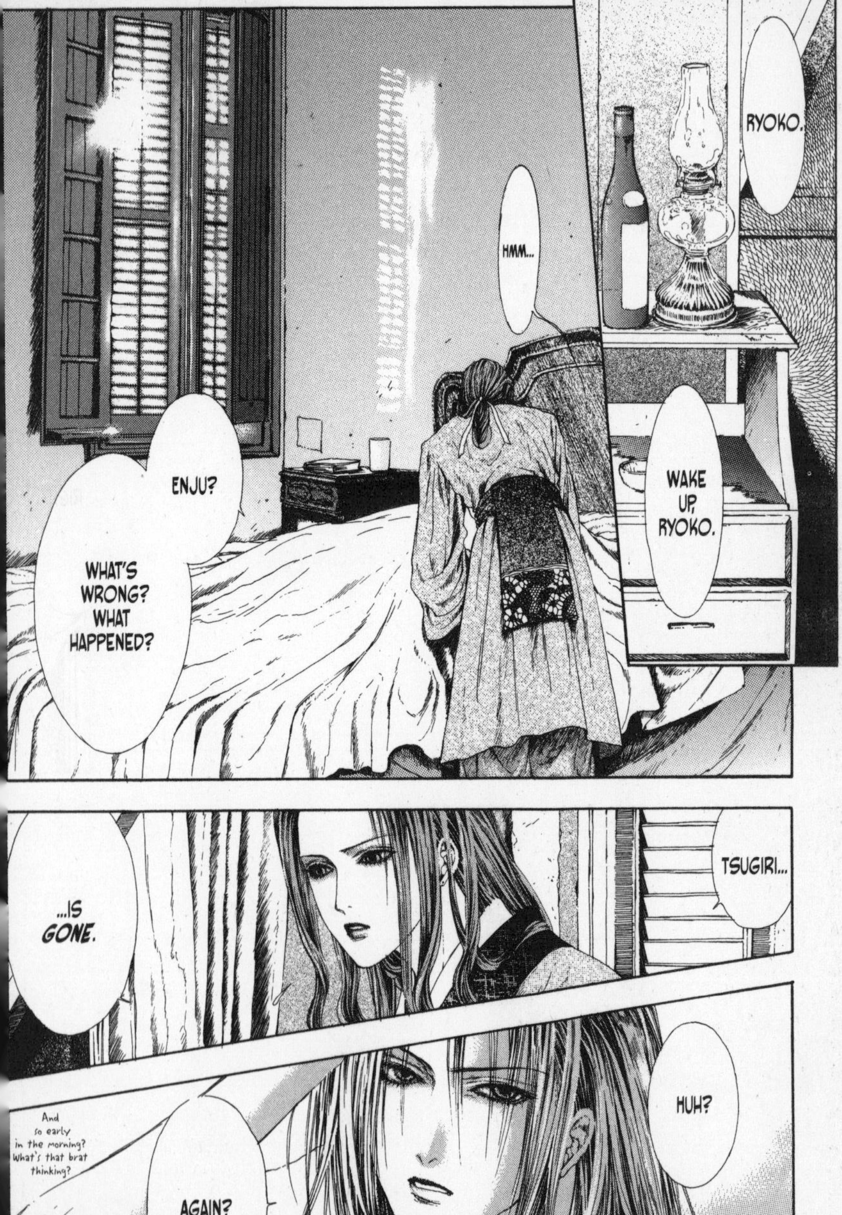
RYOKO.
WAKE UP, RYOKO.
HMM...
ENJU?
WHAT'S WRONG? WHAT HAPPENED?
TSUGIRI...
...IS GONE.
HUH?
AGAIN?
And so early in the morning? What's that brat thinking?

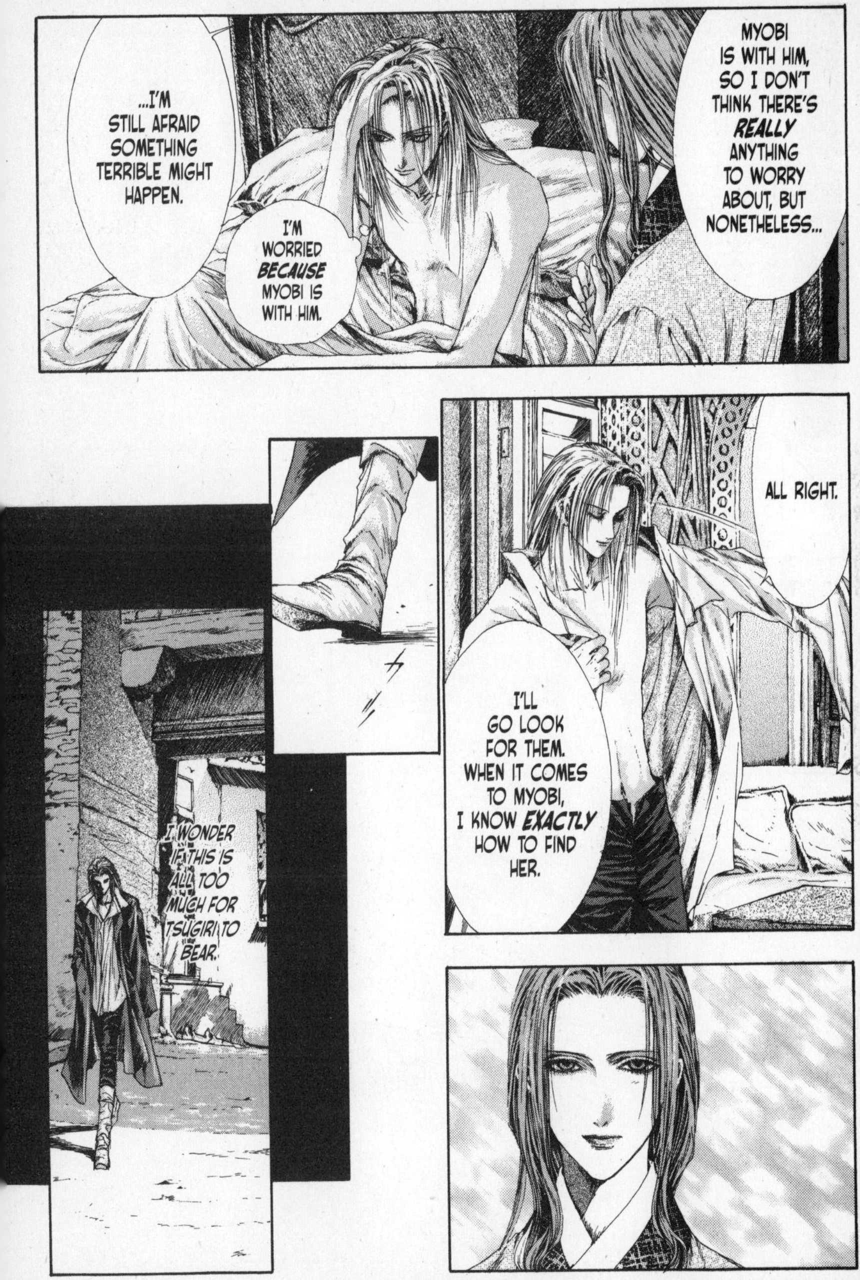
MYOBI IS WITH HIM, SO I DON'T THINK THERE'S *REALLY* ANYTHING TO WORRY ABOUT, BUT NONETHELESS...
...I'M STILL AFRAID SOMETHING TERRIBLE MIGHT HAPPEN.
I'M WORRIED *BECAUSE* MYOBI IS WITH HIM.
ALL RIGHT.
I'LL GO LOOK FOR THEM. WHEN IT COMES TO MYOBI, I KNOW *EXACTLY* HOW TO FIND HER.
I WONDER IF THIS IS ALL TOO MUCH FOR TSUGIRI TO BEAR.

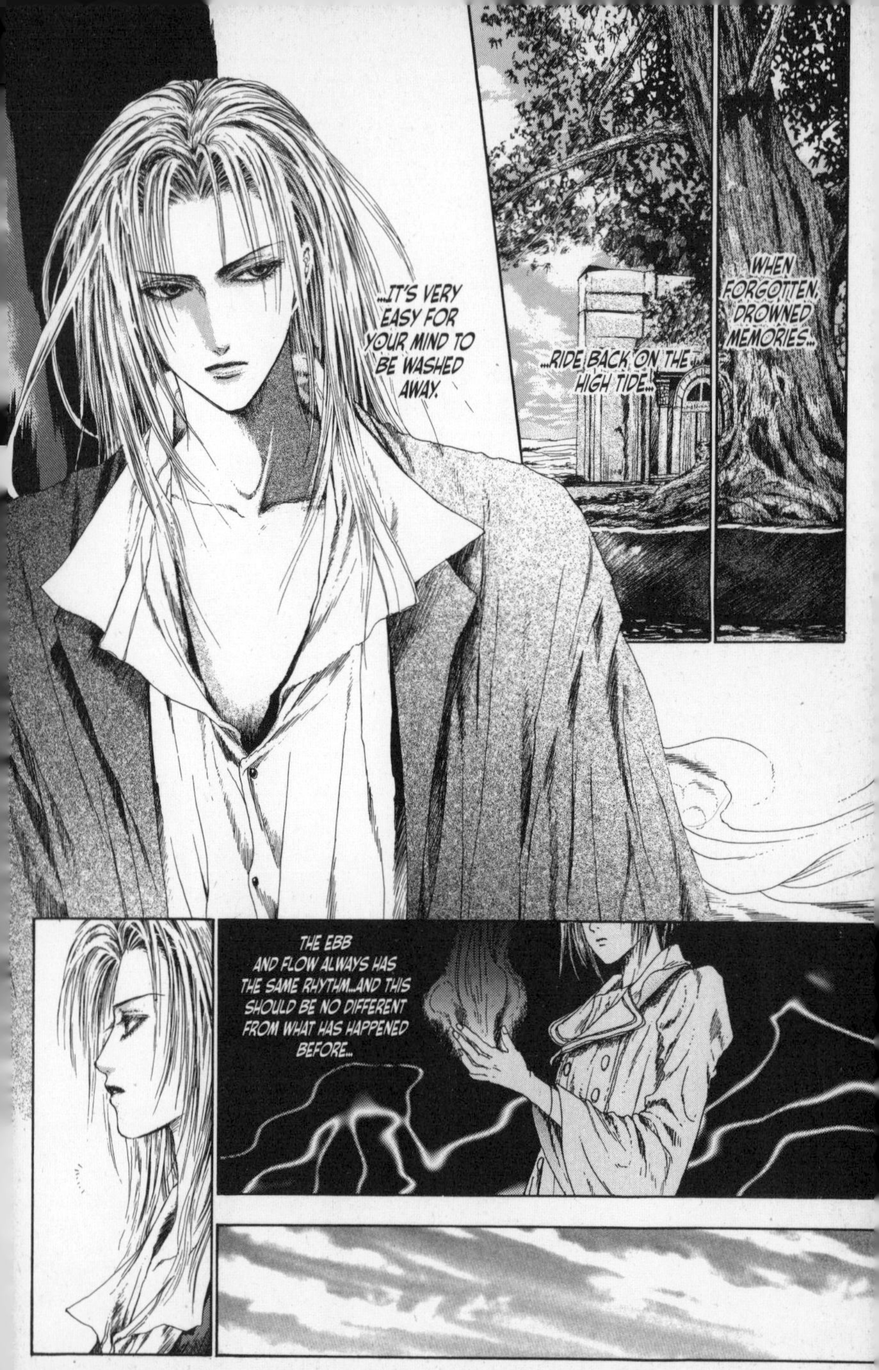
WHEN FORGOTTEN, DROWNED MEMORIES...
...RIDE BACK ON THE HIGH TIDE...
...IT'S VERY EASY FOR YOUR MIND TO BE WASHED AWAY.
THE EBB AND FLOW ALWAYS HAS THE SAME RHYTHM...AND THIS SHOULD BE NO DIFFERENT FROM WHAT HAS HAPPENED BEFORE...

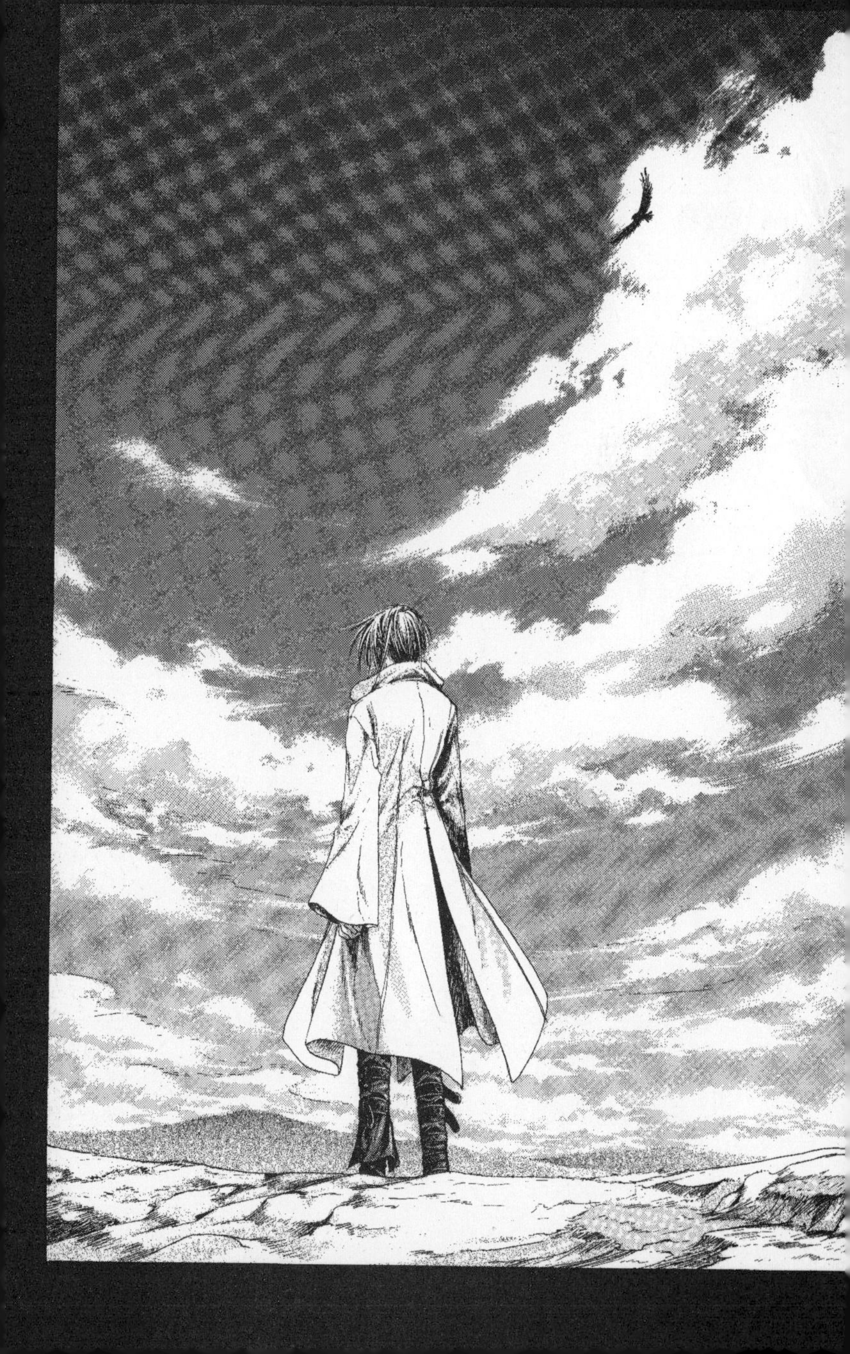

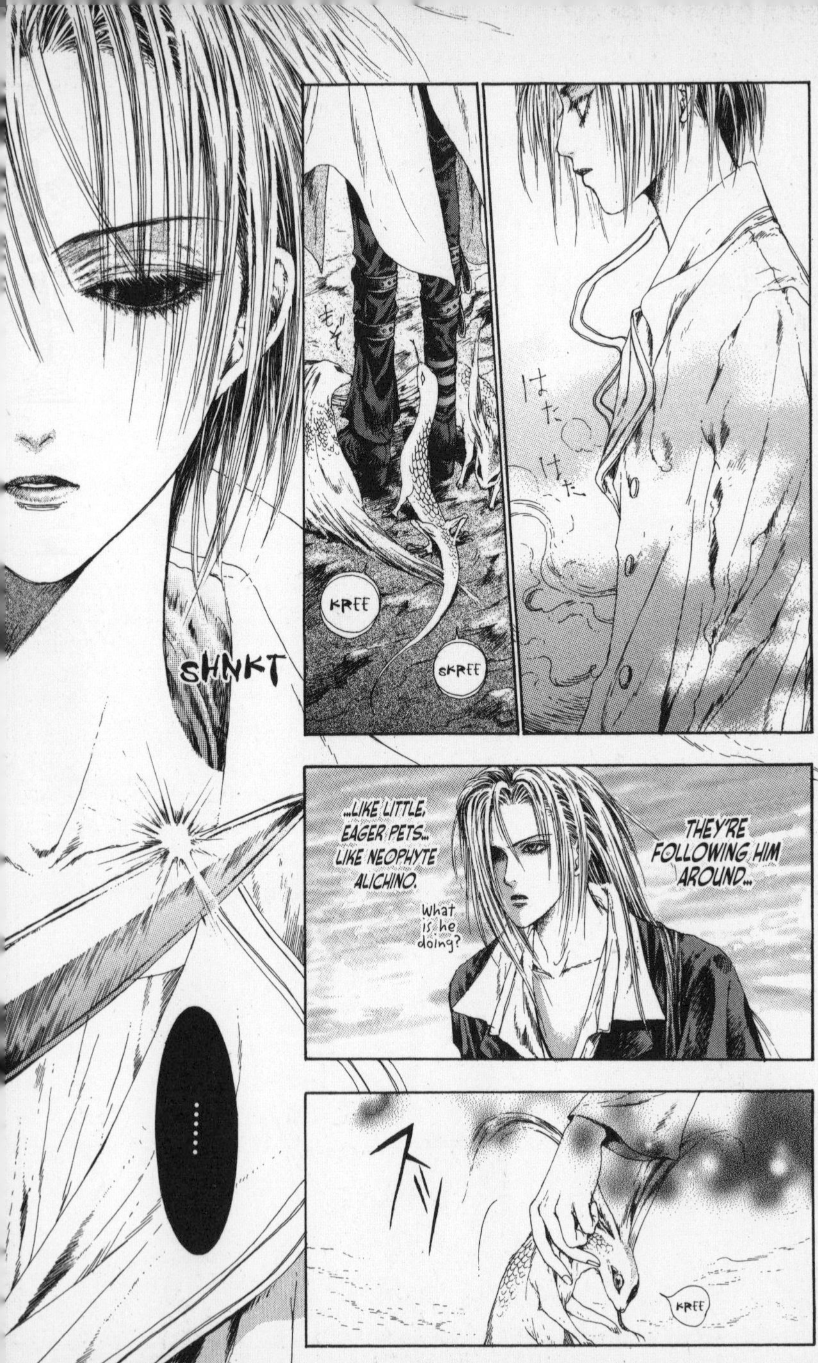
はた
はた
もぞ
KREE
SKREE
THEY'RE FOLLOWING HIM AROUND...
...LIKE LITTLE, EAGER PETS... LIKE NEOPHYTE ALICHINO.
What is he doing?
スッ
KREE
SHNKT
......

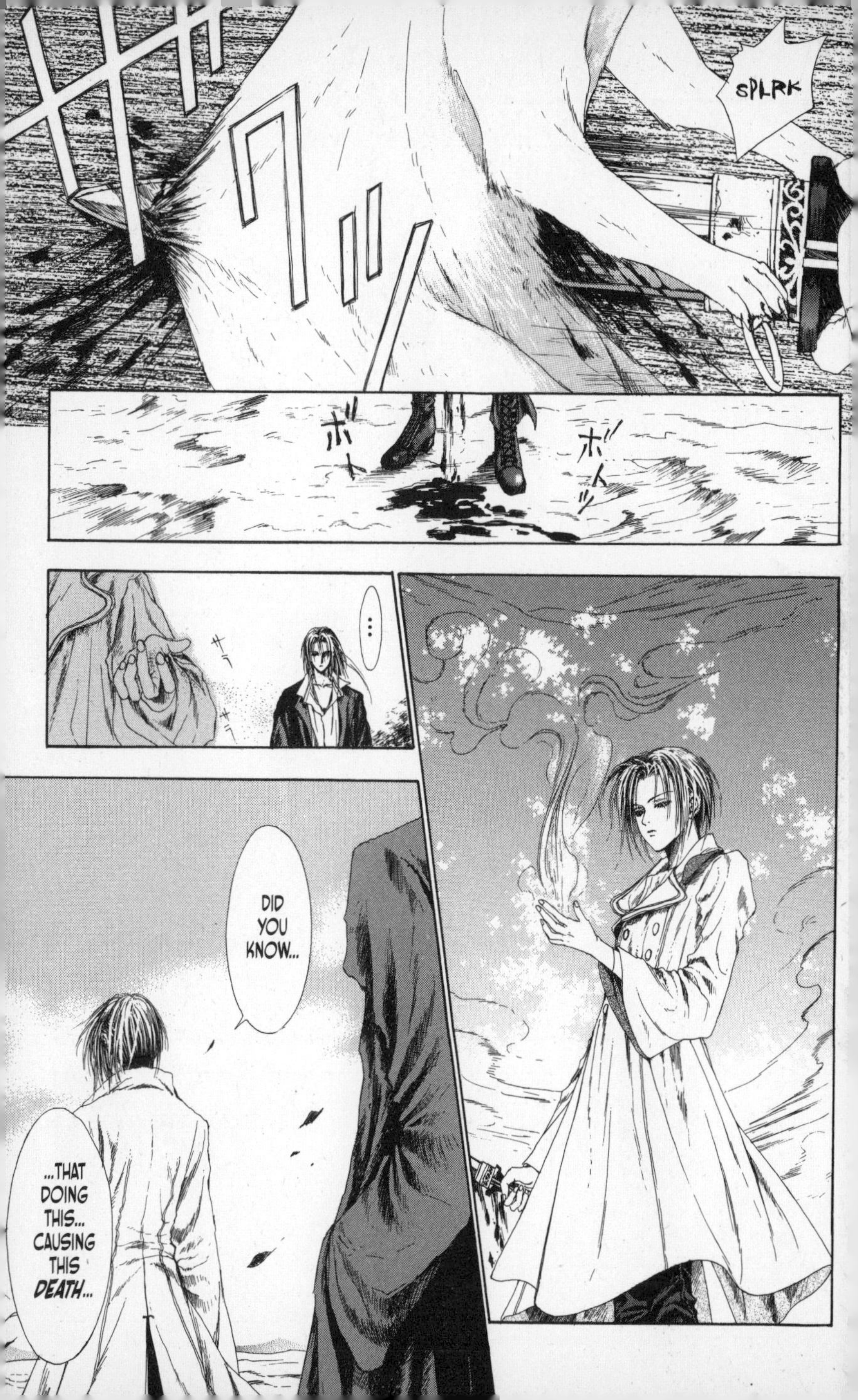
SPLRK
ボトッ
ボト
...
サラ
サラ
DID YOU KNOW...
...THAT DOING THIS... CAUSING THIS DEATH...

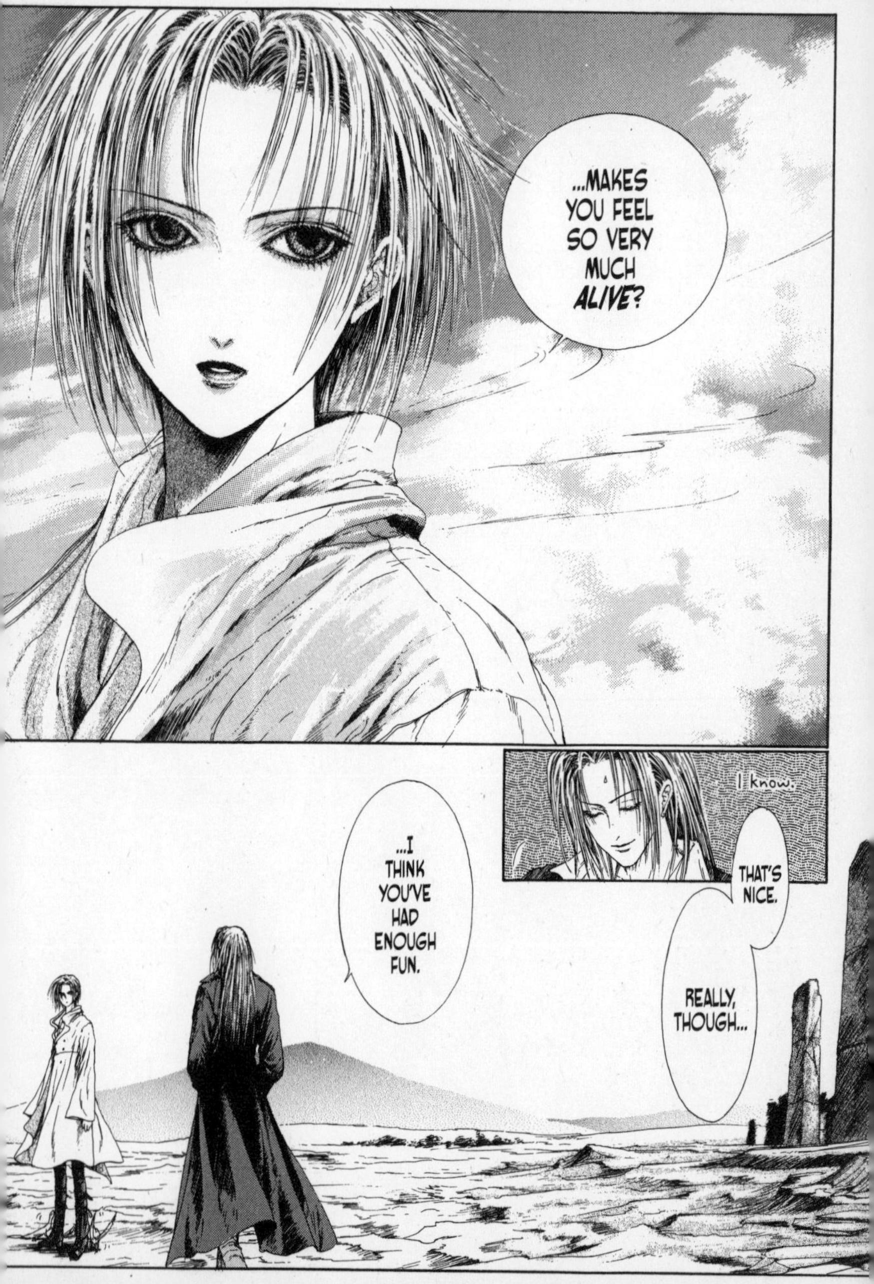
...MAKES YOU FEEL SO VERY MUCH *ALIVE*?
I know.
THAT'S NICE.
REALLY, THOUGH...
...I THINK YOU'VE HAD ENOUGH FUN.

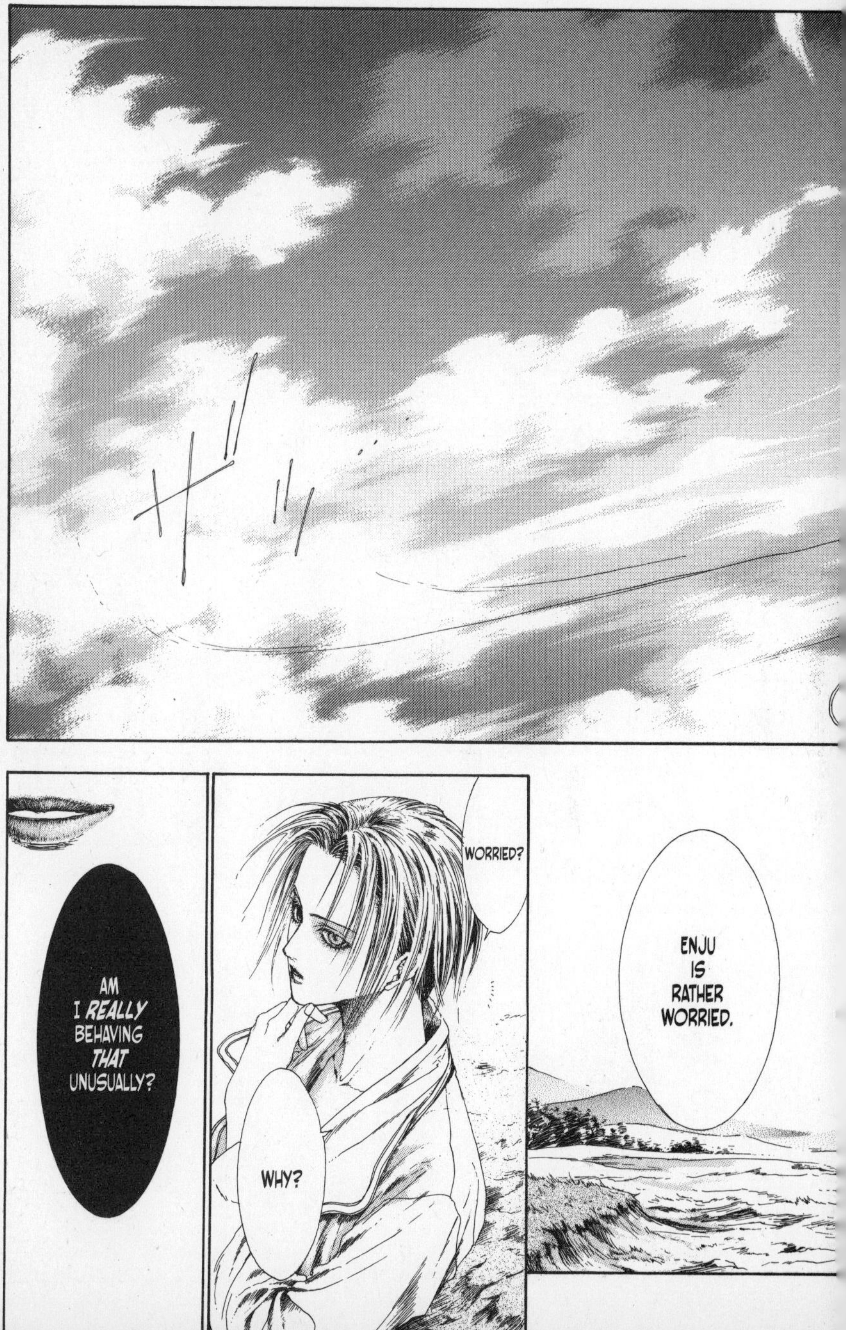
ENJU IS RATHER WORRIED.
WORRIED?
WHY?
AM I REALLY BEHAVING THAT UNUSUALLY?

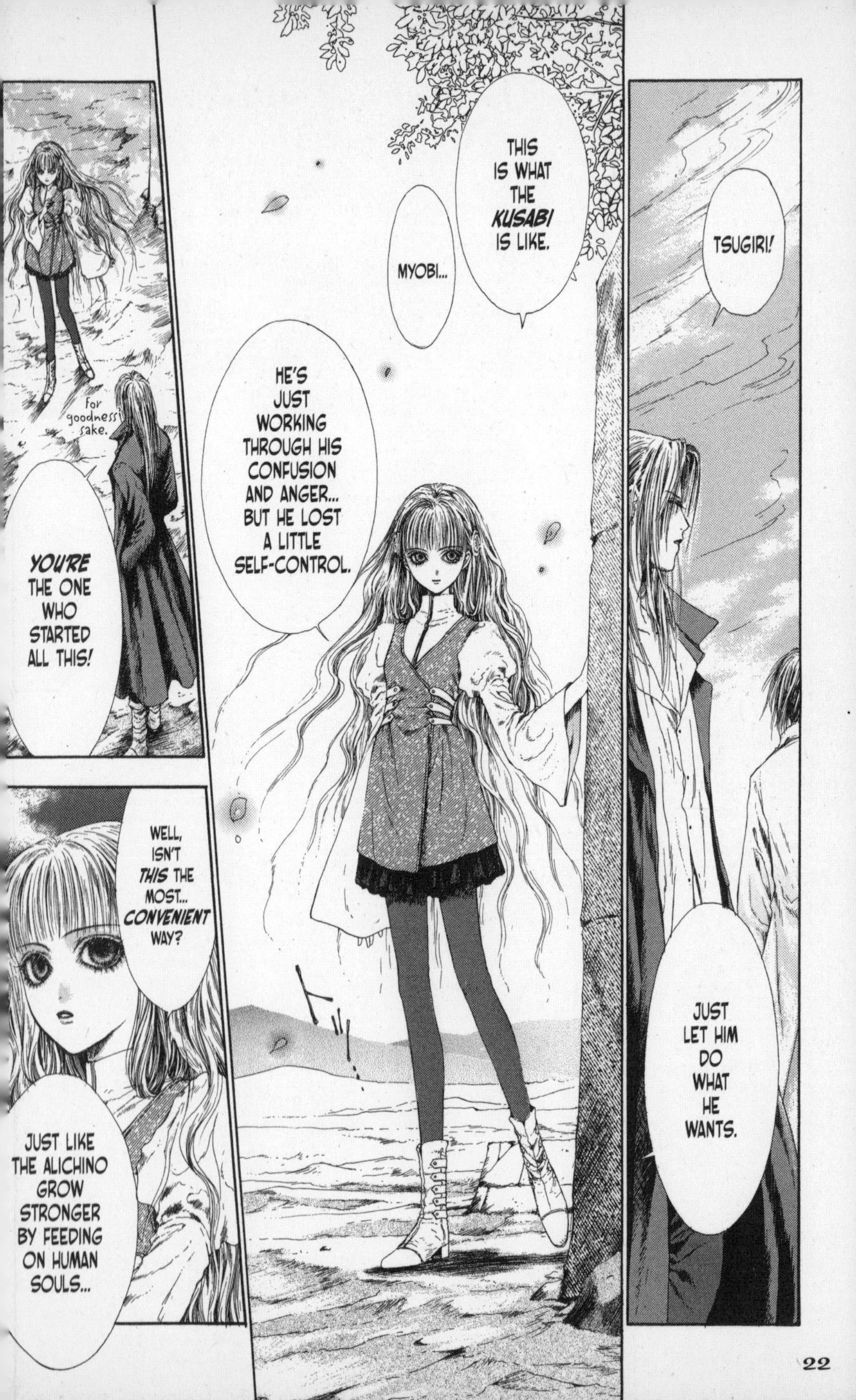
TSUGIRI!
JUST LET HIM DO WHAT HE WANTS.
THIS IS WHAT THE *KUSABI* IS LIKE.
MYOBI...
HE'S JUST WORKING THROUGH HIS CONFUSION AND ANGER... BUT HE LOST A LITTLE SELF-CONTROL.
for goodness' sake.
YOU'RE THE ONE WHO STARTED ALL THIS!
WELL, ISN'T *THIS* THE MOST... *CONVENIENT* WAY?
JUST LIKE THE ALICHINO GROW STRONGER BY FEEDING ON HUMAN SOULS...

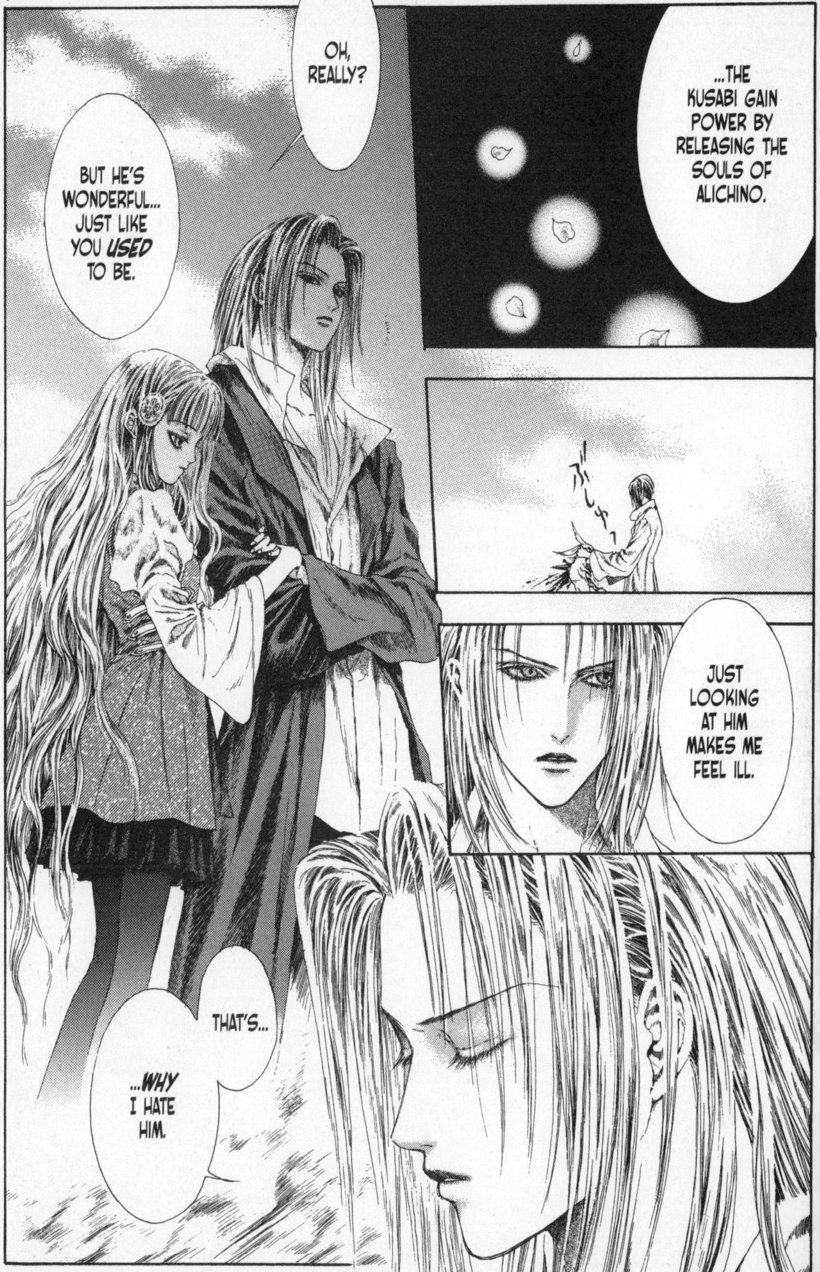
...THE KUSABI GAIN POWER BY RELEASING THE SOULS OF ALICHINO.
ぶしゃっ
JUST LOOKING AT HIM MAKES ME FEEL ILL.
OH, REALLY?
BUT HE'S WONDERFUL... JUST LIKE YOU *USED* TO BE.
THAT'S...
...*WHY* I HATE HIM.

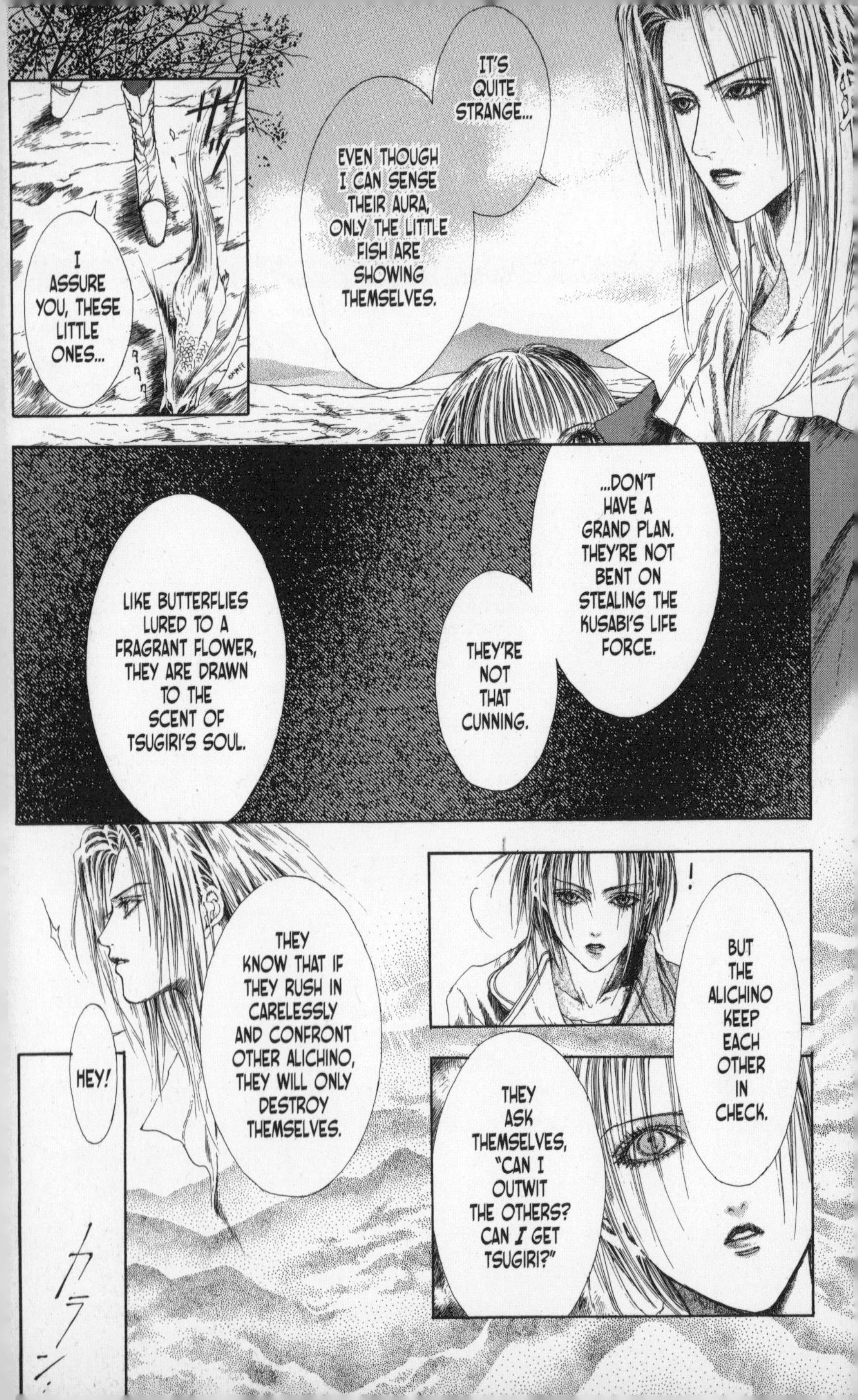
IT'S QUITE STRANGE...
EVEN THOUGH I CAN SENSE THEIR AURA, ONLY THE LITTLE FISH ARE SHOWING THEMSELVES.
I ASSURE YOU, THESE LITTLE ONES...
...DON'T HAVE A GRAND PLAN. THEY'RE NOT BENT ON STEALING THE KUSABI'S LIFE FORCE.
THEY'RE NOT THAT CUNNING.
LIKE BUTTERFLIES LURED TO A FRAGRANT FLOWER, THEY ARE DRAWN TO THE SCENT OF TSUGIRI'S SOUL.
!
BUT THE ALICHINO KEEP EACH OTHER IN CHECK.
THEY ASK THEMSELVES, "CAN I OUTWIT THE OTHERS? CAN *I* GET TSUGIRI?"
THEY KNOW THAT IF THEY RUSH IN CARELESSLY AND CONFRONT OTHER ALICHINO, THEY WILL ONLY DESTROY THEMSELVES.
HEY!

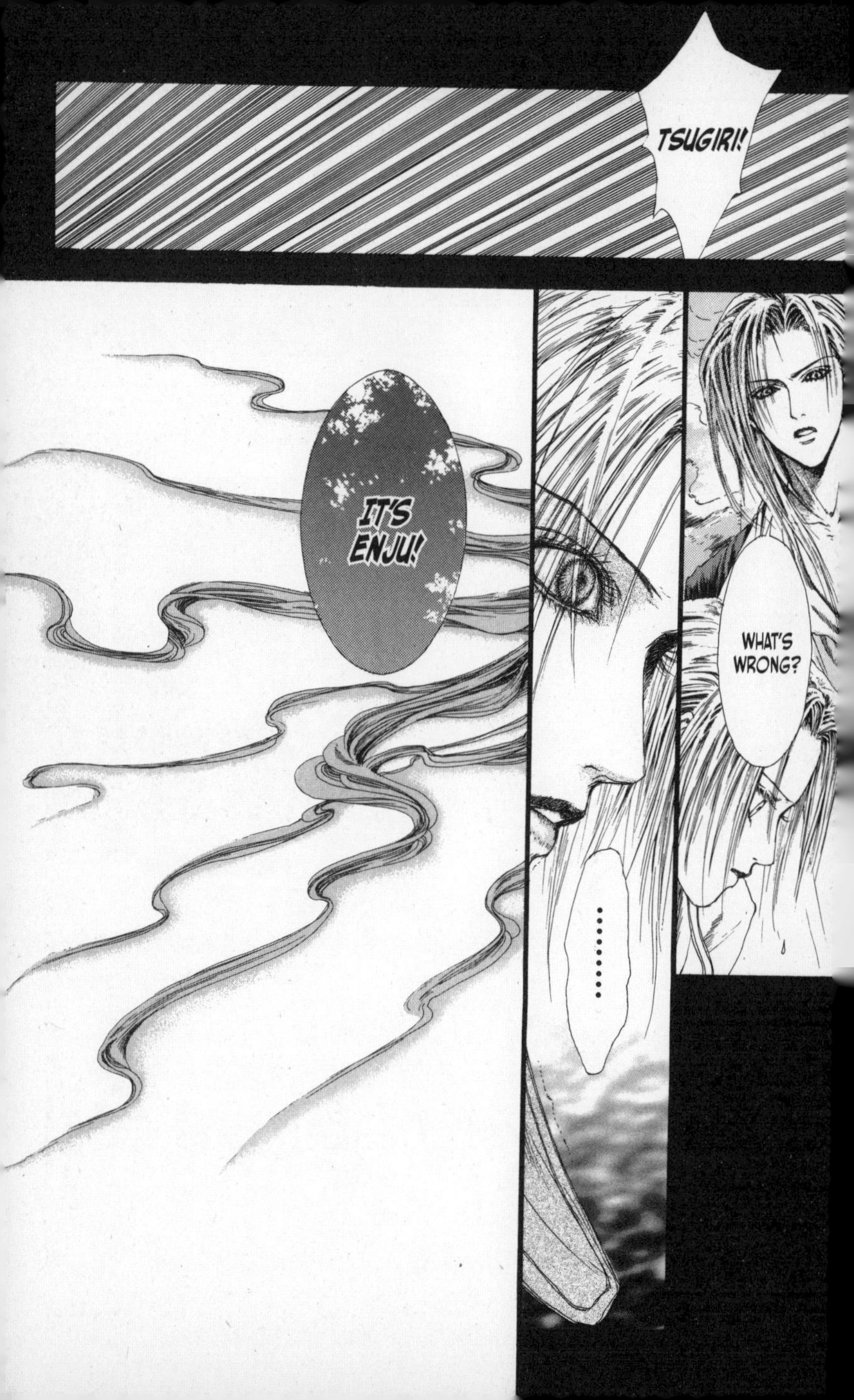
TSUGIRI!!
WHAT'S WRONG?
......
IT'S ENJU!

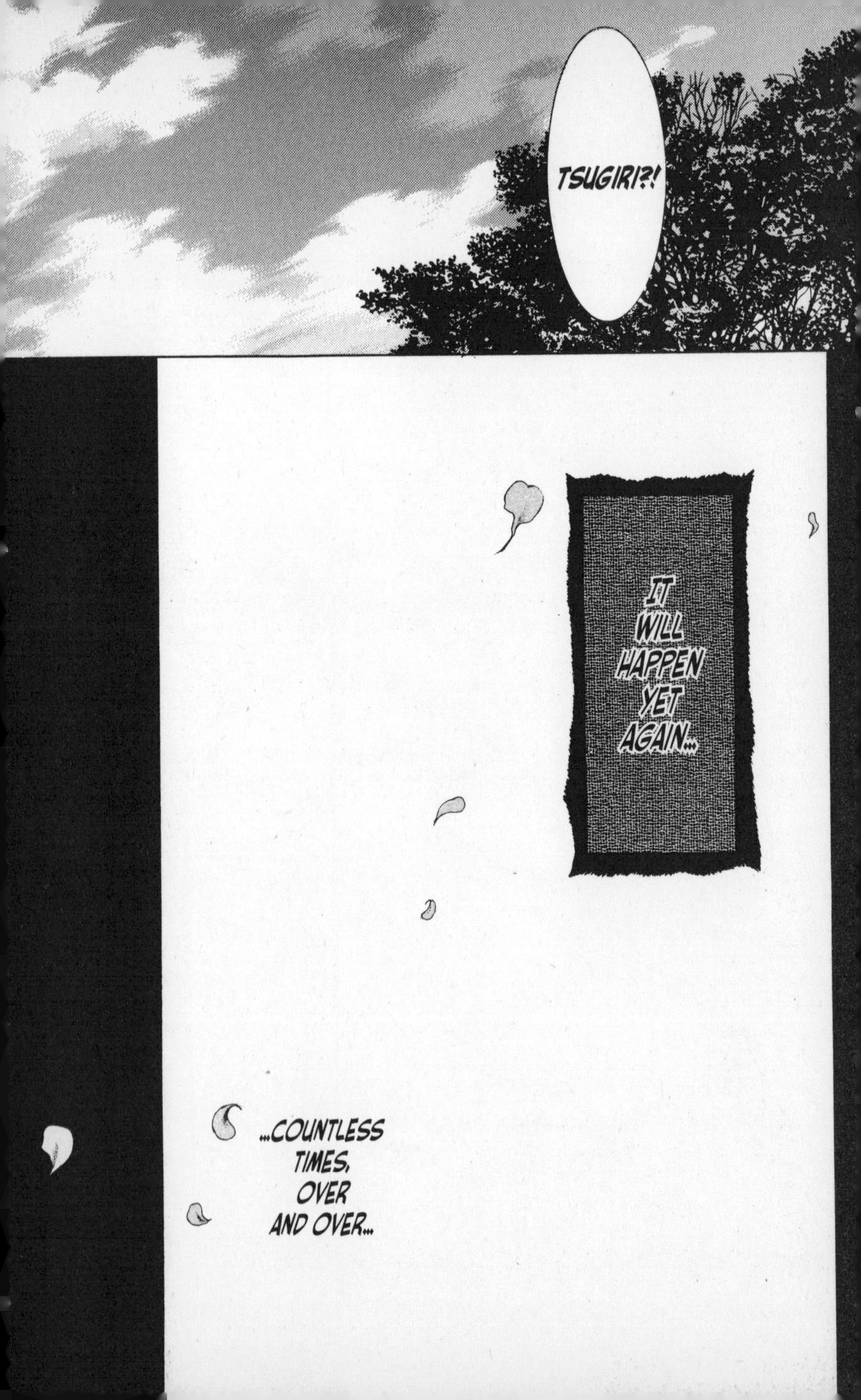
TSUGIRI?!
IT WILL HAPPEN YET AGAIN...
...COUNTLESS TIMES, OVER AND OVER...

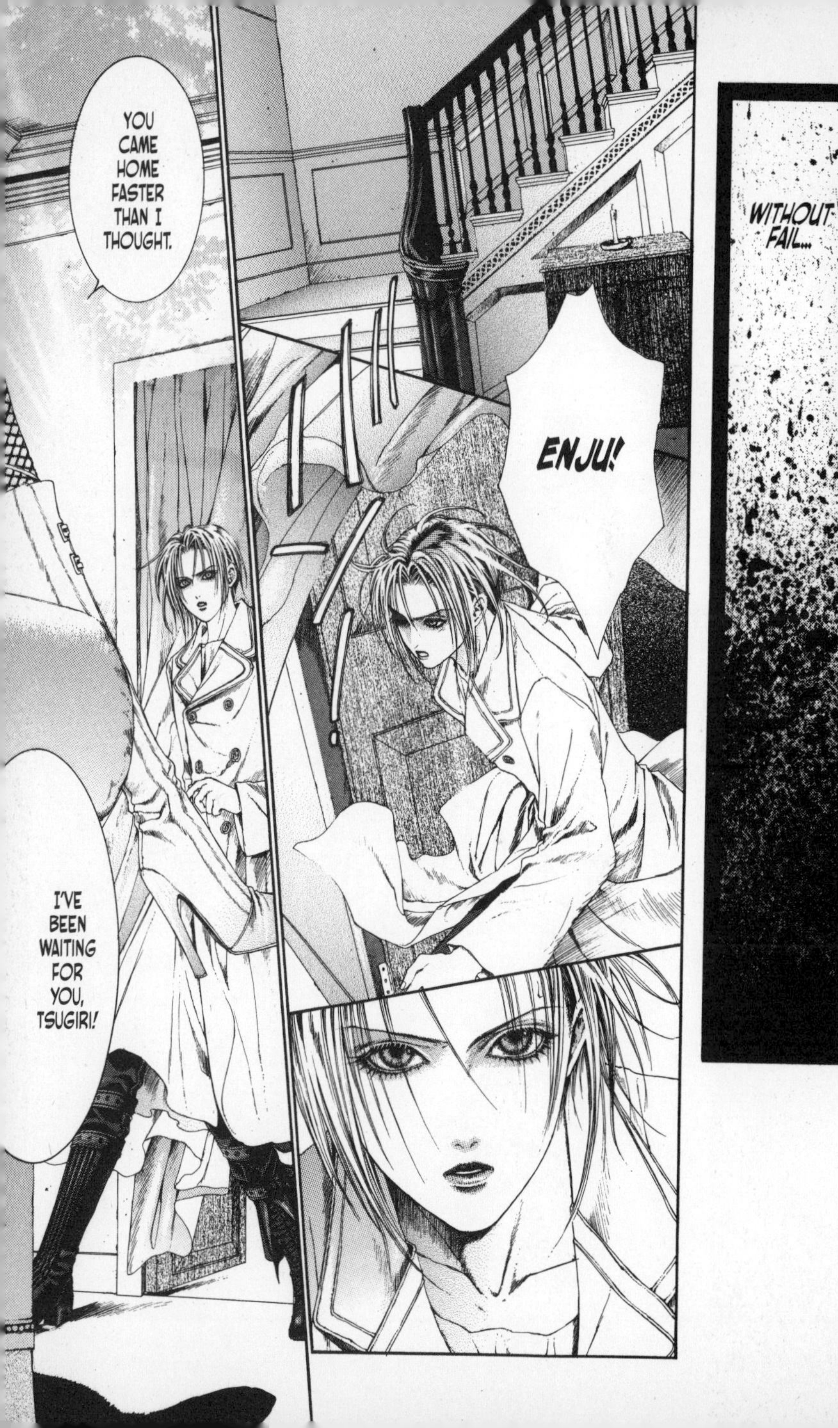
WITHOUT FAIL...
ENJU!
YOU CAME HOME FASTER THAN I THOUGHT.
I'VE BEEN WAITING FOR YOU, TSUGIRI!

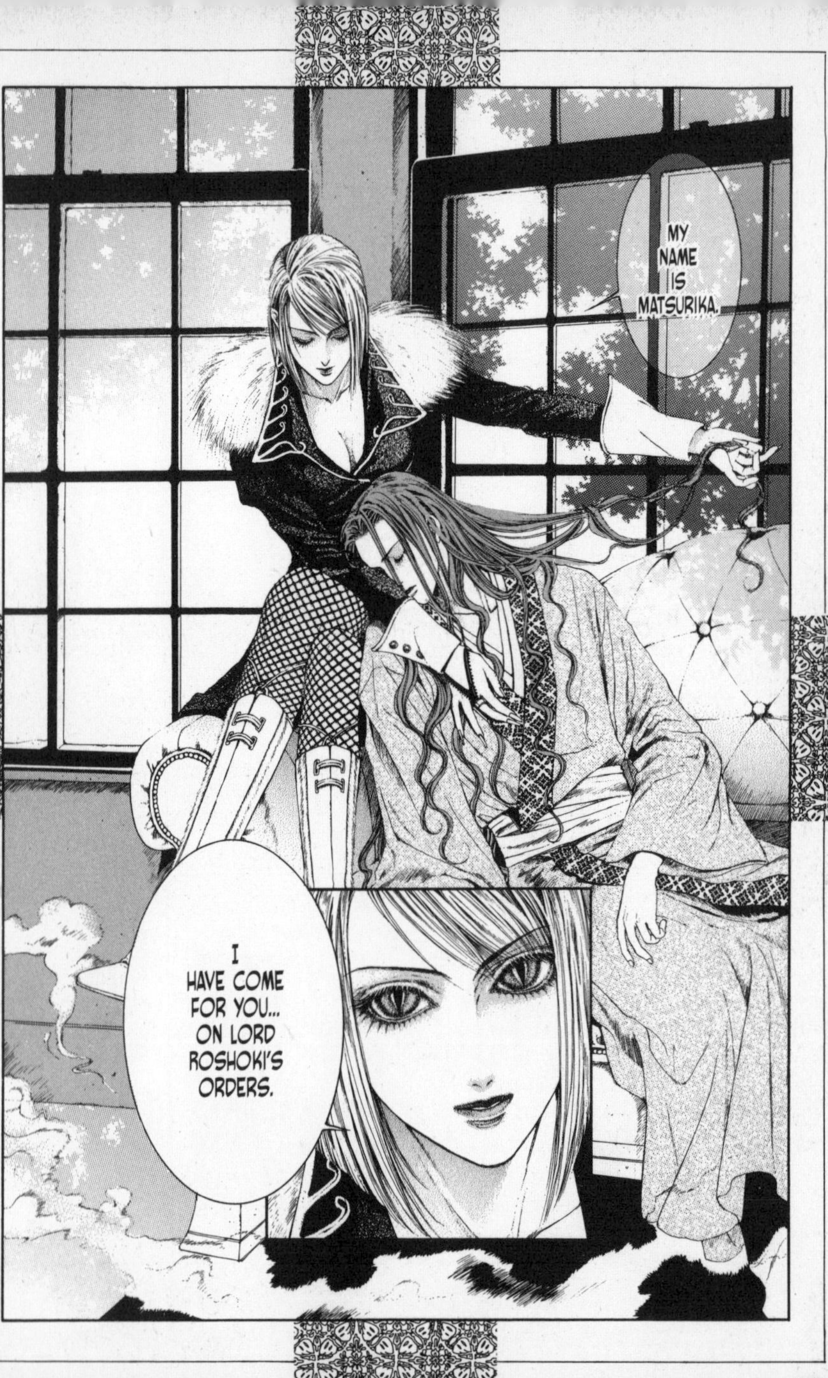
MY NAME IS MATSURIKA.
I HAVE COME FOR YOU... ON LORD ROSHOKI'S ORDERS.

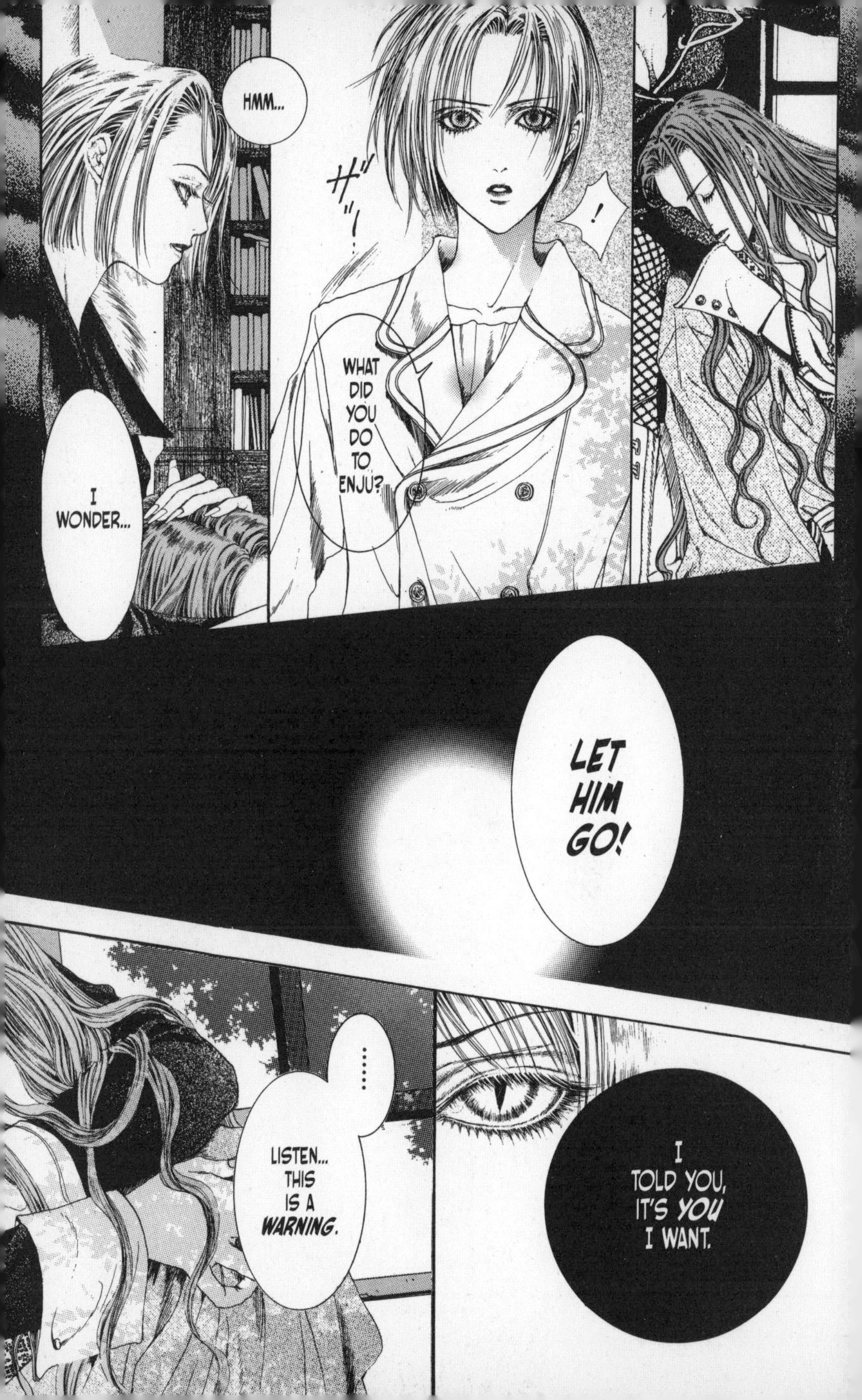
!
WHAT DID YOU DO TO ENJU?
HMM...
I WONDER...
LET HIM GO!
I TOLD YOU, IT'S *YOU* I WANT.
......
LISTEN... THIS IS A *WARNING*.

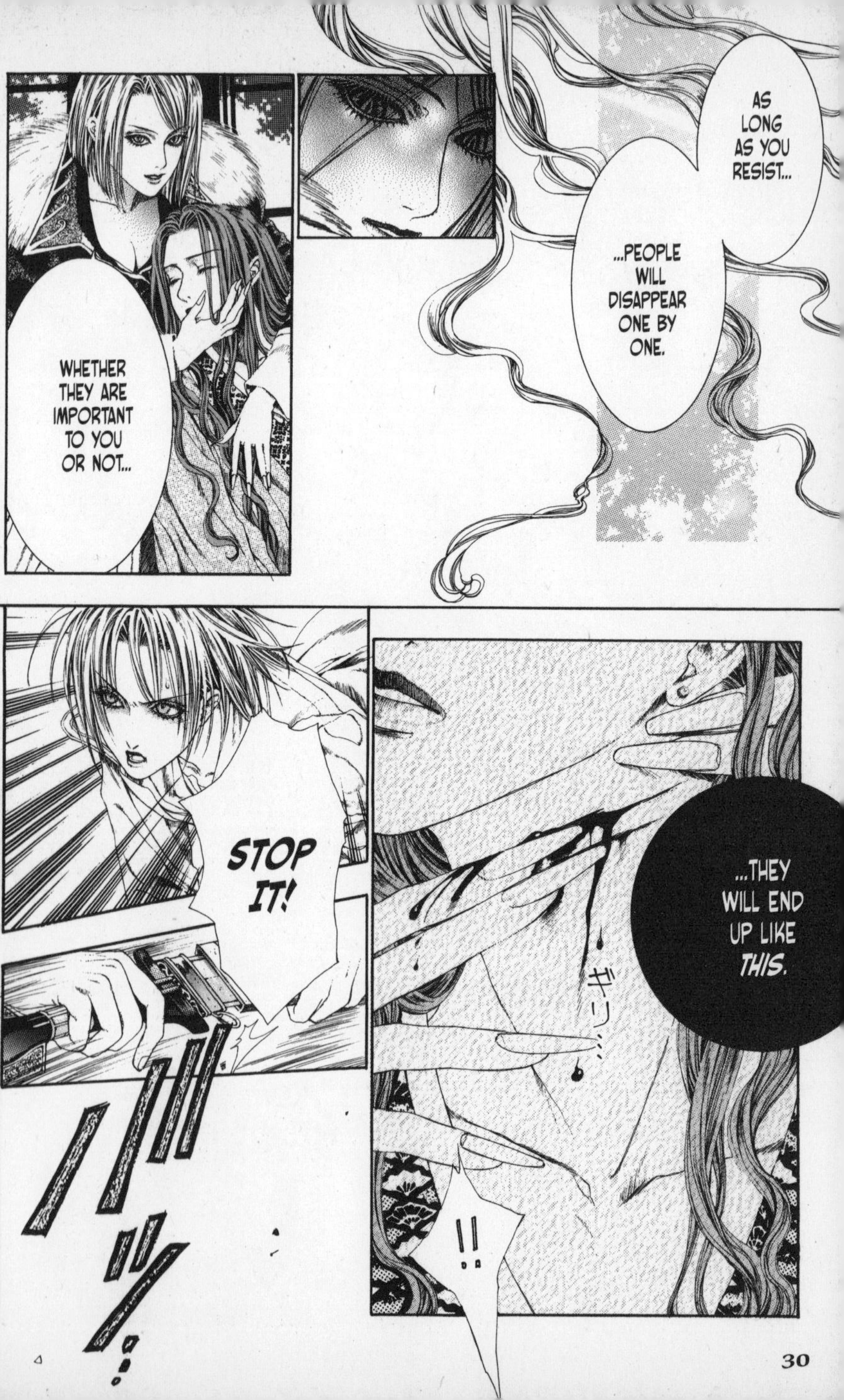
AS LONG AS YOU RESIST...
...PEOPLE WILL DISAPPEAR ONE BY ONE.
WHETHER THEY ARE IMPORTANT TO YOU OR NOT...
...THEY WILL END UP LIKE *THIS.*
ギリ
!!
STOP IT!

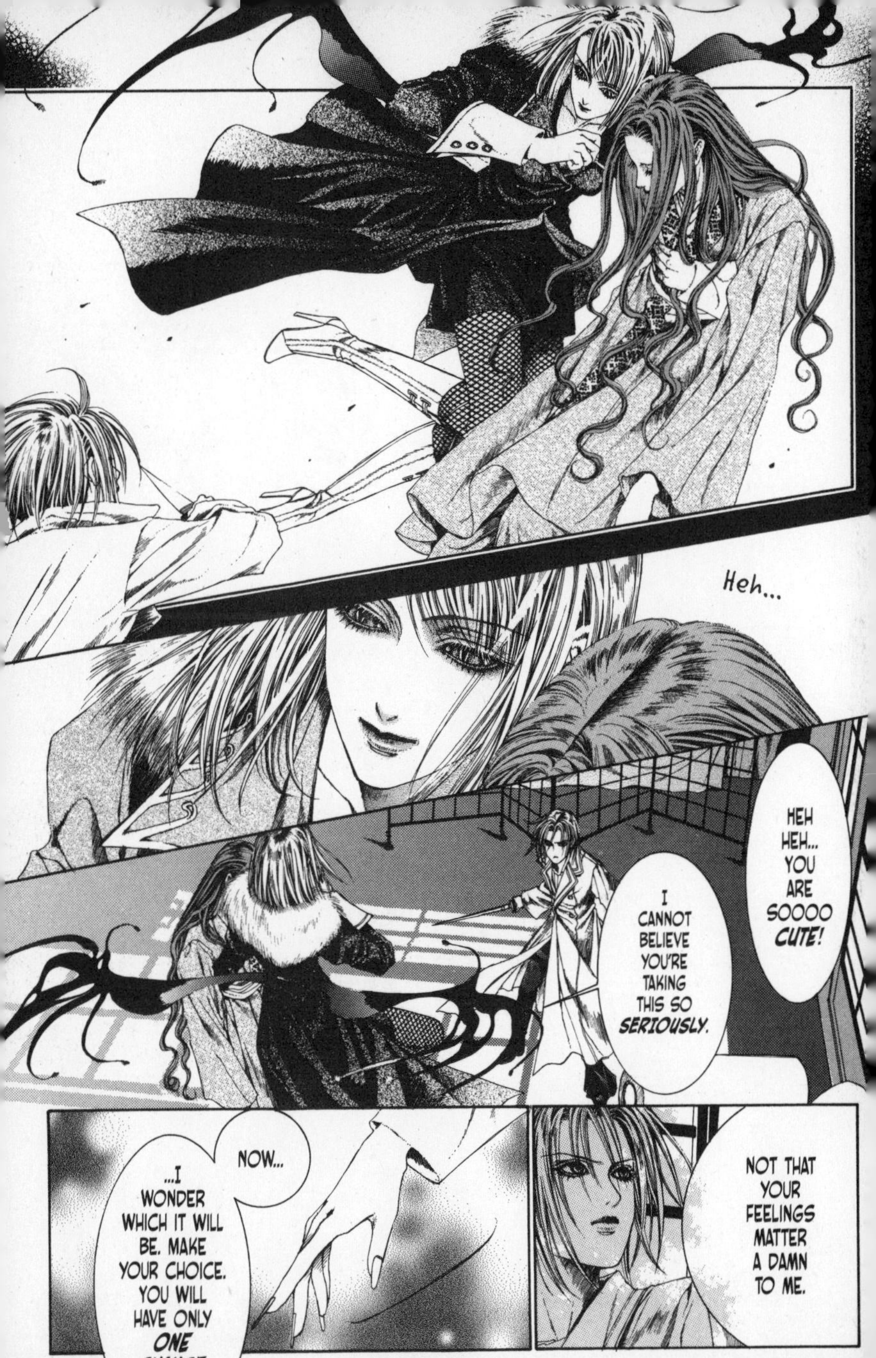
Heh...
HEH HEH... YOU ARE SOOOO ***CUTE!***
I CANNOT BELIEVE YOU'RE TAKING THIS SO ***SERIOUSLY.***
NOT THAT YOUR FEELINGS MATTER A DAMN TO ME.
NOW...
...I WONDER WHICH IT WILL BE. MAKE YOUR CHOICE. YOU WILL HAVE ONLY ***ONE CHANCE.***

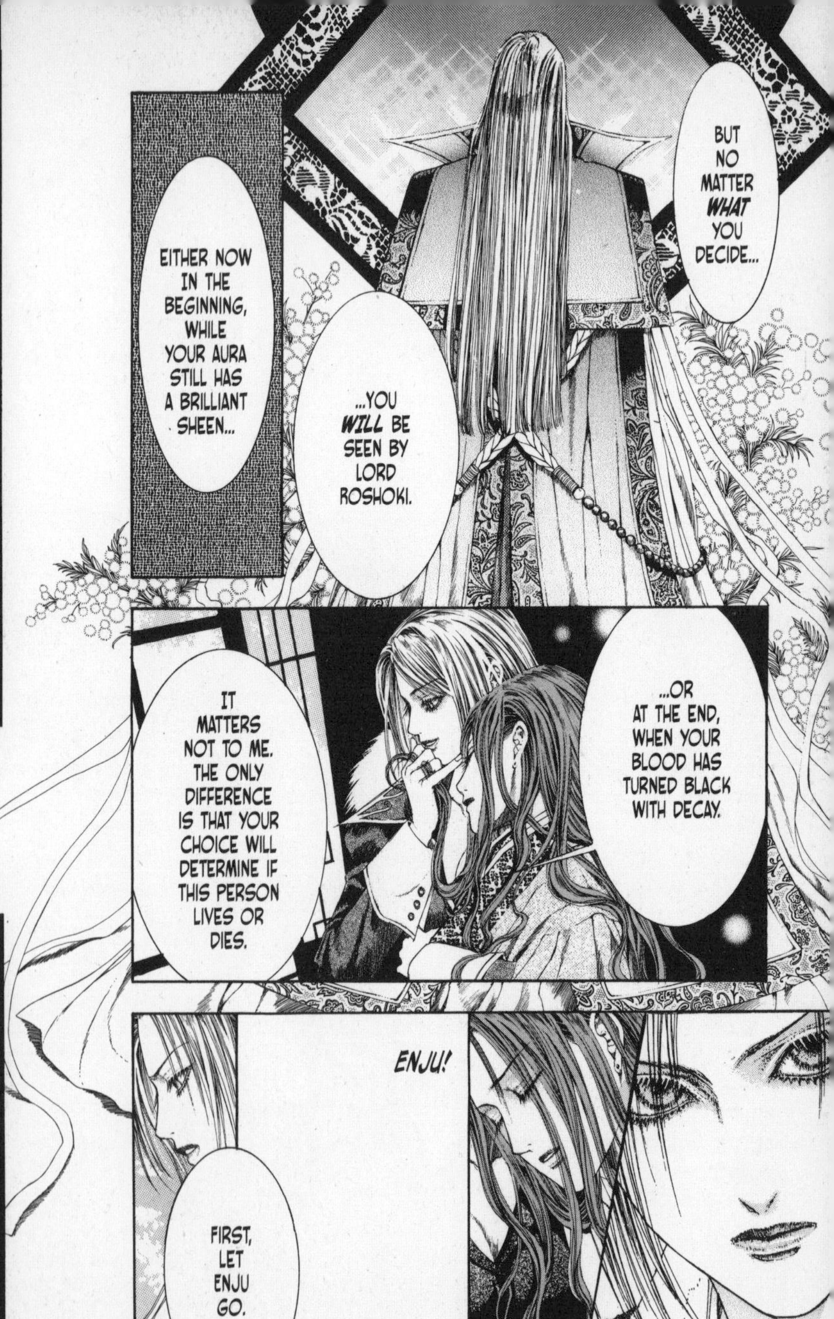
BUT NO MATTER WHAT YOU DECIDE...
...YOU WILL BE SEEN BY LORD ROSHOKI.
EITHER NOW IN THE BEGINNING, WHILE YOUR AURA STILL HAS A BRILLIANT SHEEN...
...OR AT THE END, WHEN YOUR BLOOD HAS TURNED BLACK WITH DECAY.
IT MATTERS NOT TO ME. THE ONLY DIFFERENCE IS THAT YOUR CHOICE WILL DETERMINE IF THIS PERSON LIVES OR DIES.
ENJU!
FIRST, LET ENJU GO.

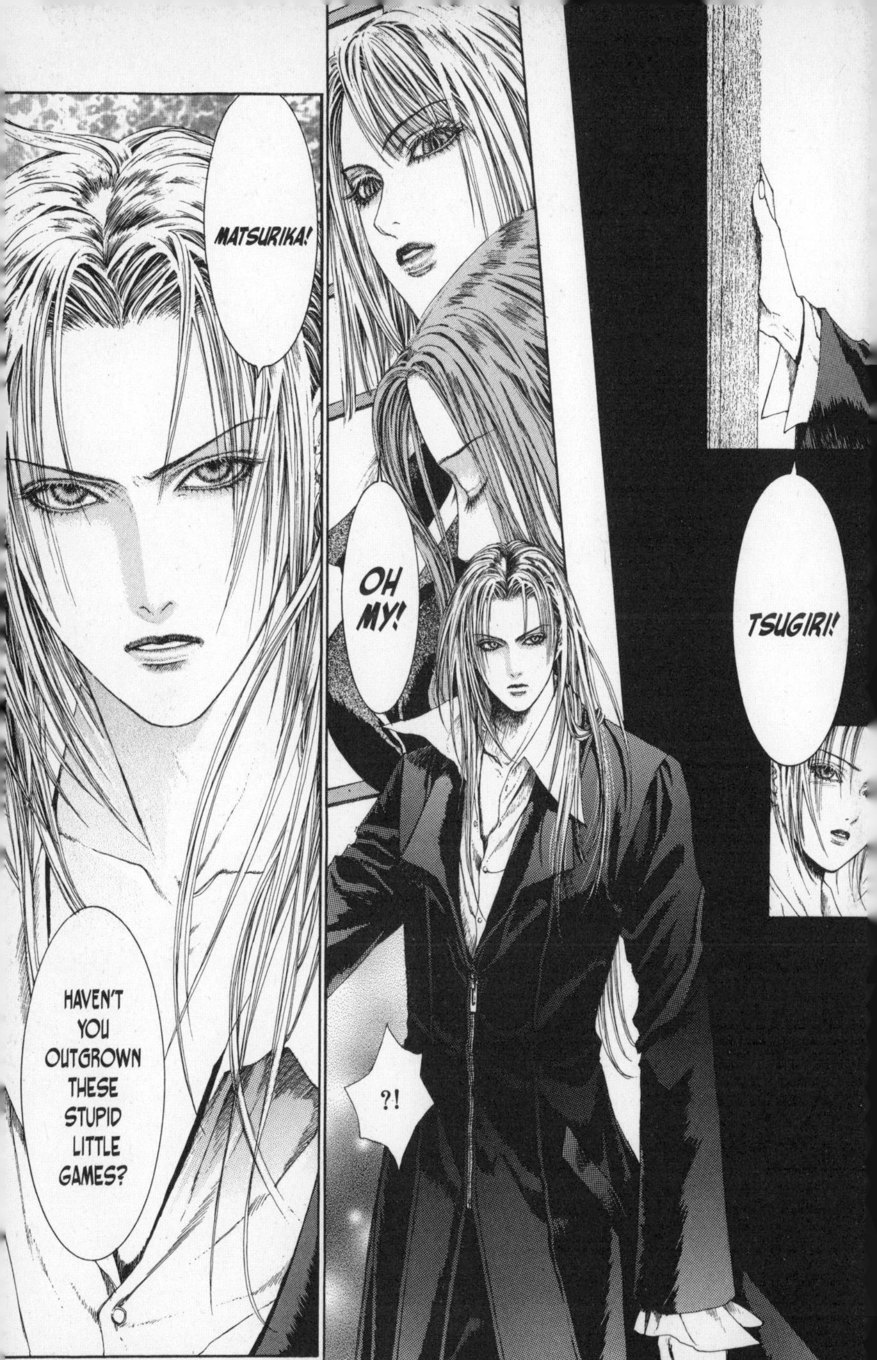
TSUGIRI!
OH MY!
?!
MATSURIKA!
HAVEN'T YOU OUTGROWN THESE STUPID LITTLE GAMES?

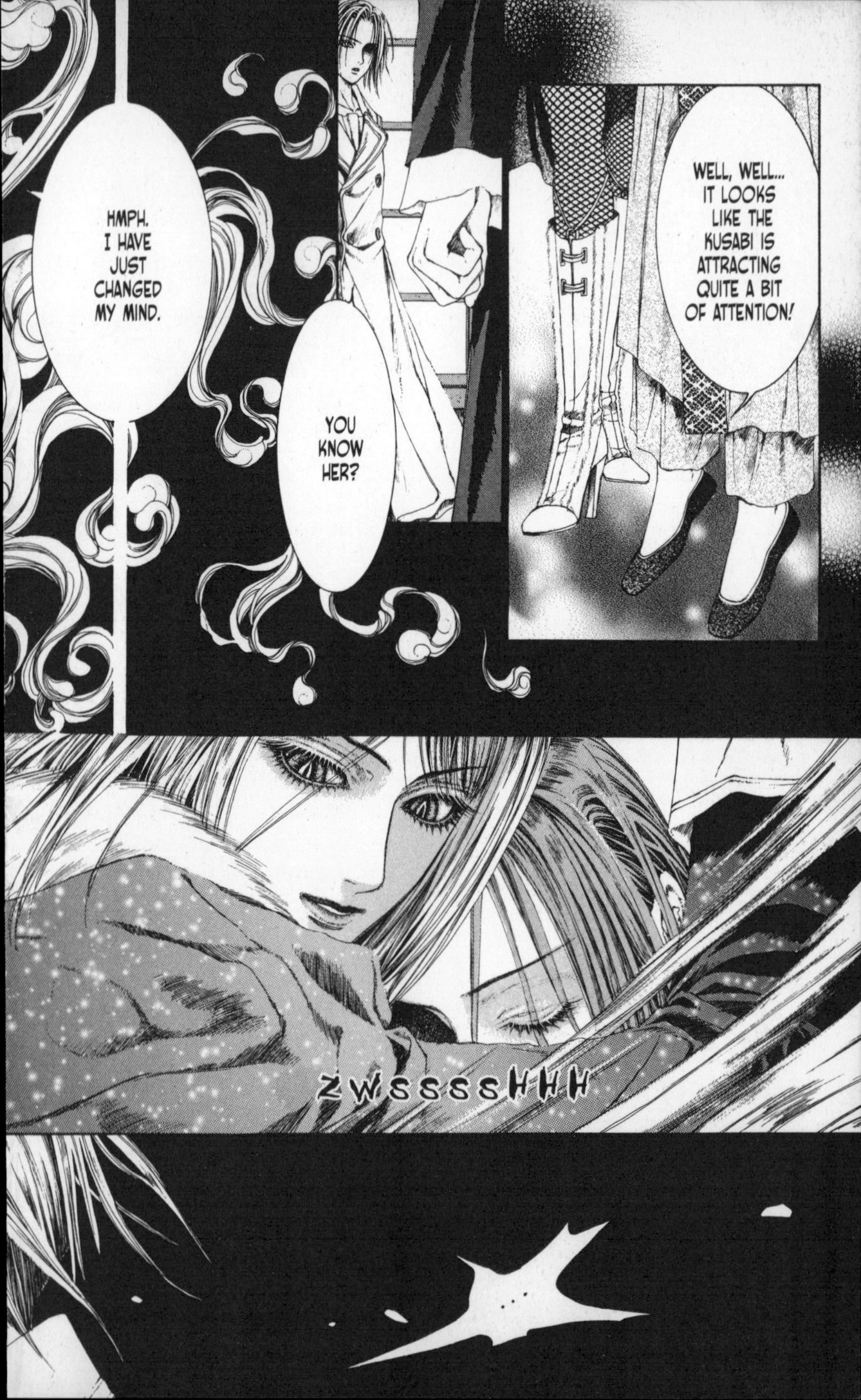
WELL, WELL... IT LOOKS LIKE THE KUSABI IS ATTRACTING QUITE A BIT OF ATTENTION!
YOU KNOW HER?
HMPH. I HAVE JUST CHANGED MY MIND.
ZWSSSSSHHH

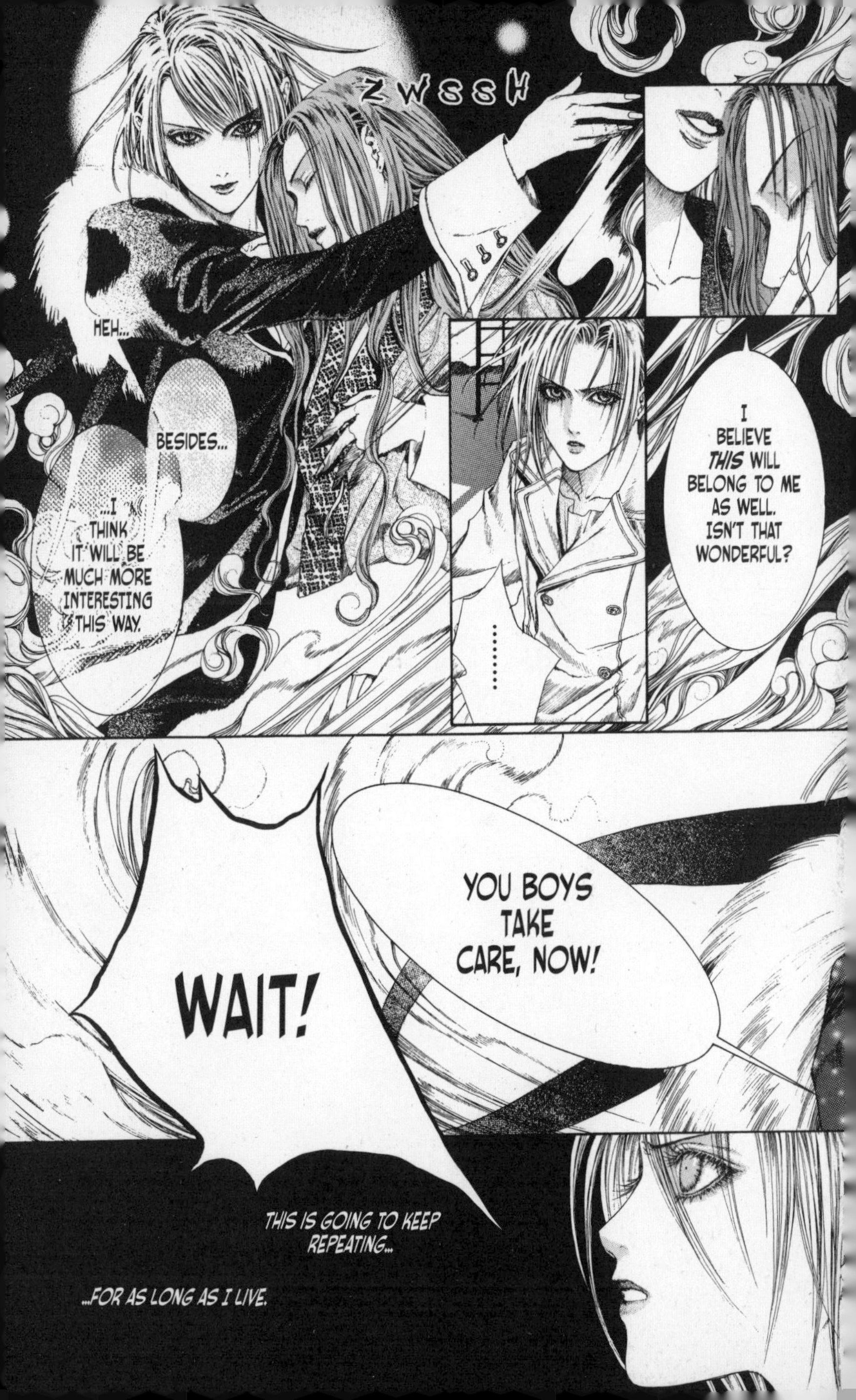
I BELIEVE THIS WILL BELONG TO ME AS WELL. ISN'T THAT WONDERFUL?
......
ZWSSH
HEH...
BESIDES...
...I THINK IT WILL BE MUCH MORE INTERESTING THIS WAY.
YOU BOYS TAKE CARE, NOW!
WAIT!
THIS IS GOING TO KEEP REPEATING...
...FOR AS LONG AS I LIVE.

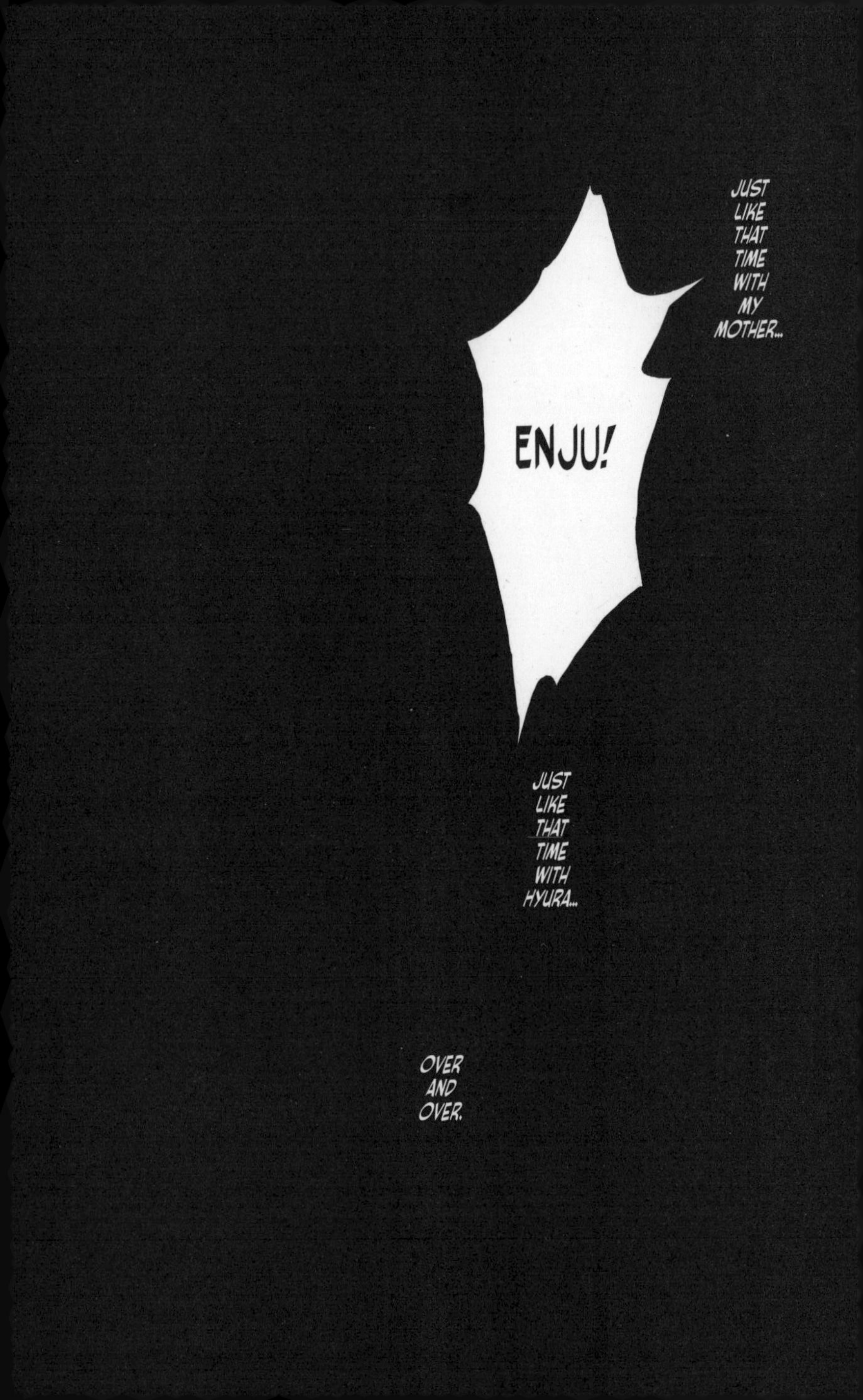
JUST LIKE THAT TIME WITH MY MOTHER...
ENJU!
JUST LIKE THAT TIME WITH HYURA...
OVER AND OVER.

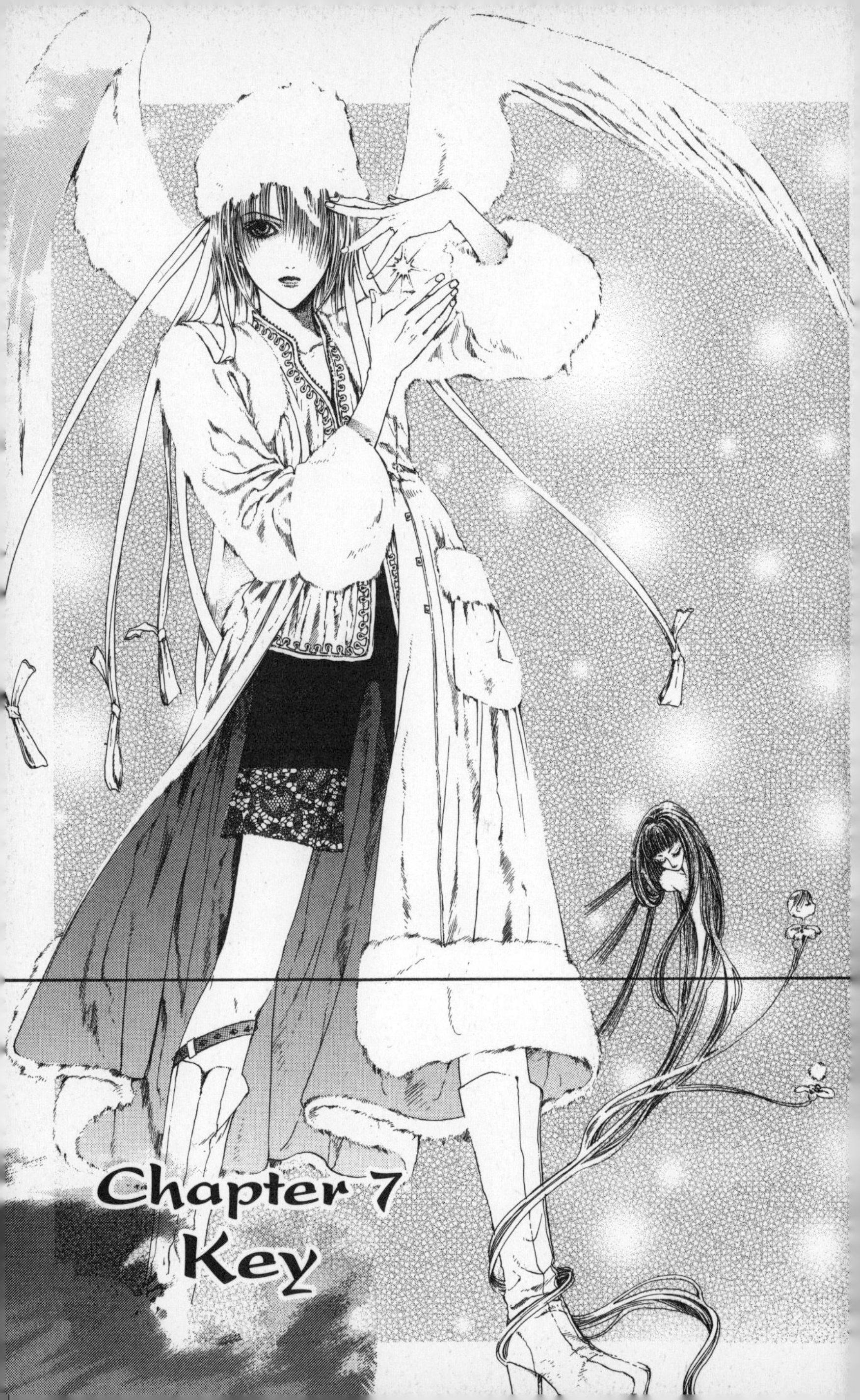
Chapter 7
Key

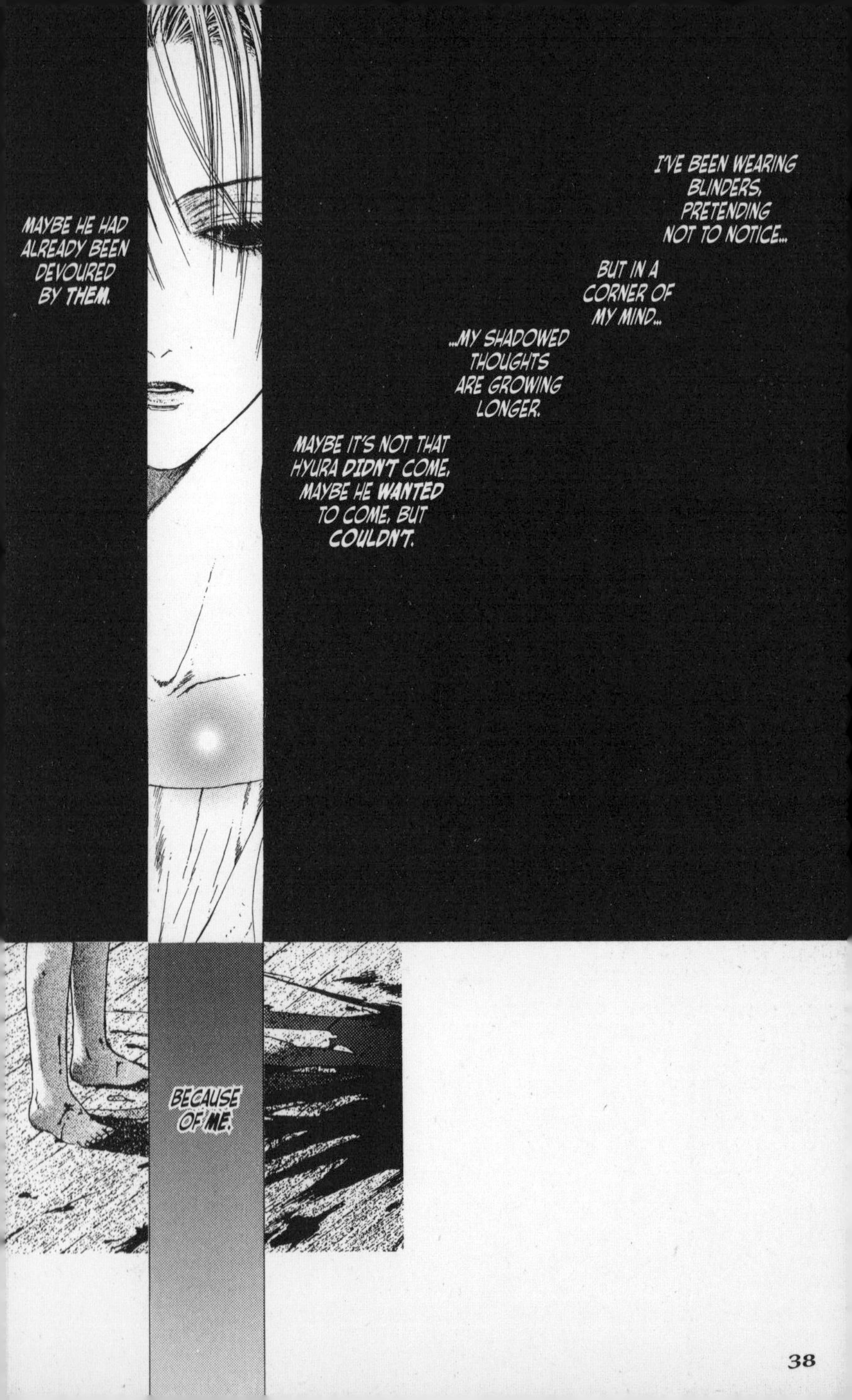
I'VE BEEN WEARING BLINDERS, PRETENDING NOT TO NOTICE...
BUT IN A CORNER OF MY MIND...
...MY SHADOWED THOUGHTS ARE GROWING LONGER.
MAYBE IT'S NOT THAT HYURA **DIDN'T** COME. MAYBE HE **WANTED** TO COME, BUT **COULDN'T**.
MAYBE HE HAD ALREADY BEEN DEVOURED BY **THEM**.
BECAUSE OF **ME**.

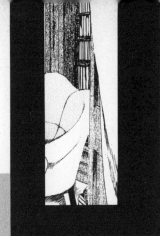

I COULDN'T PROTECT HIM.

EVEN THOUGH I WAS RIGHT THERE.

ENJU...

I HATE WAITING LIKE THIS... WAITING FOR THE END TO COME.

I DON'T WANT TO RELIVE THAT ALL OVER AGAIN.

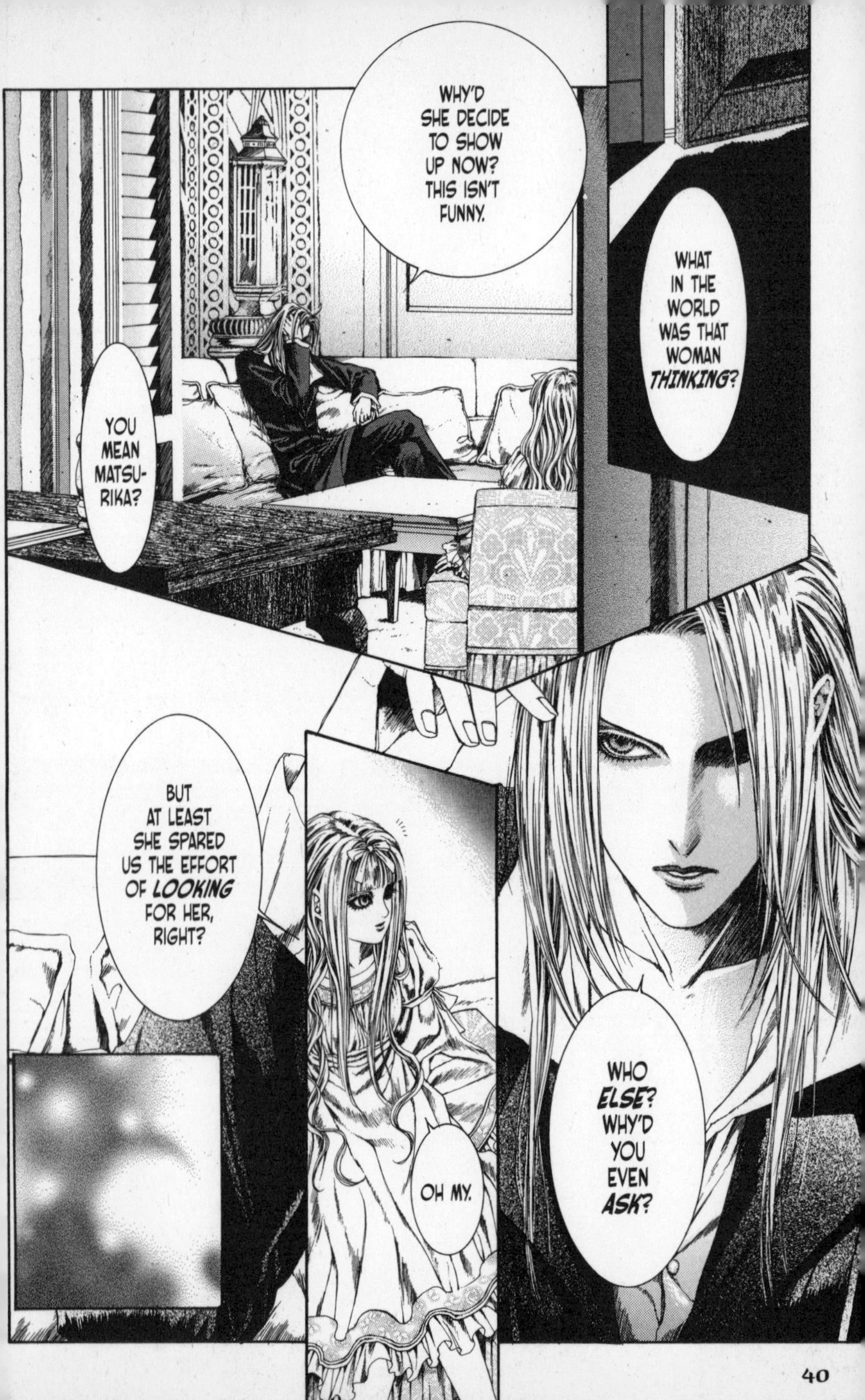
WHY'D SHE DECIDE TO SHOW UP NOW? THIS ISN'T FUNNY.
WHAT IN THE WORLD WAS THAT WOMAN *THINKING*?
YOU MEAN MATSU-RIKA?
WHO *ELSE*? WHY'D YOU EVEN *ASK*?
OH MY.
BUT AT LEAST SHE SPARED US THE EFFORT OF *LOOKING* FOR HER, RIGHT?

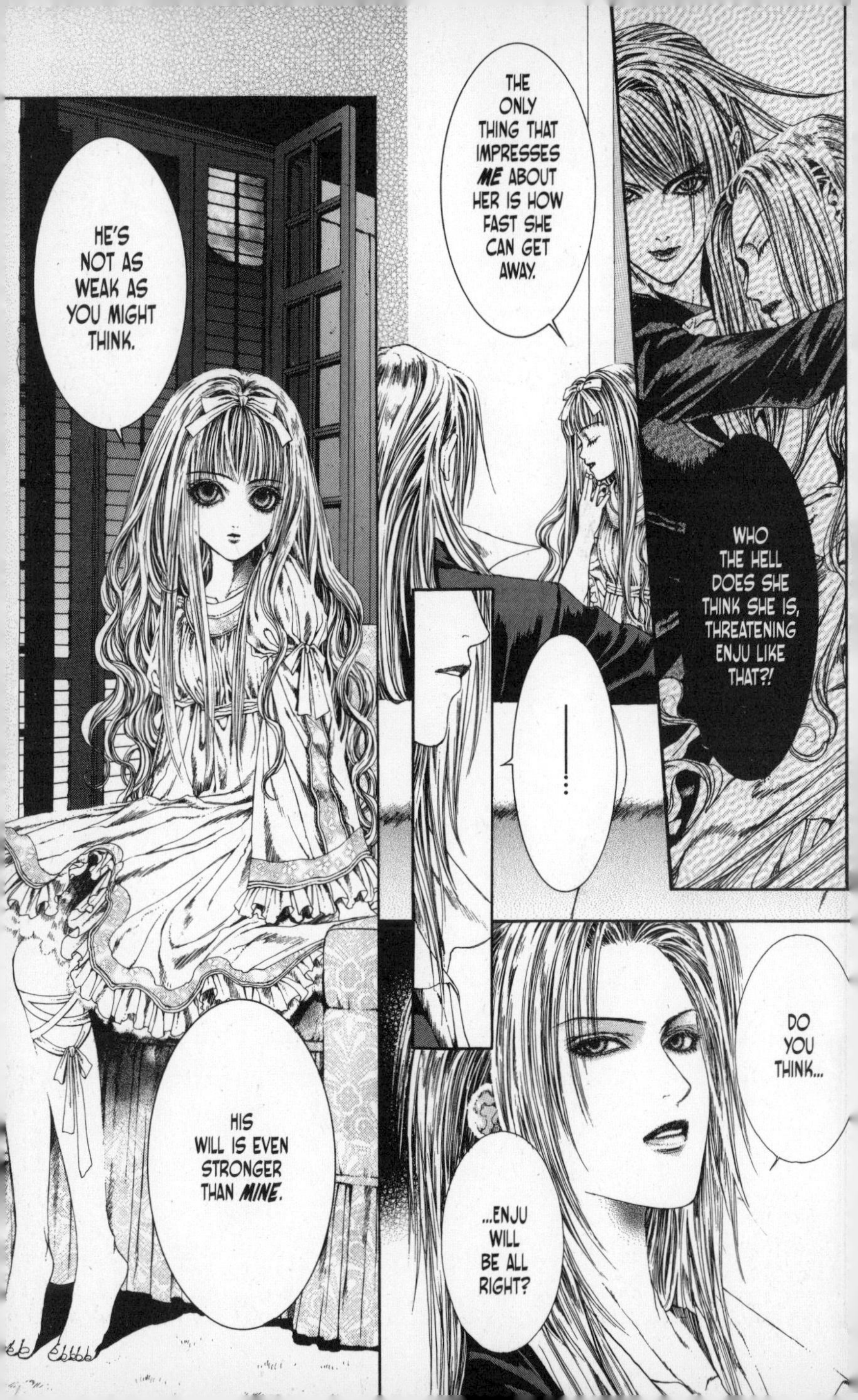
WHO THE HELL DOES SHE THINK SHE IS, THREATENING ENJU LIKE THAT?!
THE ONLY THING THAT IMPRESSES *ME* ABOUT HER IS HOW FAST SHE CAN GET AWAY.
......
DO YOU THINK...
...ENJU WILL BE ALL RIGHT?
HE'S NOT AS WEAK AS YOU MIGHT THINK.
HIS WILL IS EVEN STRONGER THAN *MINE*.

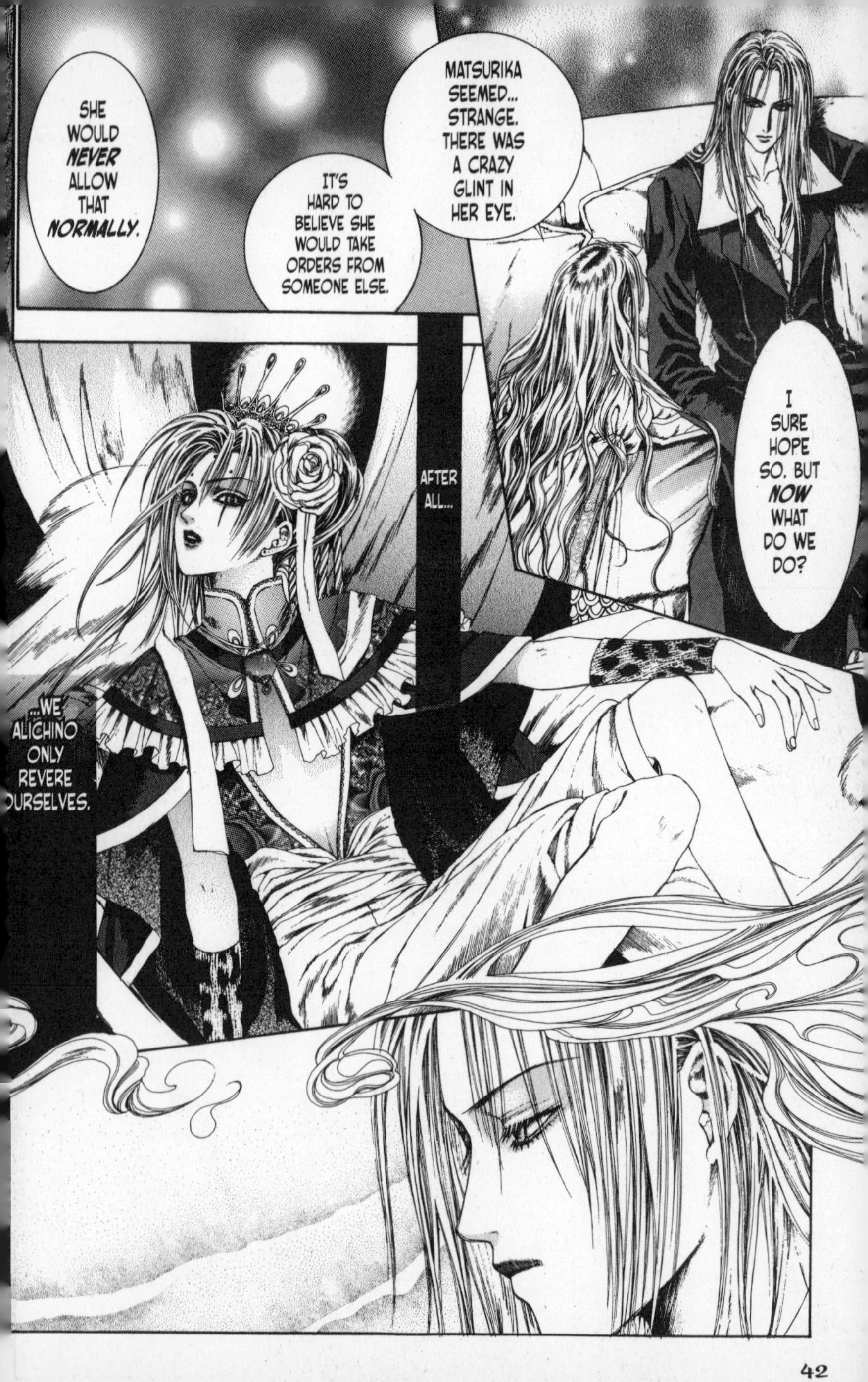
MATSURIKA SEEMED... STRANGE. THERE WAS A CRAZY GLINT IN HER EYE.
IT'S HARD TO BELIEVE SHE WOULD TAKE ORDERS FROM SOMEONE ELSE.
SHE WOULD *NEVER* ALLOW THAT *NORMALLY*.
I SURE HOPE SO. BUT *NOW* WHAT DO WE DO?
AFTER ALL...
...WE ALICHINO ONLY REVERE OURSELVES.

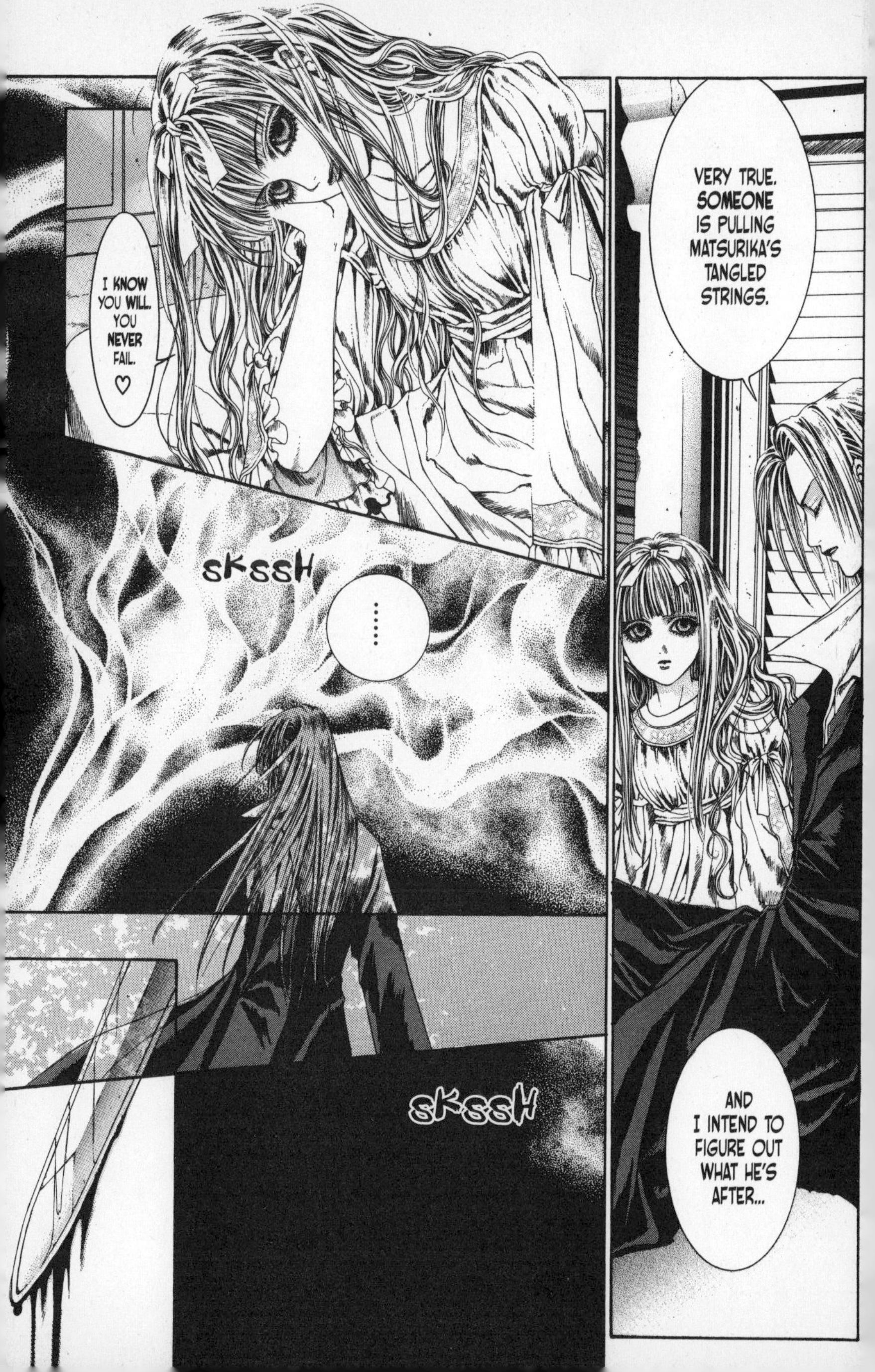
VERY TRUE. SOMEONE IS PULLING MATSURIKA'S TANGLED STRINGS.
AND I INTEND TO FIGURE OUT WHAT HE'S AFTER...
I KNOW YOU WILL. YOU NEVER FAIL. ♡
SKSSH
......
SKSSH

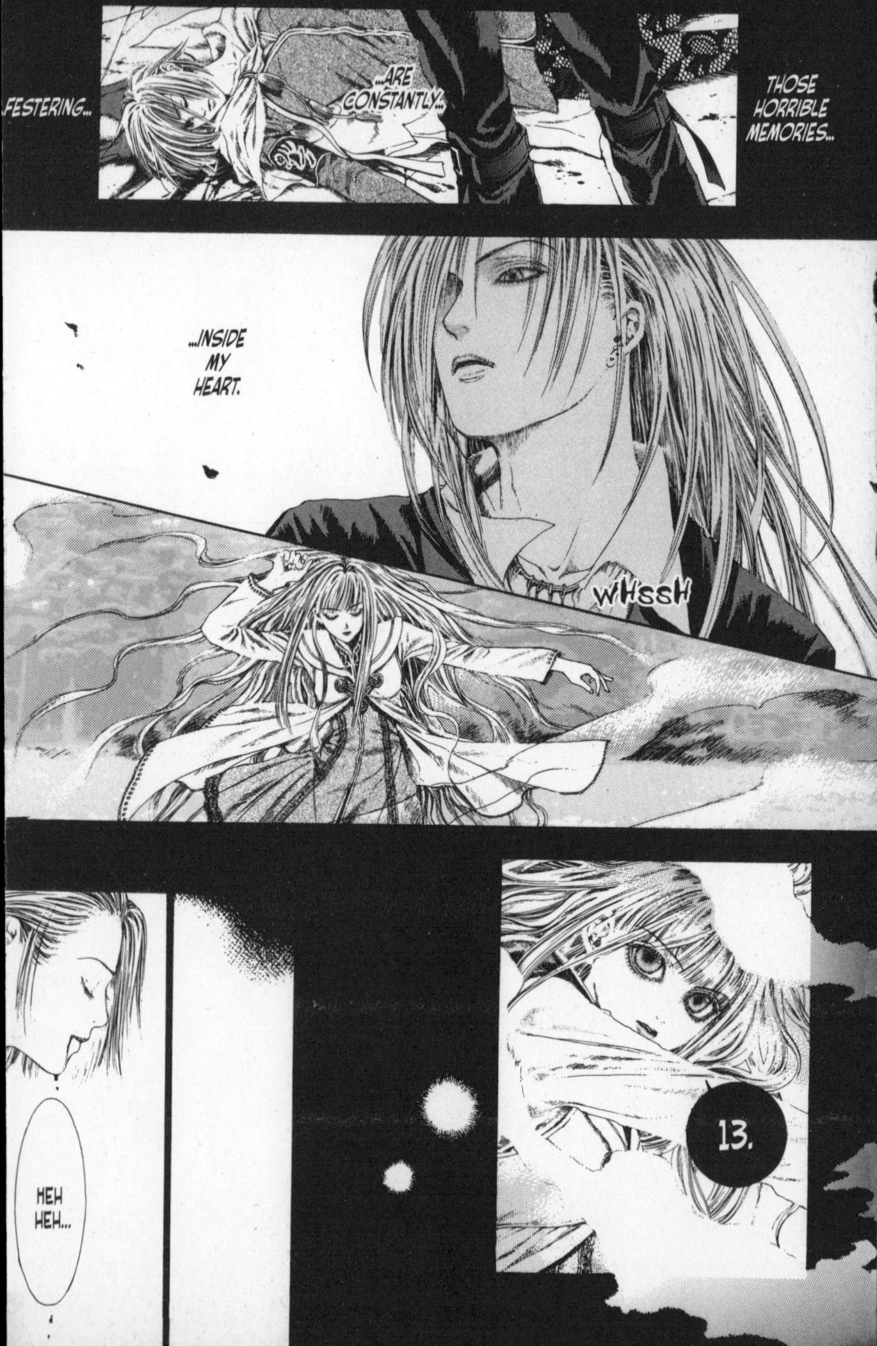
THOSE HORRIBLE MEMORIES...
...ARE CONSTANTLY...
FESTERING...
...INSIDE MY HEART.
WHSSH
13.
HEH HEH...

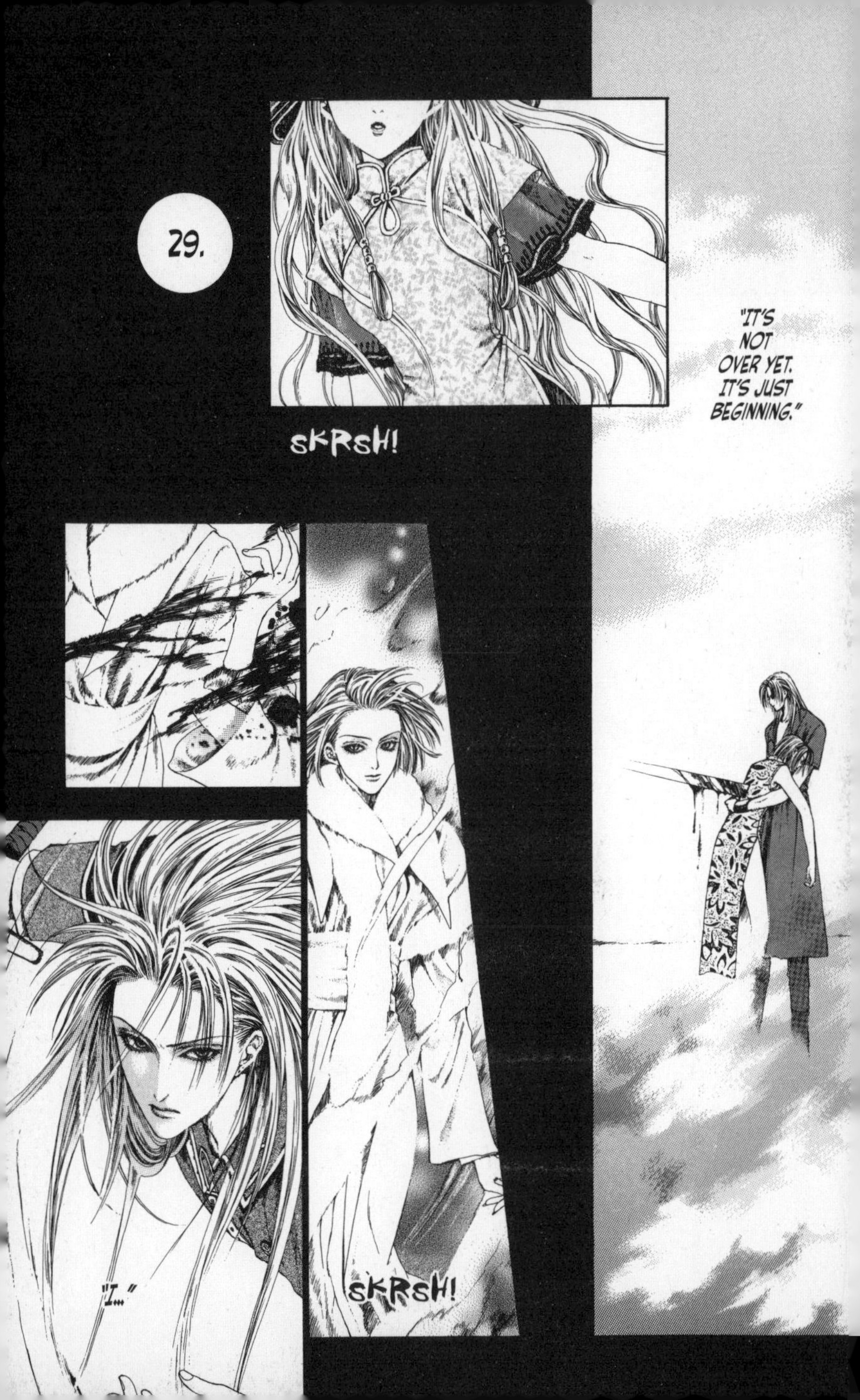
"IT'S NOT OVER YET. IT'S JUST BEGINNING."
29.
SKRSH!
SKRSH!
"I..."

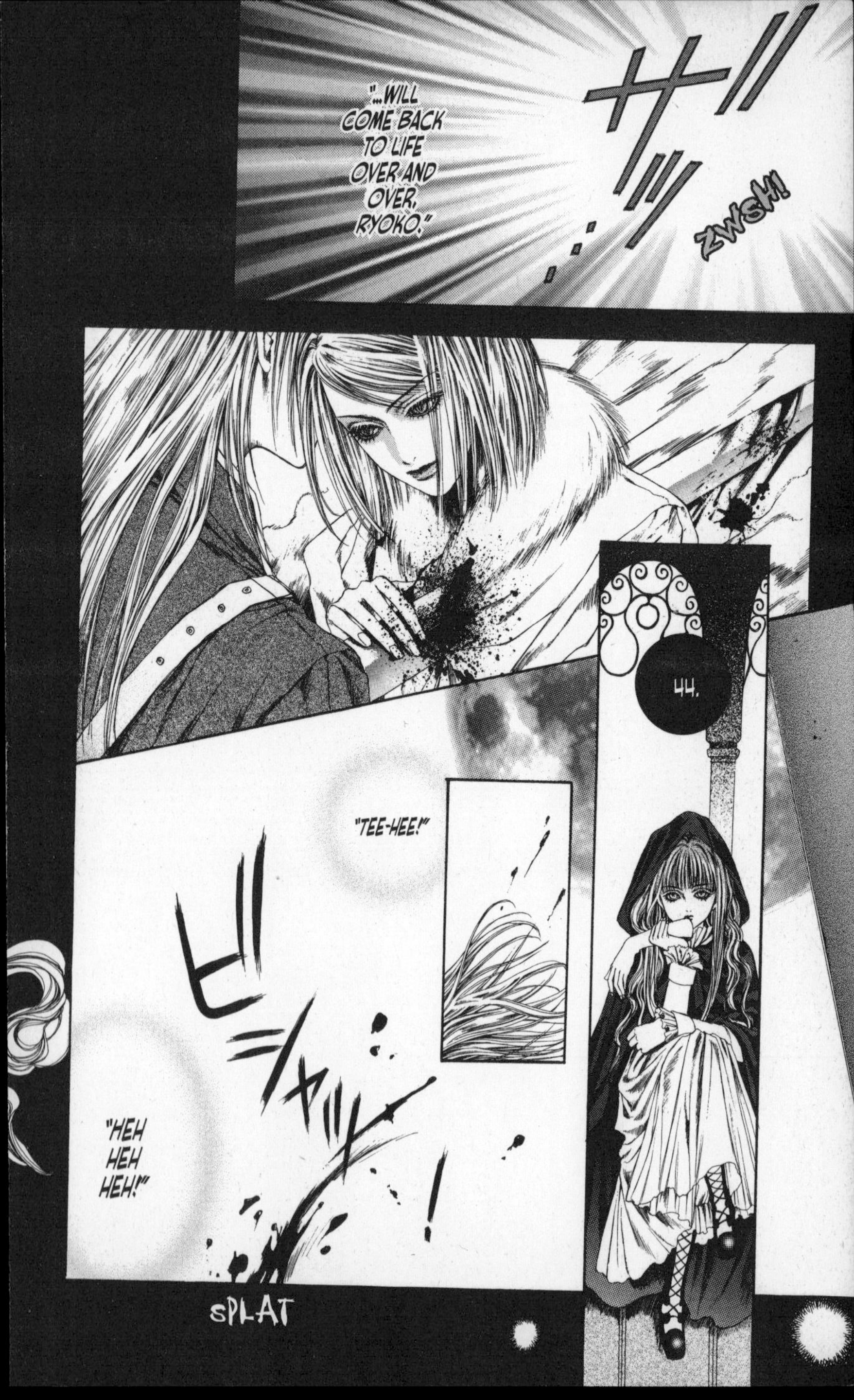

"...WILL COME BACK TO LIFE OVER AND OVER, RYOKO."
ZWSH!
44.
"TEE-HEE!"
"HEH HEH HEH!"
SPLAT

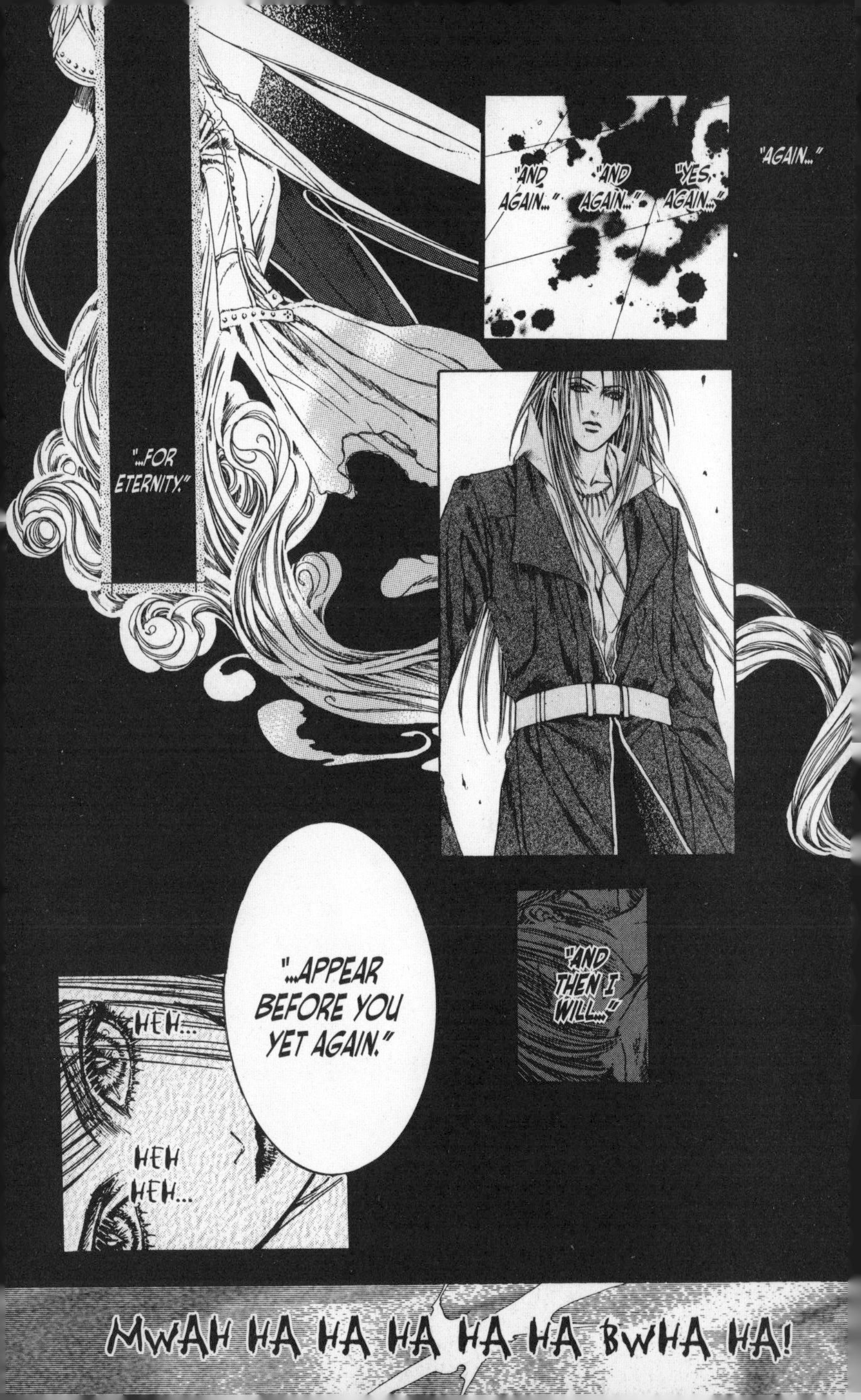
"AGAIN..."
"YES, AGAIN..."
"AND AGAIN..."
"AND AGAIN..."
"...FOR ETERNITY."
"AND THEN I WILL..."
"...APPEAR BEFORE YOU YET AGAIN."
HEH...
HEH HEH...
MWAH HA HA HA HA HA BWHA HA!

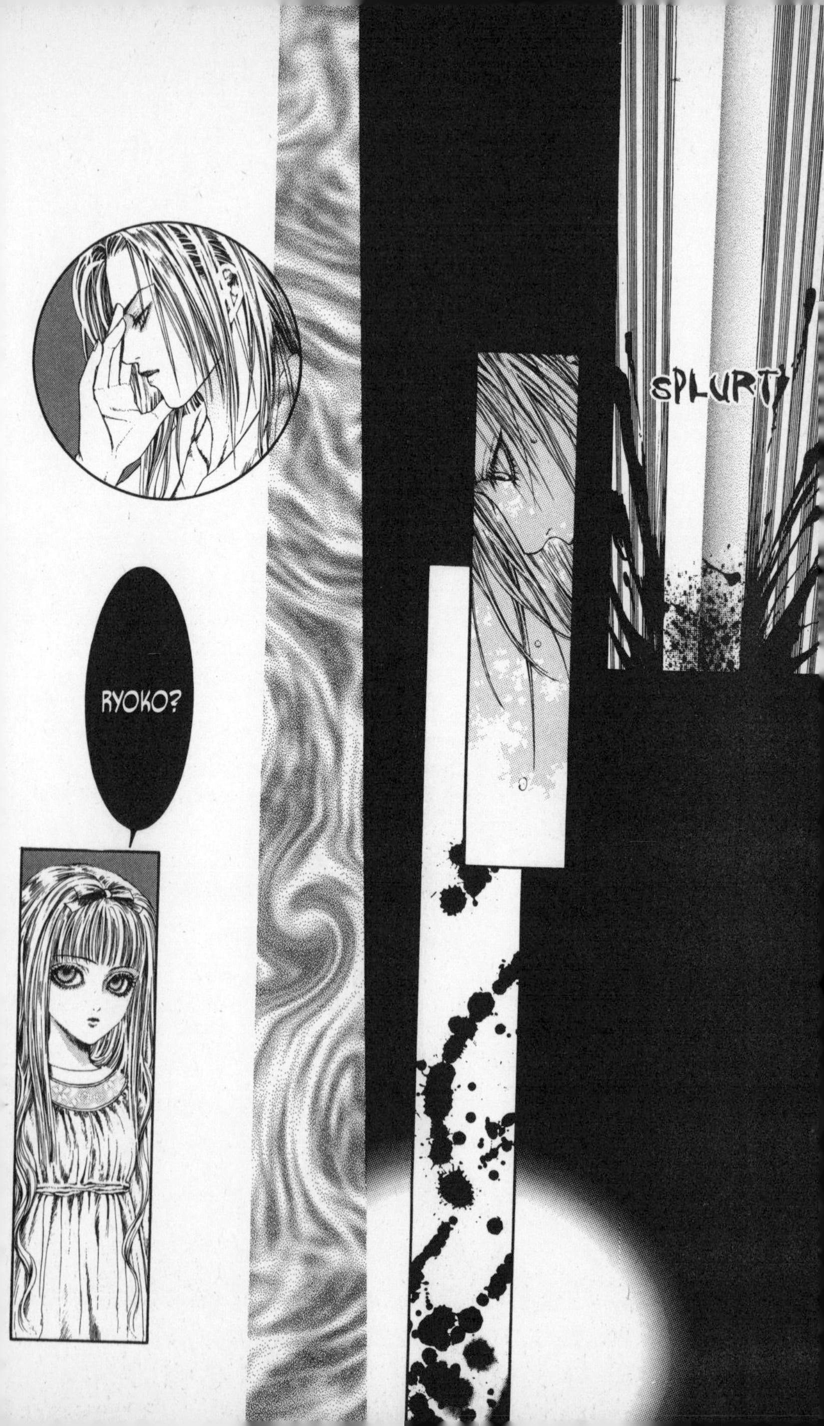
SPLURT
RYOKO?

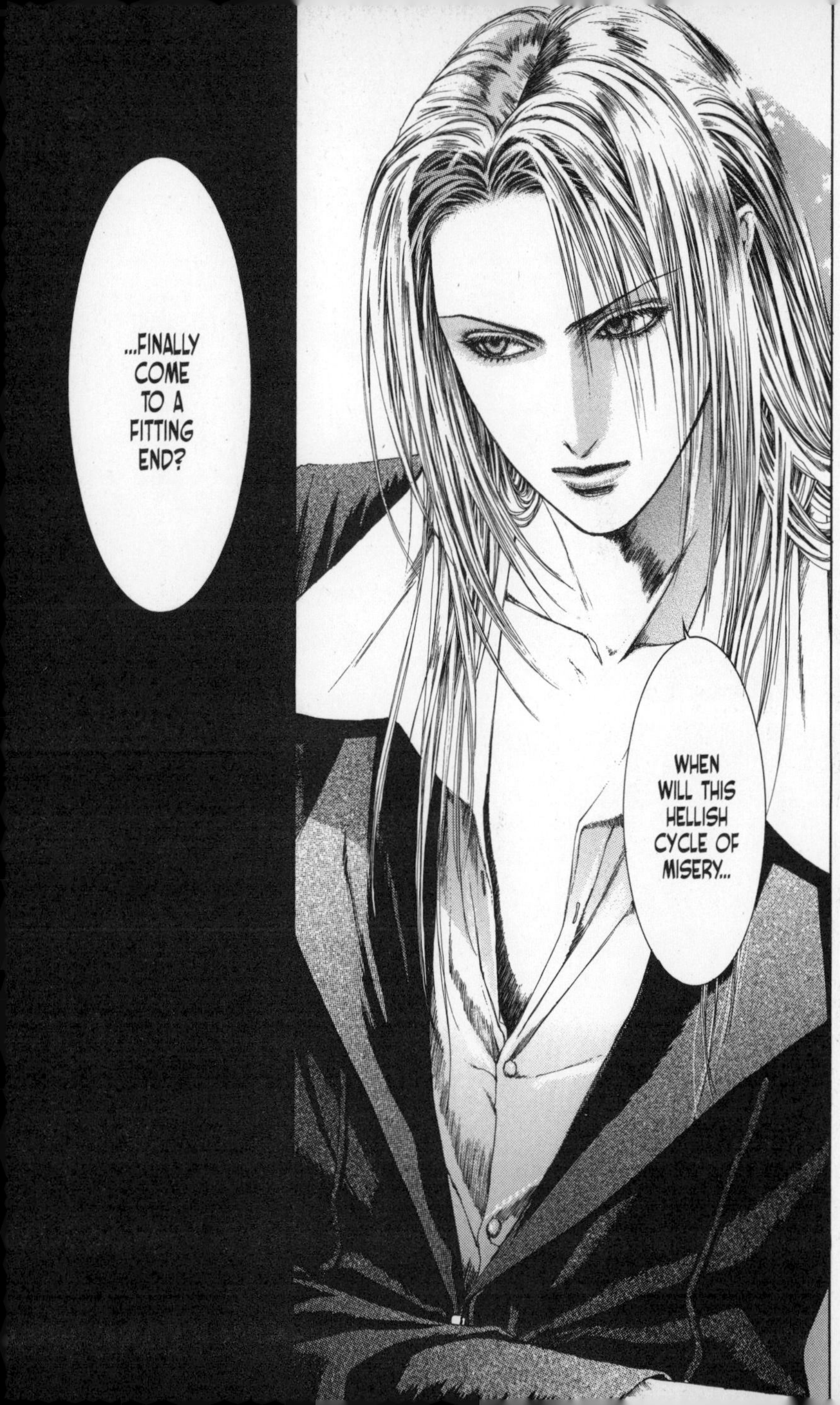
WHEN WILL THIS HELLISH CYCLE OF MISERY...
...FINALLY COME TO A FITTING END?

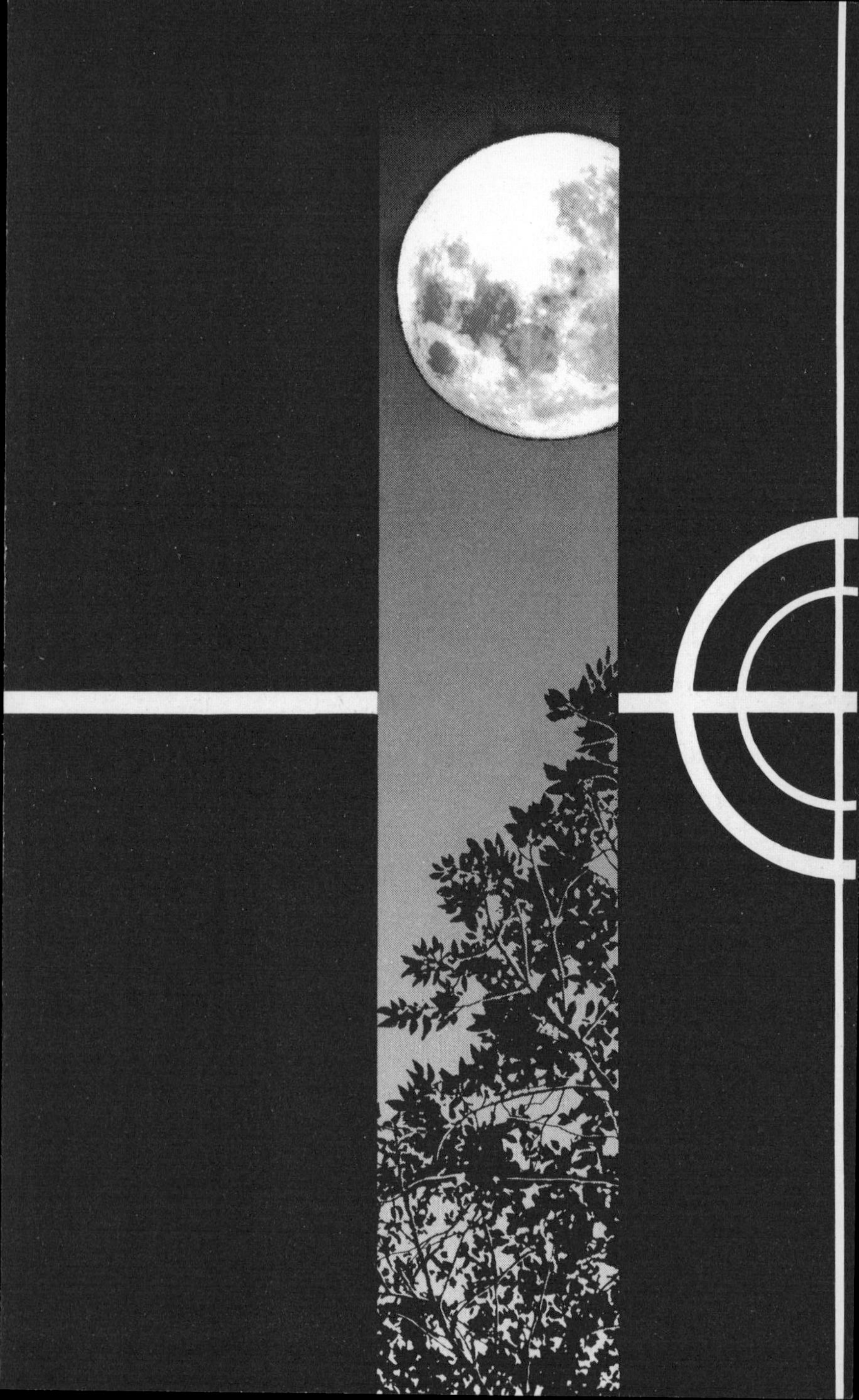

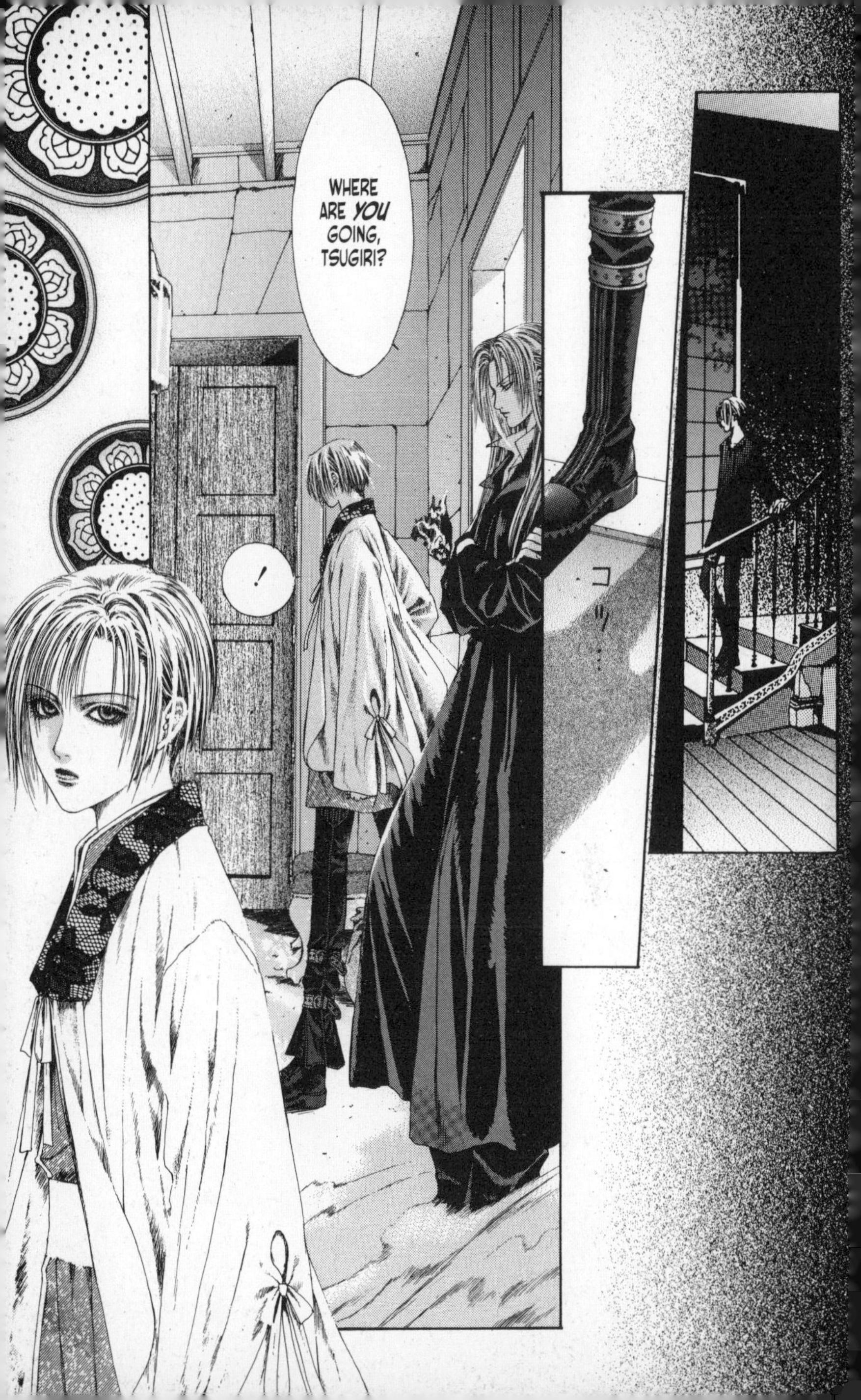
WHERE ARE *YOU* GOING, TSUGIRI?
!

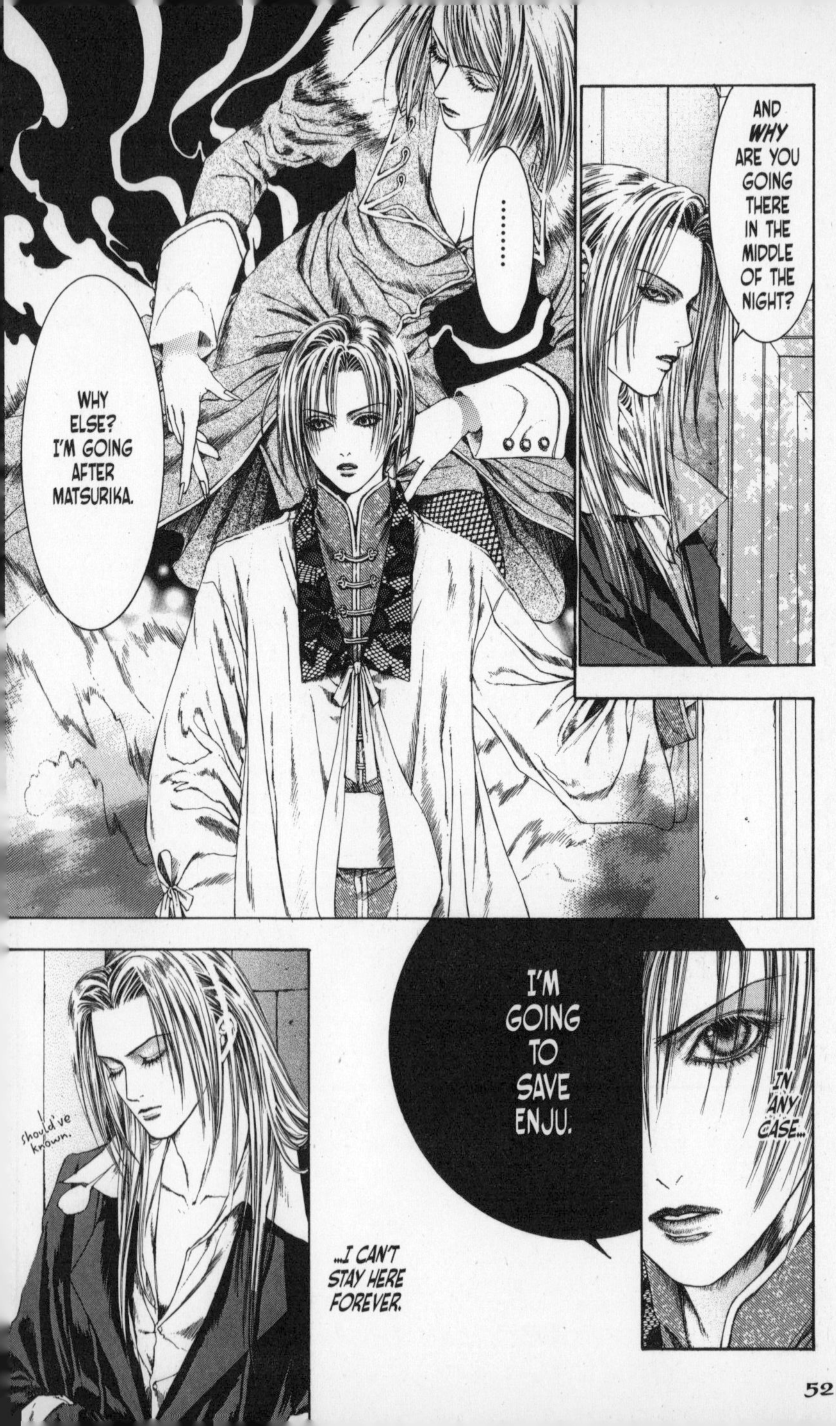
AND WHY ARE YOU GOING THERE IN THE MIDDLE OF THE NIGHT?
......
WHY ELSE? I'M GOING AFTER MATSURIKA.
IN ANY CASE...
I'M GOING TO SAVE ENJU.
...I CAN'T STAY HERE FOREVER.
I should've known.

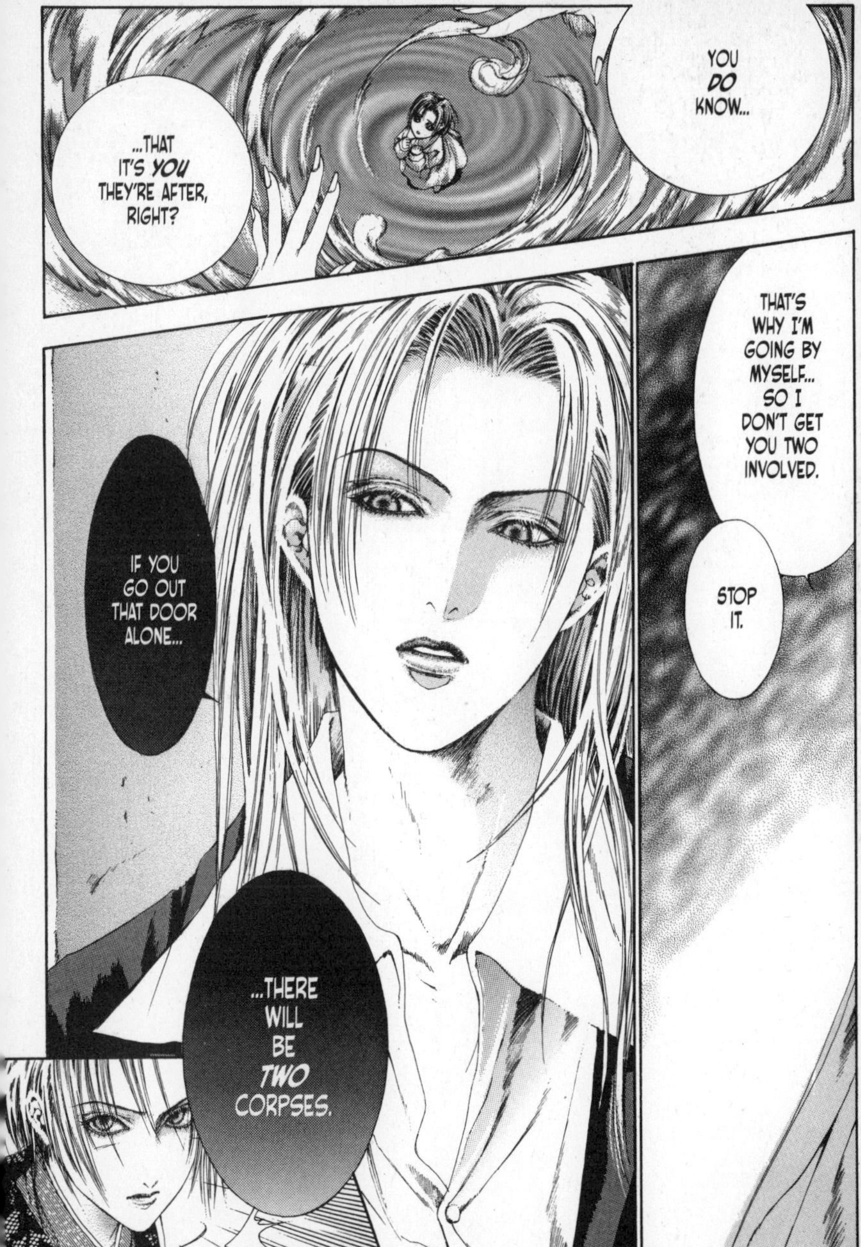
YOU DO KNOW...
...THAT IT'S YOU THEY'RE AFTER, RIGHT?
THAT'S WHY I'M GOING BY MYSELF... SO I DON'T GET YOU TWO INVOLVED.
STOP IT.
IF YOU GO OUT THAT DOOR ALONE...
...THERE WILL BE TWO CORPSES.

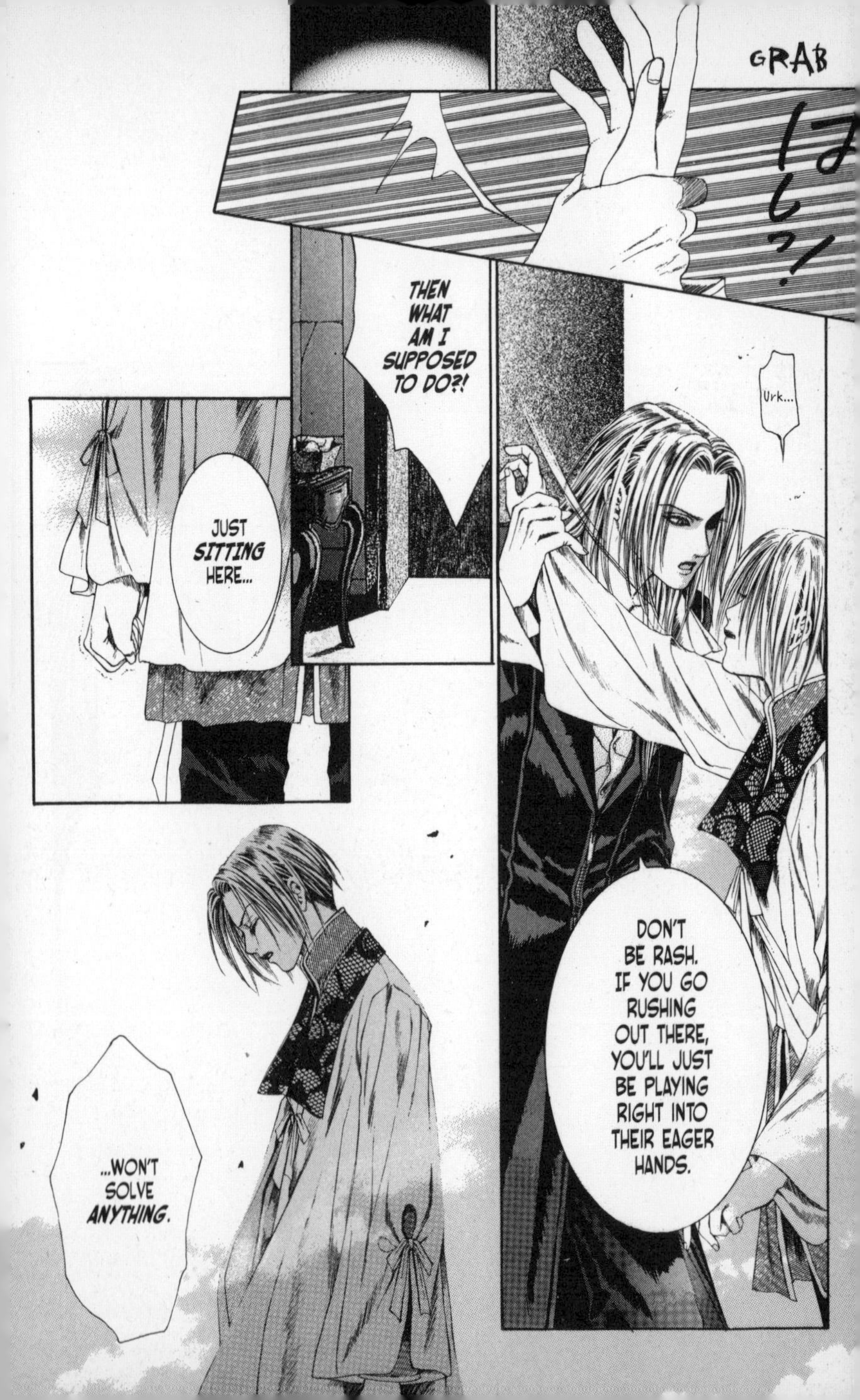
GRAB
はしっ!
Urk...
DON'T BE RASH. IF YOU GO RUSHING OUT THERE, YOU'LL JUST BE PLAYING RIGHT INTO THEIR EAGER HANDS.
THEN WHAT AM I SUPPOSED TO DO?!
JUST SITTING HERE...
...WON'T SOLVE ANYTHING.

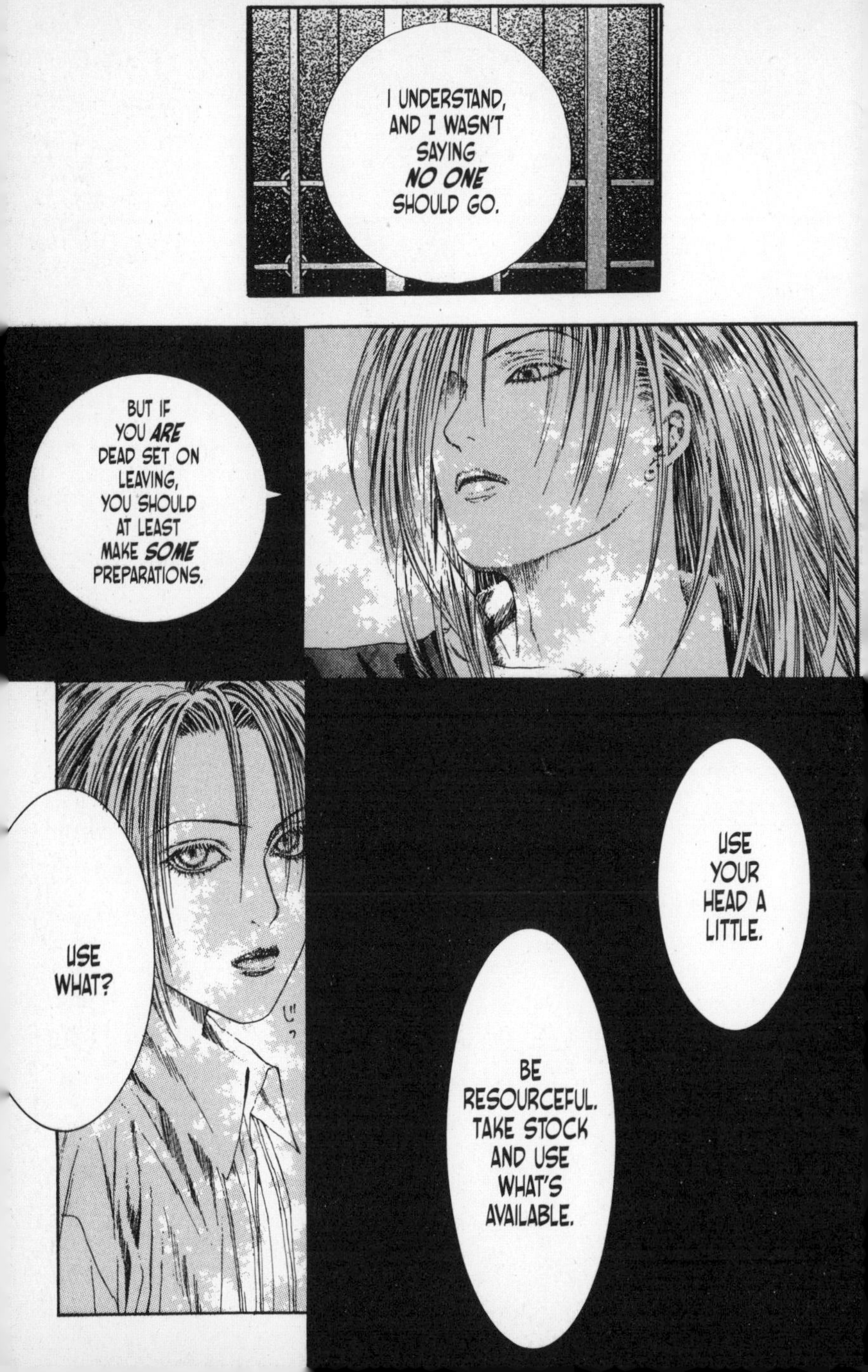
I UNDERSTAND, AND I WASN'T SAYING NO ONE SHOULD GO.
BUT IF YOU ARE DEAD SET ON LEAVING, YOU SHOULD AT LEAST MAKE SOME PREPARATIONS.
USE YOUR HEAD A LITTLE.
BE RESOURCEFUL. TAKE STOCK AND USE WHAT'S AVAILABLE.
USE WHAT?

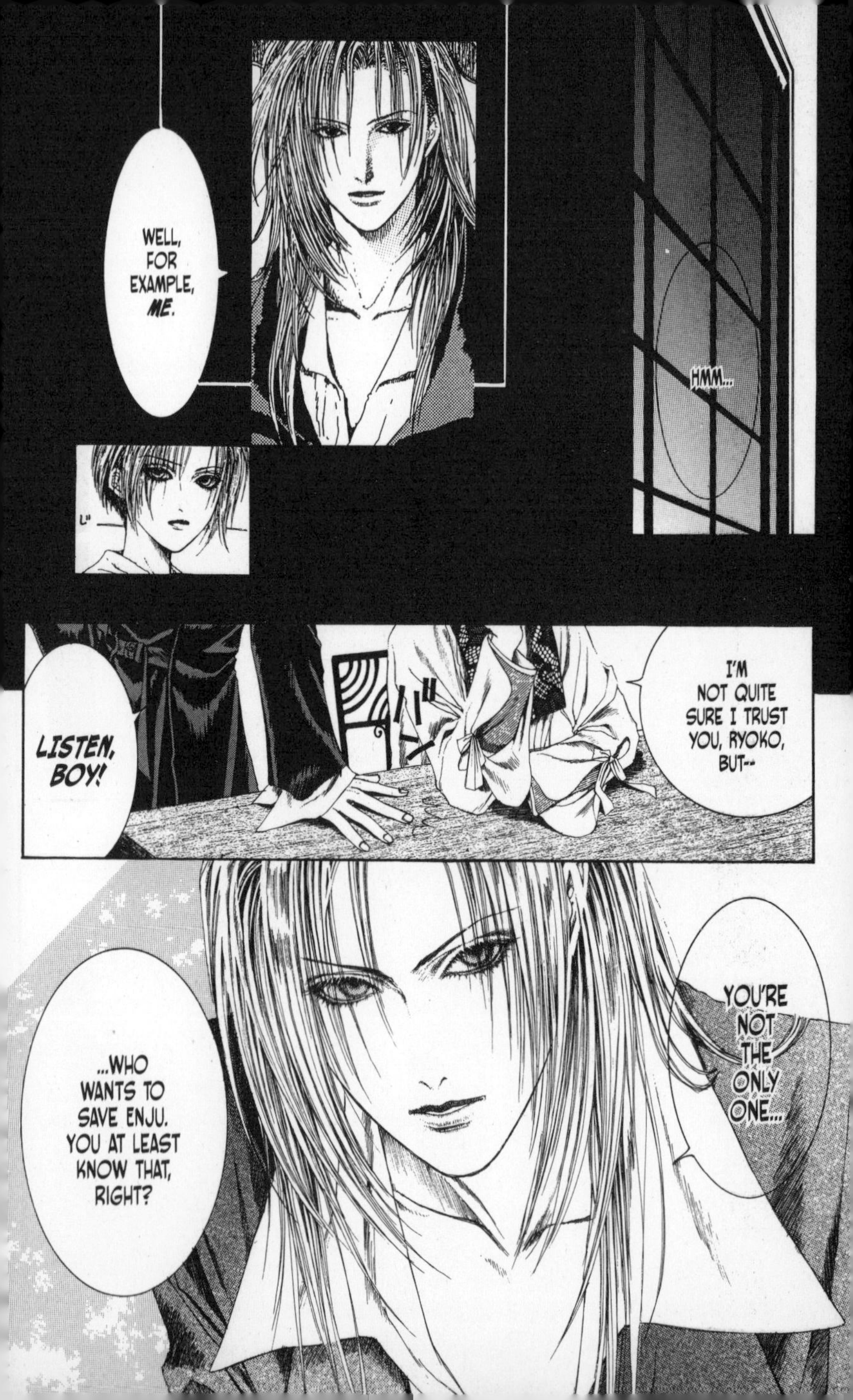
HMM...
WELL, FOR EXAMPLE, *ME*.
I'M NOT QUITE SURE I TRUST YOU, RYOKO, BUT--
LISTEN, BOY!
YOU'RE NOT THE ONLY ONE...
...WHO WANTS TO SAVE ENJU. YOU AT LEAST KNOW THAT, RIGHT?

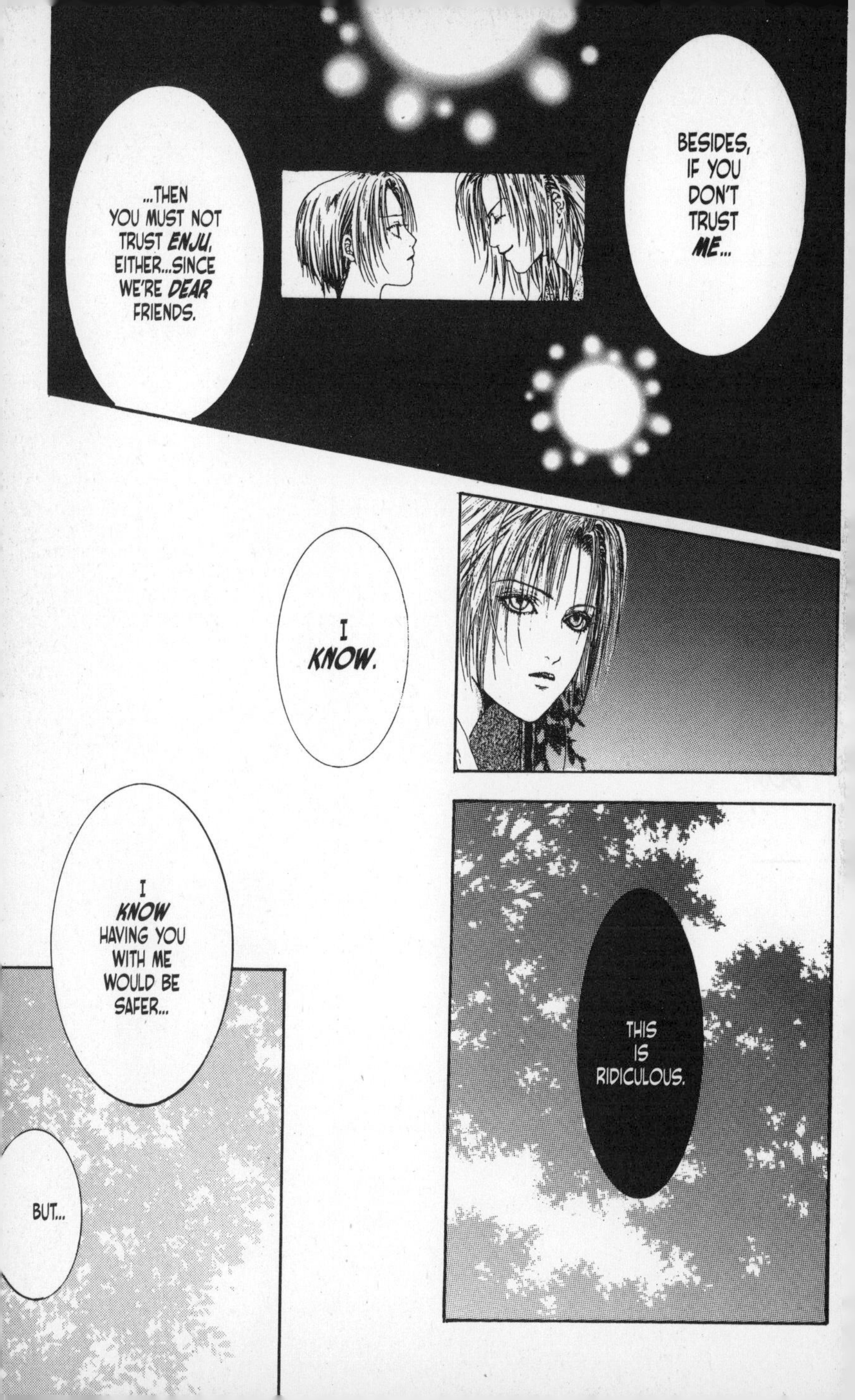
BESIDES, IF YOU DON'T TRUST ME...
...THEN YOU MUST NOT TRUST ENJU, EITHER...SINCE WE'RE DEAR FRIENDS.
I KNOW.
THIS IS RIDICULOUS.
I KNOW HAVING YOU WITH ME WOULD BE SAFER...
BUT...

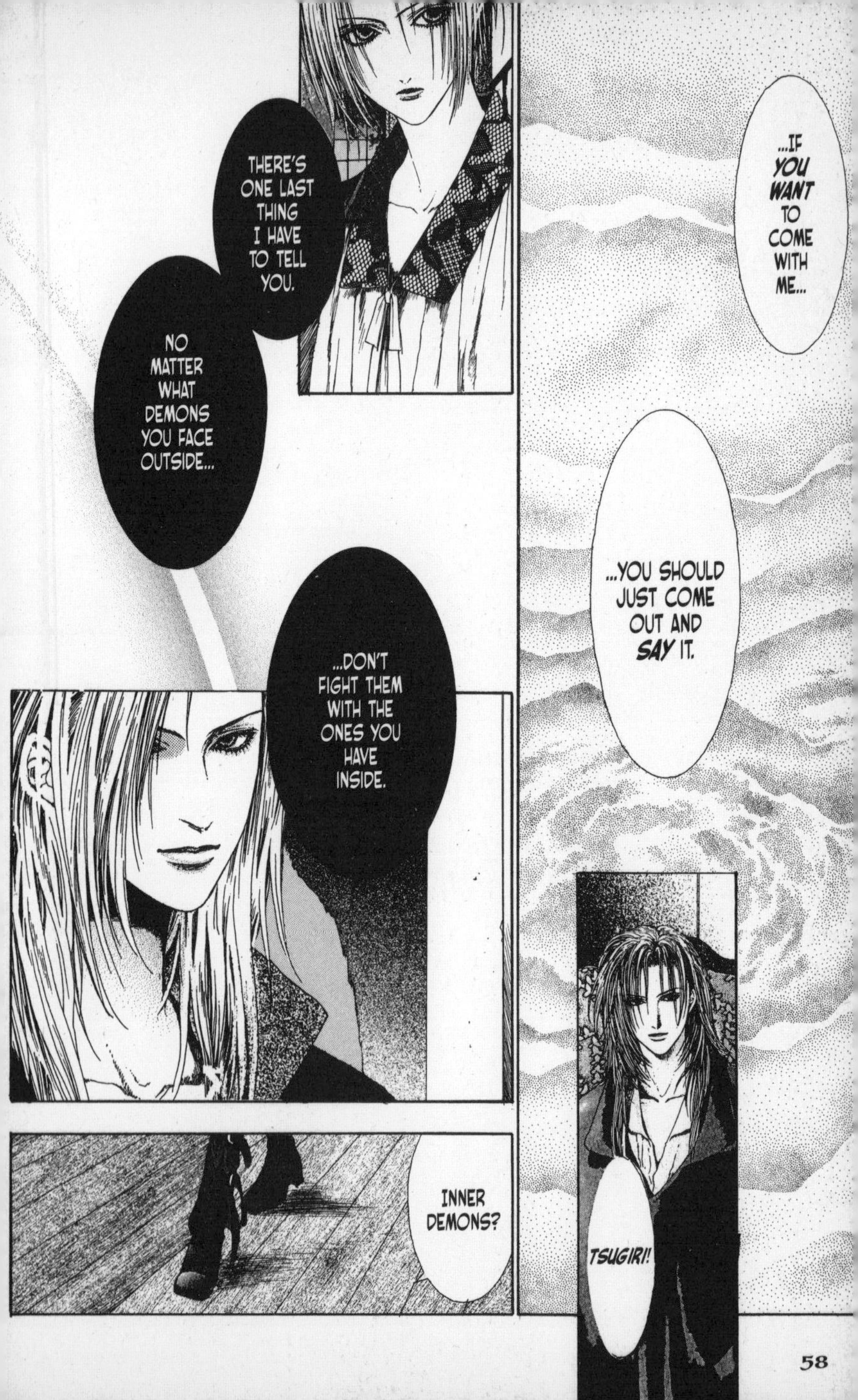
...IF *YOU WANT* TO COME WITH ME...
...YOU SHOULD JUST COME OUT AND *SAY* IT.
TSUGIRI!
THERE'S ONE LAST THING I HAVE TO TELL YOU.
NO MATTER WHAT DEMONS YOU FACE OUTSIDE...
...DON'T FIGHT THEM WITH THE ONES YOU HAVE INSIDE.
INNER DEMONS?

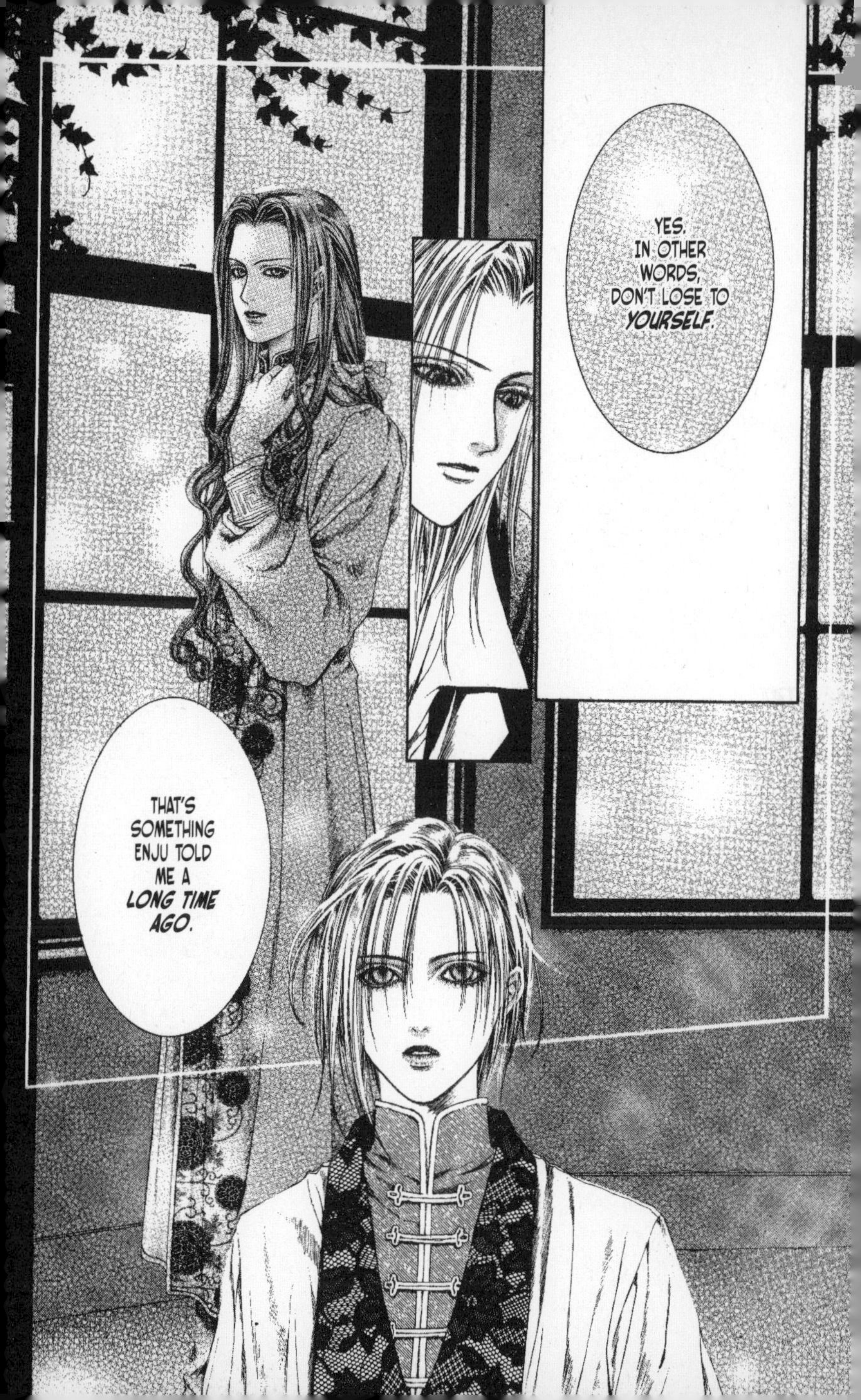
YES. IN OTHER WORDS, DON'T LOSE TO *YOURSELF*.
THAT'S SOMETHING ENJU TOLD ME A *LONG TIME AGO*.

RIGHT.
I'LL TRY NOT TO FORGET THAT.

ALTHOUGH, I HAVE A FEELING IT WOULD HAVE BEEN MORE INSPIRING COMING FROM ENJU HIMSELF.
MUMBLE
I feel like I got cheated.
UNGRATEFUL BRAT...

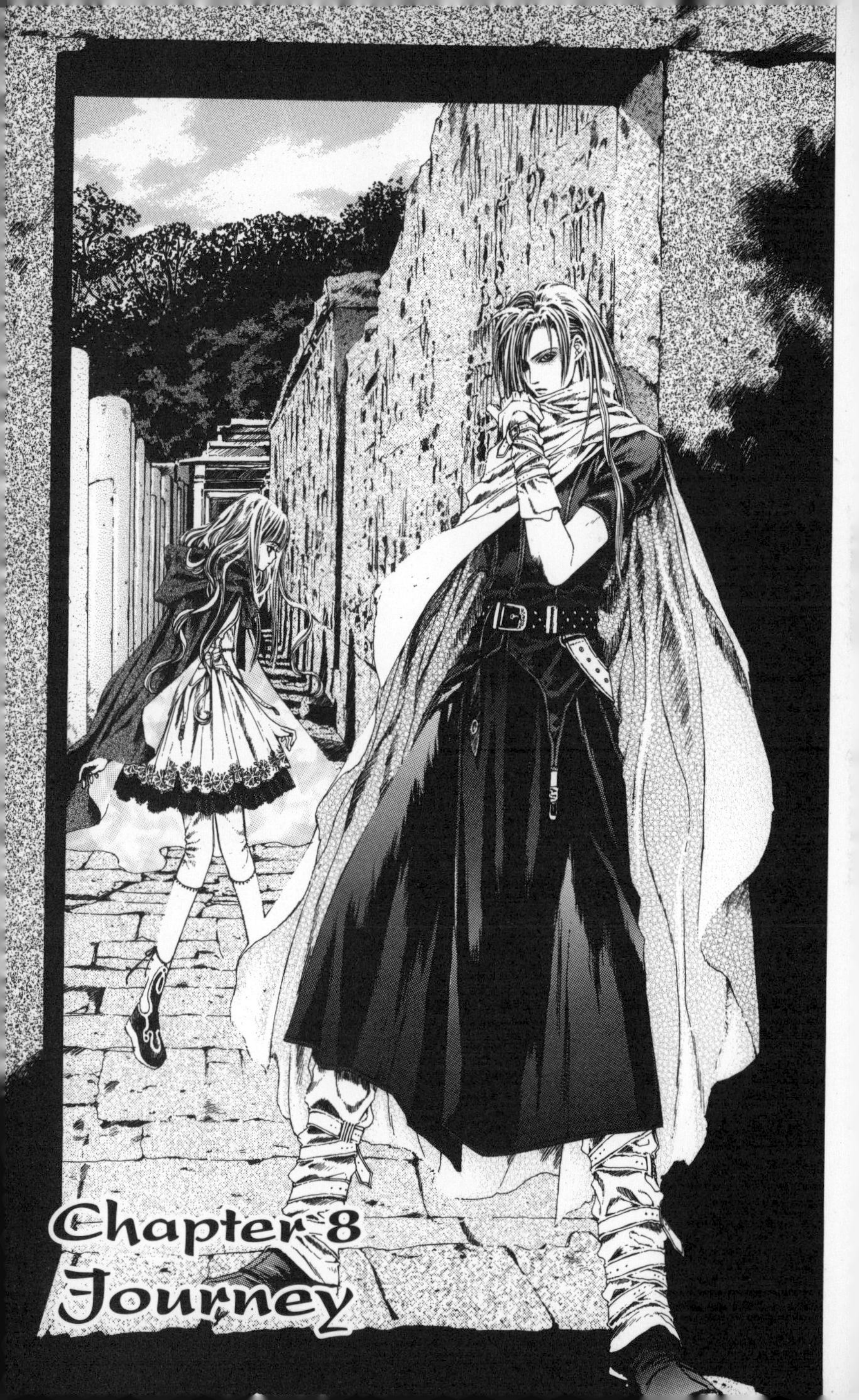
Chapter 8
Journey

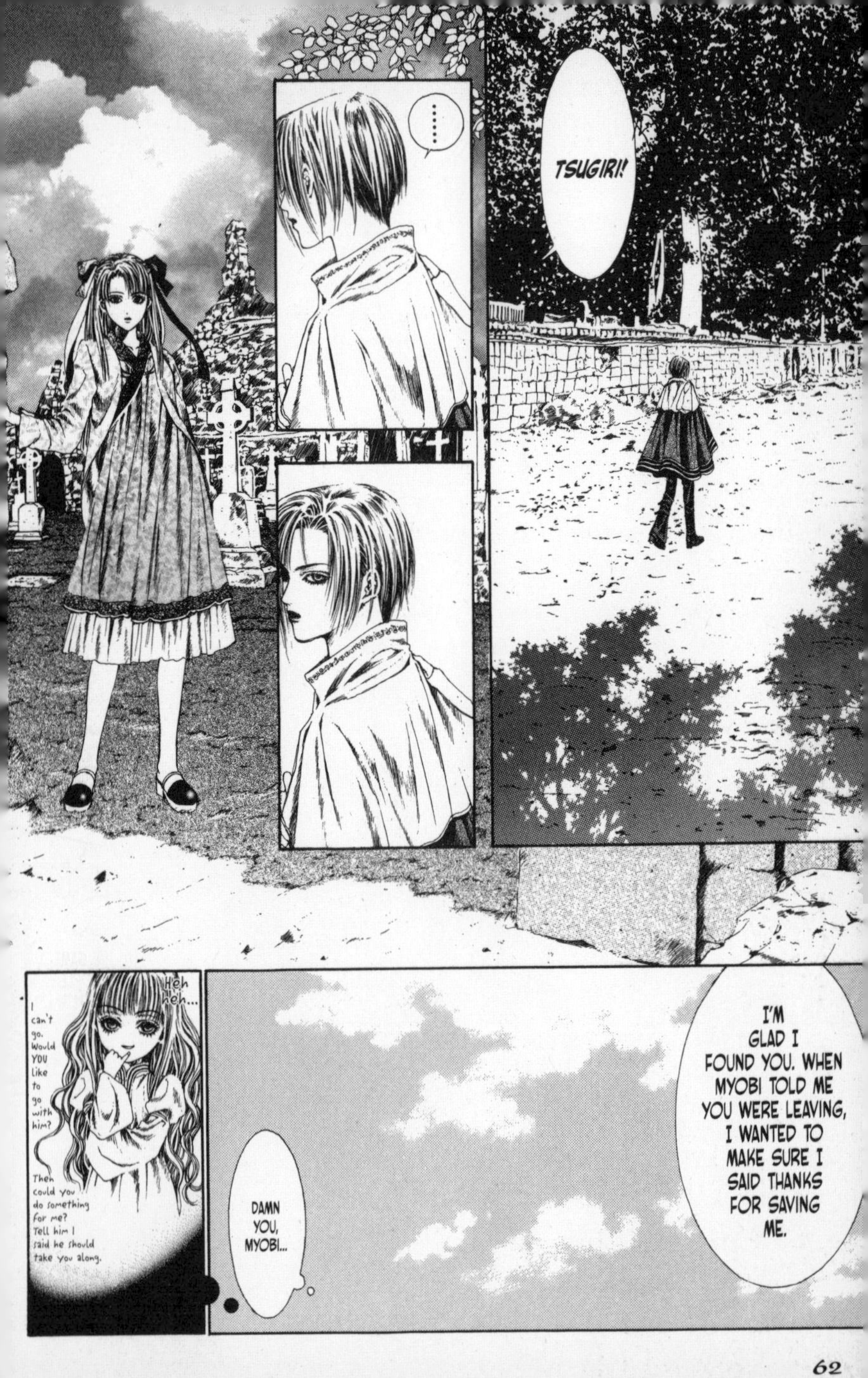
TSUGIRI!
......
I'M GLAD I FOUND YOU. WHEN MYOBI TOLD ME YOU WERE LEAVING, I WANTED TO MAKE SURE I SAID THANKS FOR SAVING ME.
DAMN YOU, MYOBI...
Heh heh...
I can't go. Would YOU like to go with him?
Then could you do something for me? Tell him I said he should take you along.

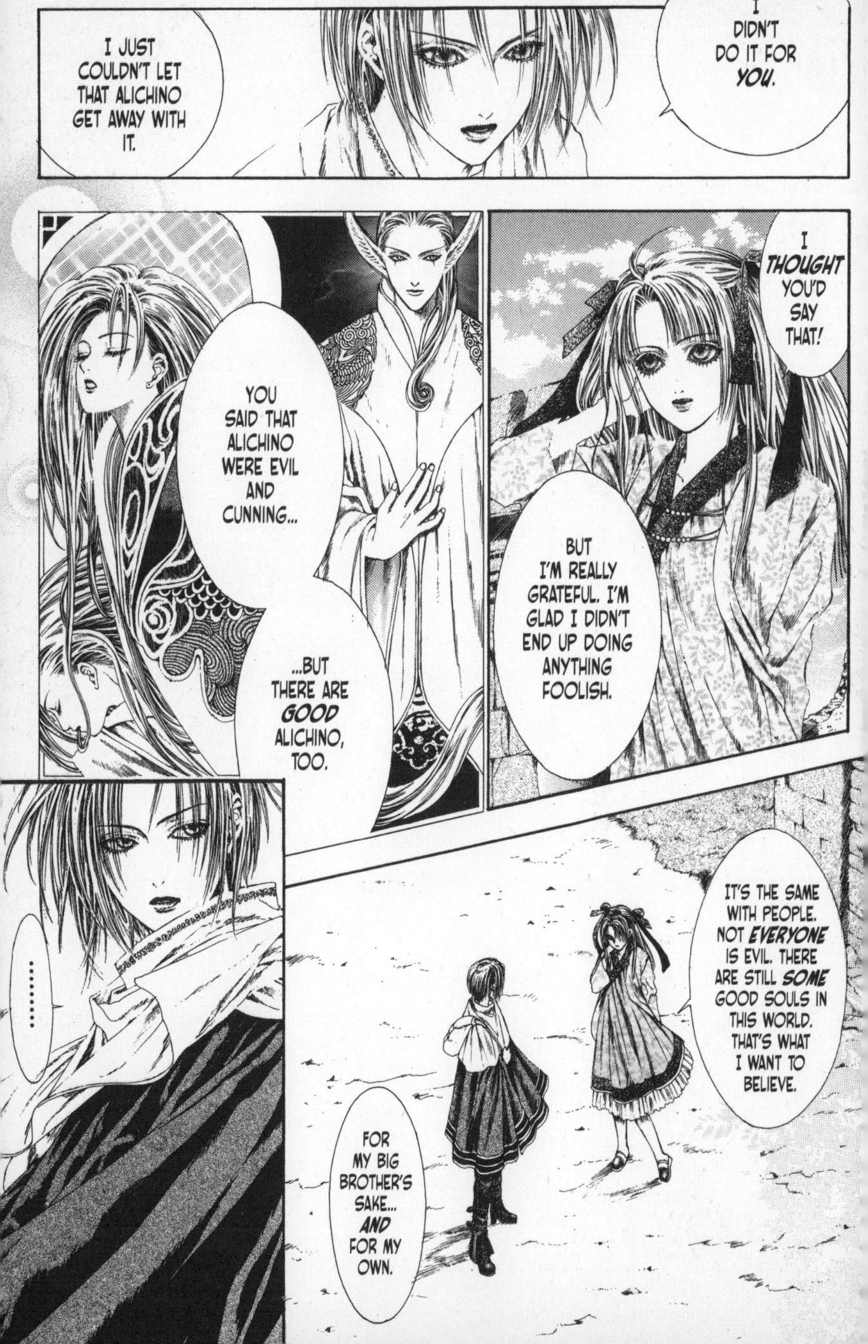
I DIDN'T DO IT FOR *YOU.*
I JUST COULDN'T LET THAT ALICHINO GET AWAY WITH IT.
I *THOUGHT* YOU'D SAY THAT!
BUT I'M REALLY GRATEFUL. I'M GLAD I DIDN'T END UP DOING ANYTHING FOOLISH.
YOU SAID THAT ALICHINO WERE EVIL AND CUNNING...
...BUT THERE ARE *GOOD* ALICHINO, TOO.
IT'S THE SAME WITH PEOPLE. NOT *EVERYONE* IS EVIL. THERE ARE STILL *SOME* GOOD SOULS IN THIS WORLD. THAT'S WHAT I WANT TO BELIEVE.
FOR MY BIG BROTHER'S SAKE... *AND* FOR MY OWN.
......

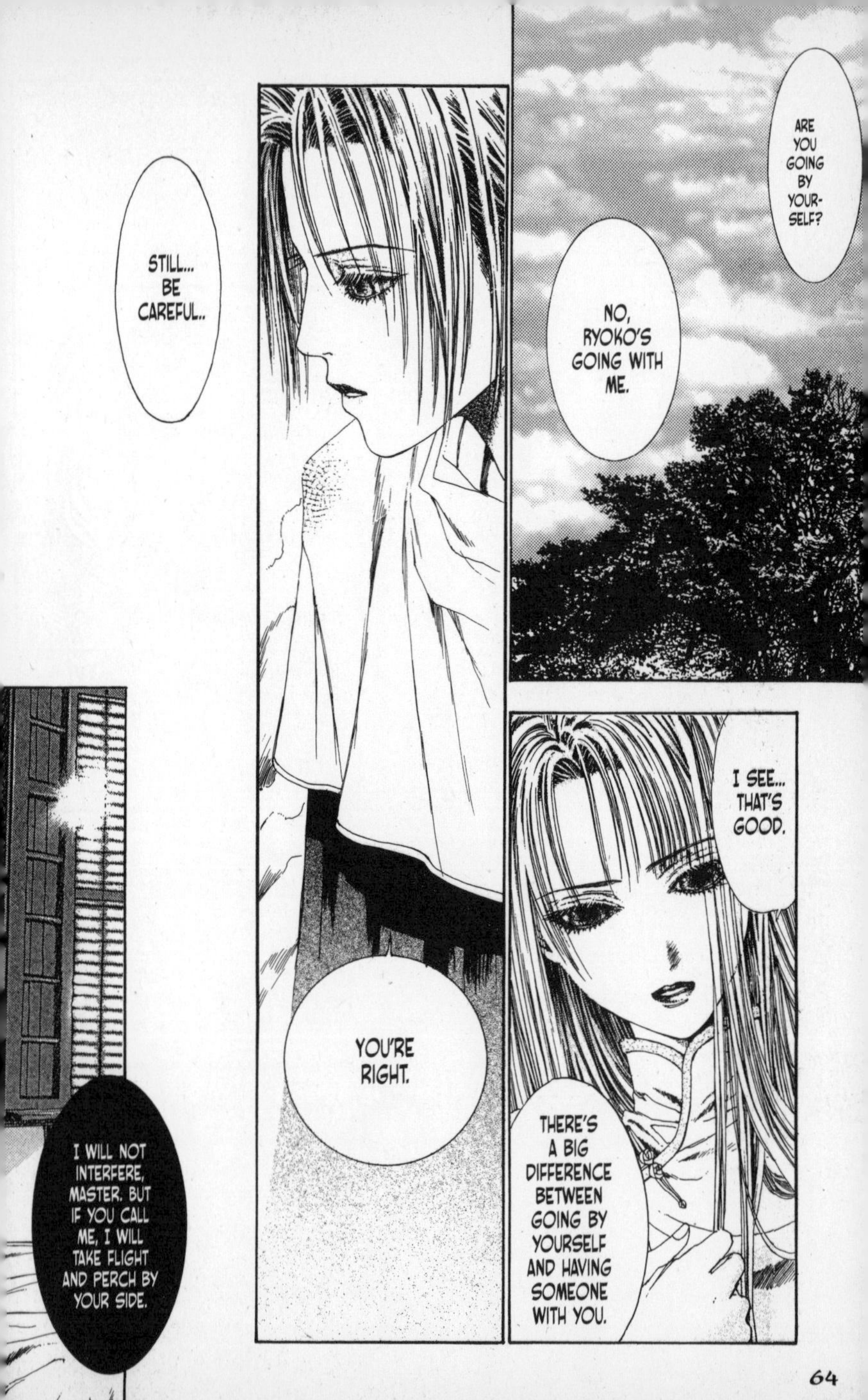
ARE YOU GOING BY YOUR-SELF?
NO, RYOKO'S GOING WITH ME.
I SEE... THAT'S GOOD.
THERE'S A BIG DIFFERENCE BETWEEN GOING BY YOURSELF AND HAVING SOMEONE WITH YOU.
YOU'RE RIGHT.
STILL... BE CAREFUL..
I WILL NOT INTERFERE, MASTER. BUT IF YOU CALL ME, I WILL TAKE FLIGHT AND PERCH BY YOUR SIDE.

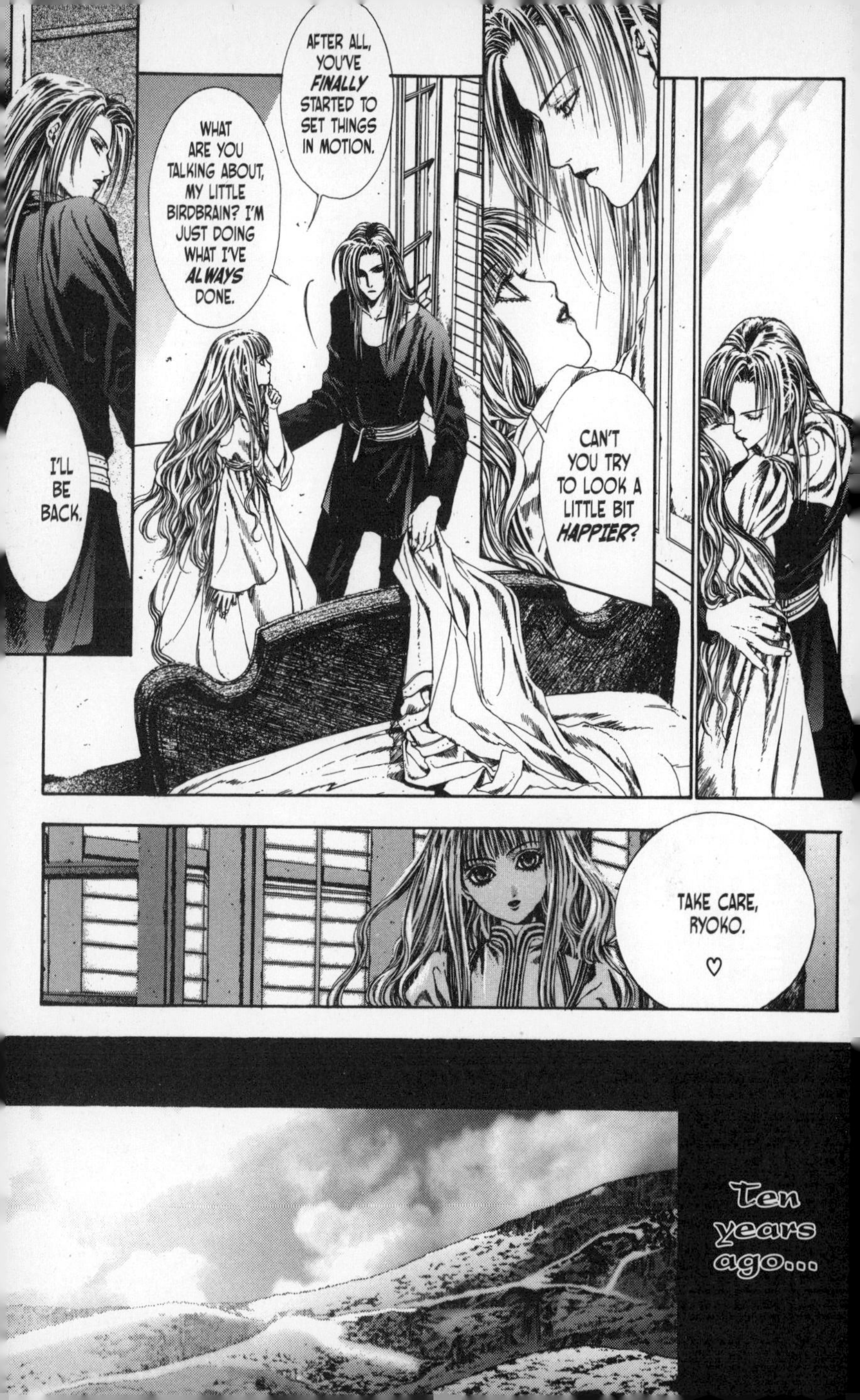
CAN'T YOU TRY TO LOOK A LITTLE BIT *HAPPIER?*
AFTER ALL, YOU'VE *FINALLY* STARTED TO SET THINGS IN MOTION.
WHAT ARE YOU TALKING ABOUT, MY LITTLE BIRDBRAIN? I'M JUST DOING WHAT I'VE *ALWAYS* DONE.
I'LL BE BACK.
TAKE CARE, RYOKO. ♡
Ten years ago...

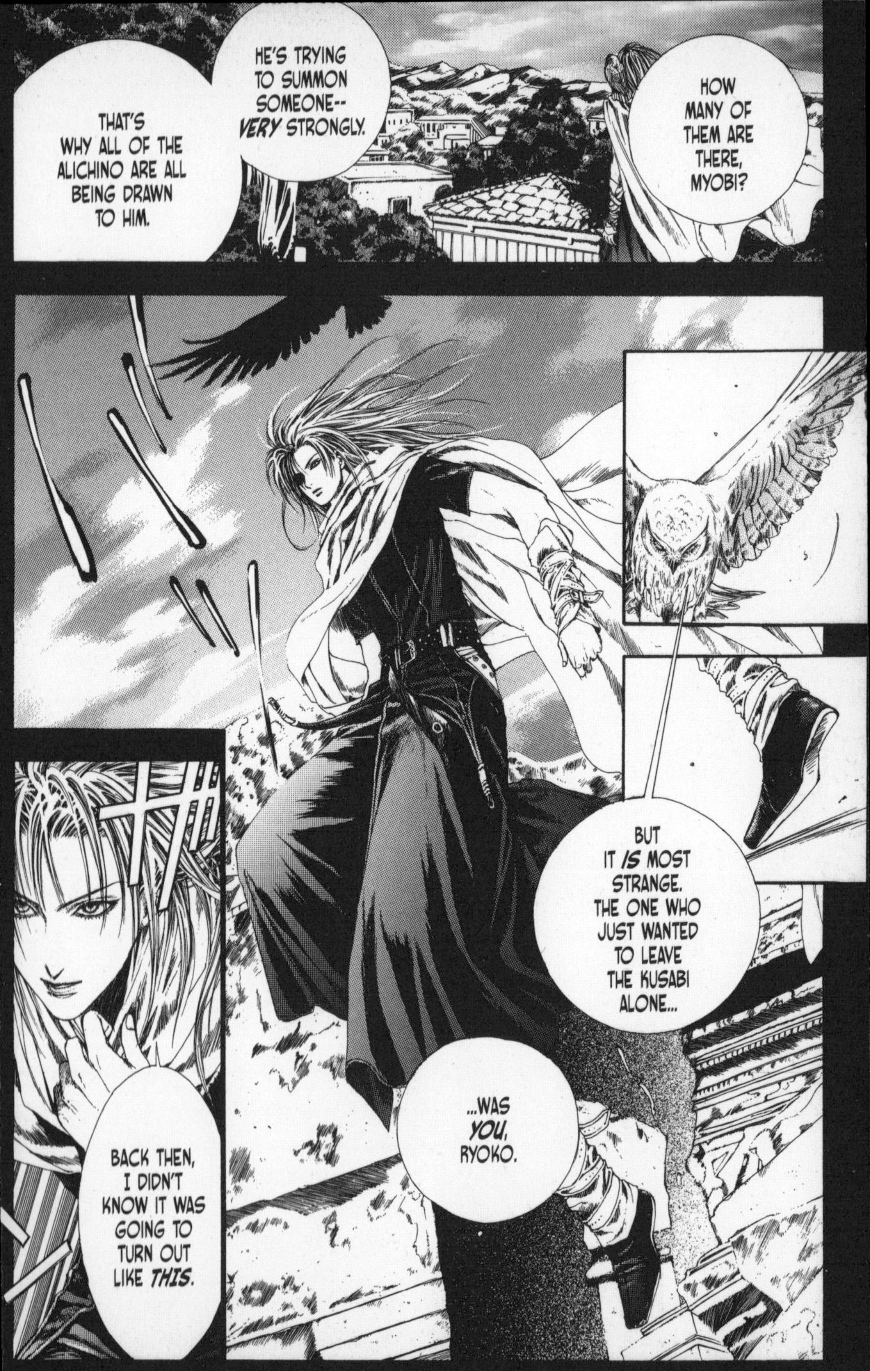
HOW MANY OF THEM ARE THERE, MYOBI?
HE'S TRYING TO SUMMON SOMEONE-- *VERY* STRONGLY.
THAT'S WHY ALL OF THE ALICHINO ARE ALL BEING DRAWN TO HIM.
BUT IT *IS* MOST STRANGE. THE ONE WHO JUST WANTED TO LEAVE THE KUSABI ALONE...
...WAS *YOU*, RYOKO.
BACK THEN, I DIDN'T KNOW IT WAS GOING TO TURN OUT LIKE *THIS*.

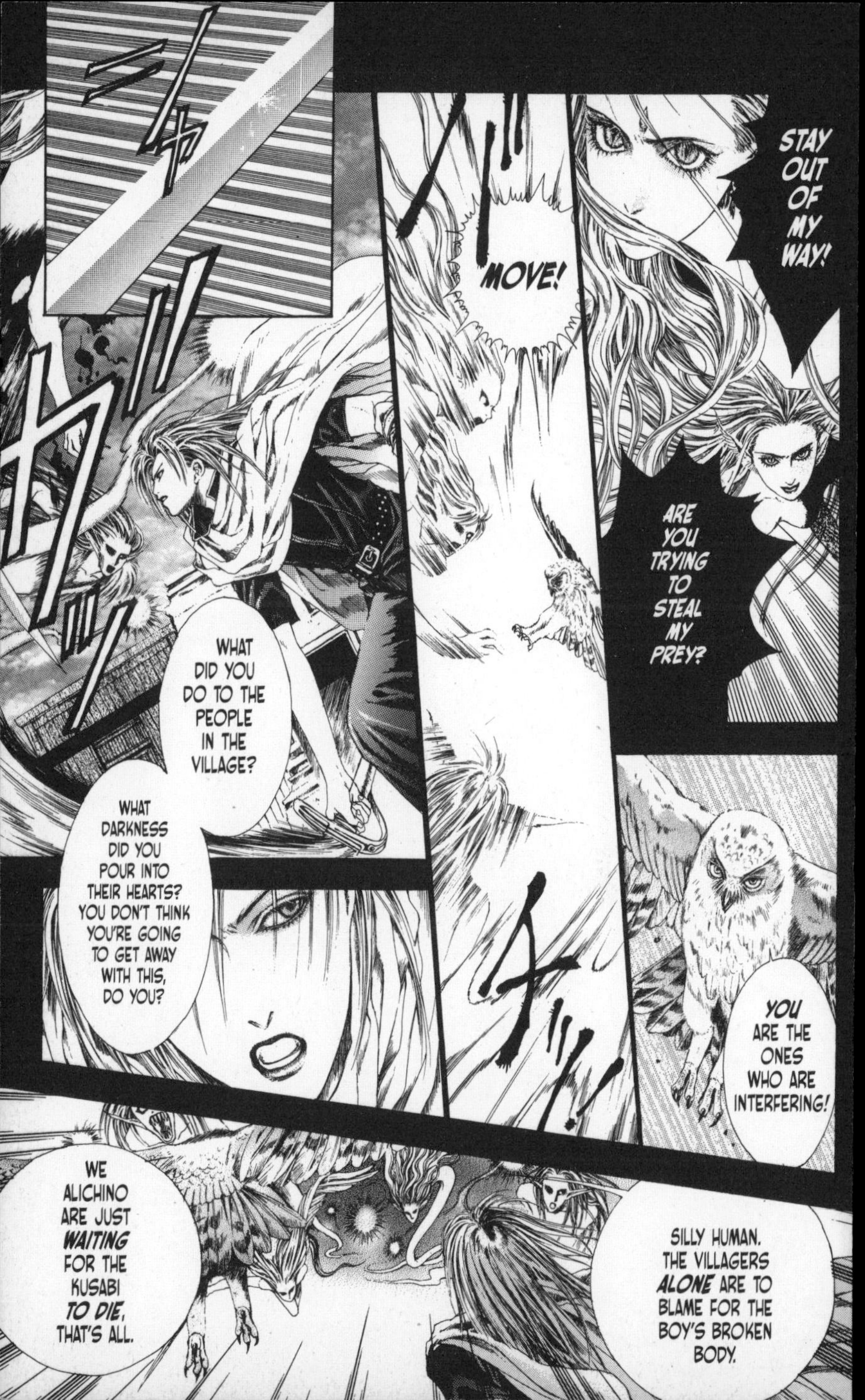
STAY OUT OF MY WAY!
ARE YOU TRYING TO STEAL MY PREY?
MOVE!
WHAT DID YOU DO TO THE PEOPLE IN THE VILLAGE?
YOU ARE THE ONES WHO ARE INTERFERING!
WHAT DARKNESS DID YOU POUR INTO THEIR HEARTS? YOU DON'T THINK YOU'RE GOING TO GET AWAY WITH THIS, DO YOU?
SILLY HUMAN. THE VILLAGERS ALONE ARE TO BLAME FOR THE BOY'S BROKEN BODY.
WE ALICHINO ARE JUST WAITING FOR THE KUSABI TO DIE, THAT'S ALL.

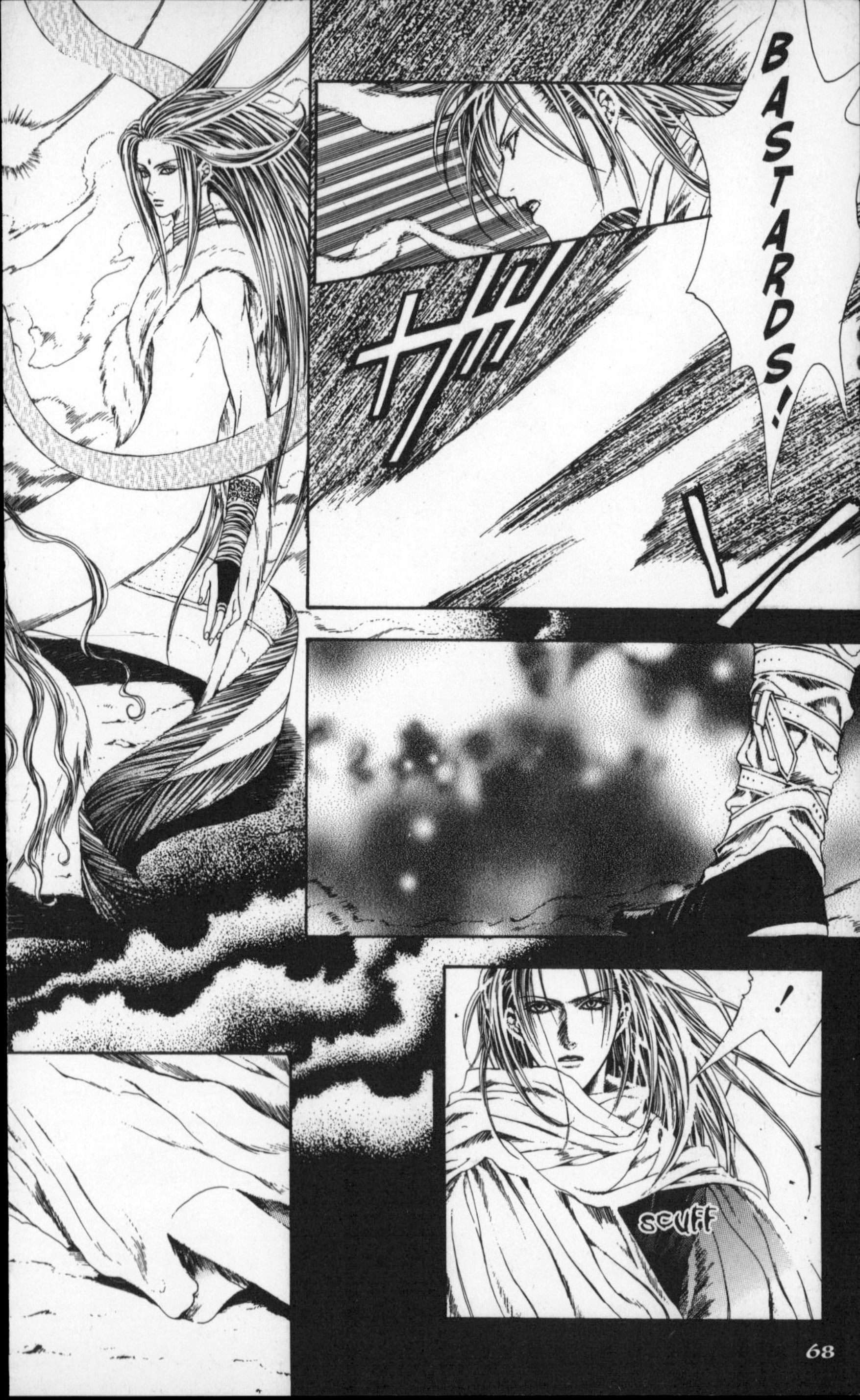
BASTARDS!!
!
SCUFF

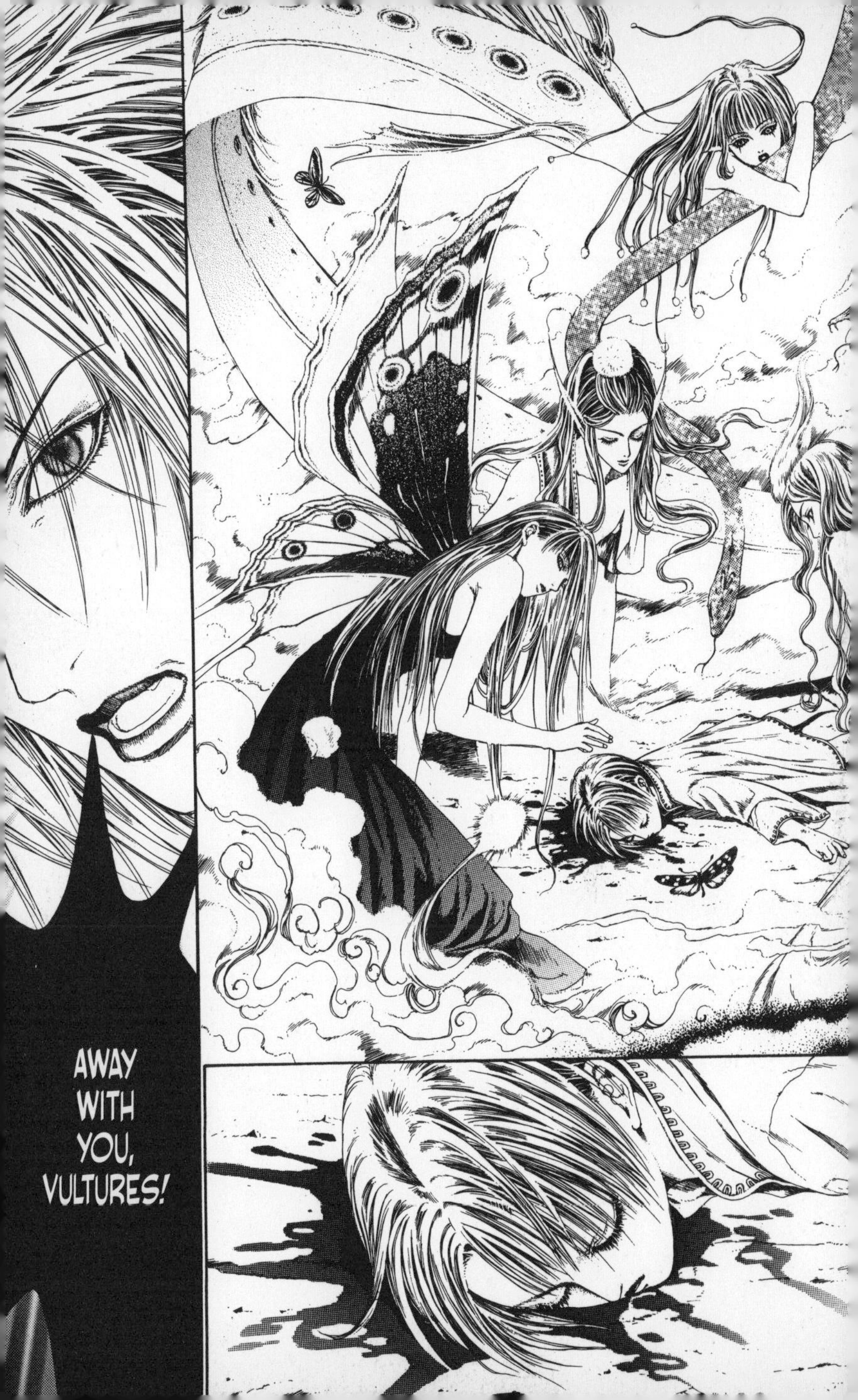
AWAY WITH YOU, VULTURES!

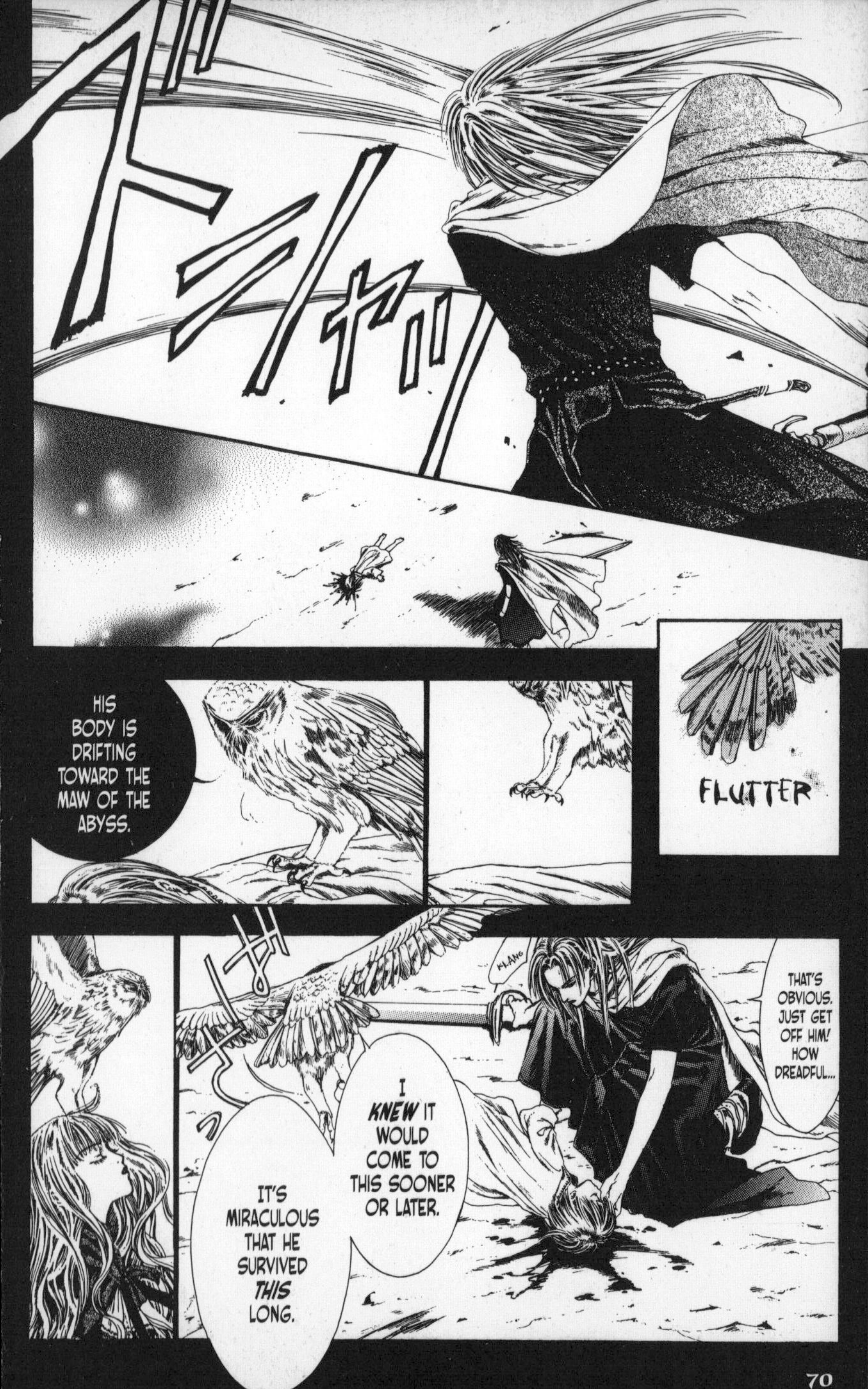
ドシャッ
FLUTTER
HIS BODY IS DRIFTING TOWARD THE MAW OF THE ABYSS.
KLANG
THAT'S OBVIOUS. JUST GET OFF HIM! HOW DREADFUL...
I *KNEW* IT WOULD COME TO THIS SOONER OR LATER.
IT'S MIRACULOUS THAT HE SURVIVED *THIS* LONG.

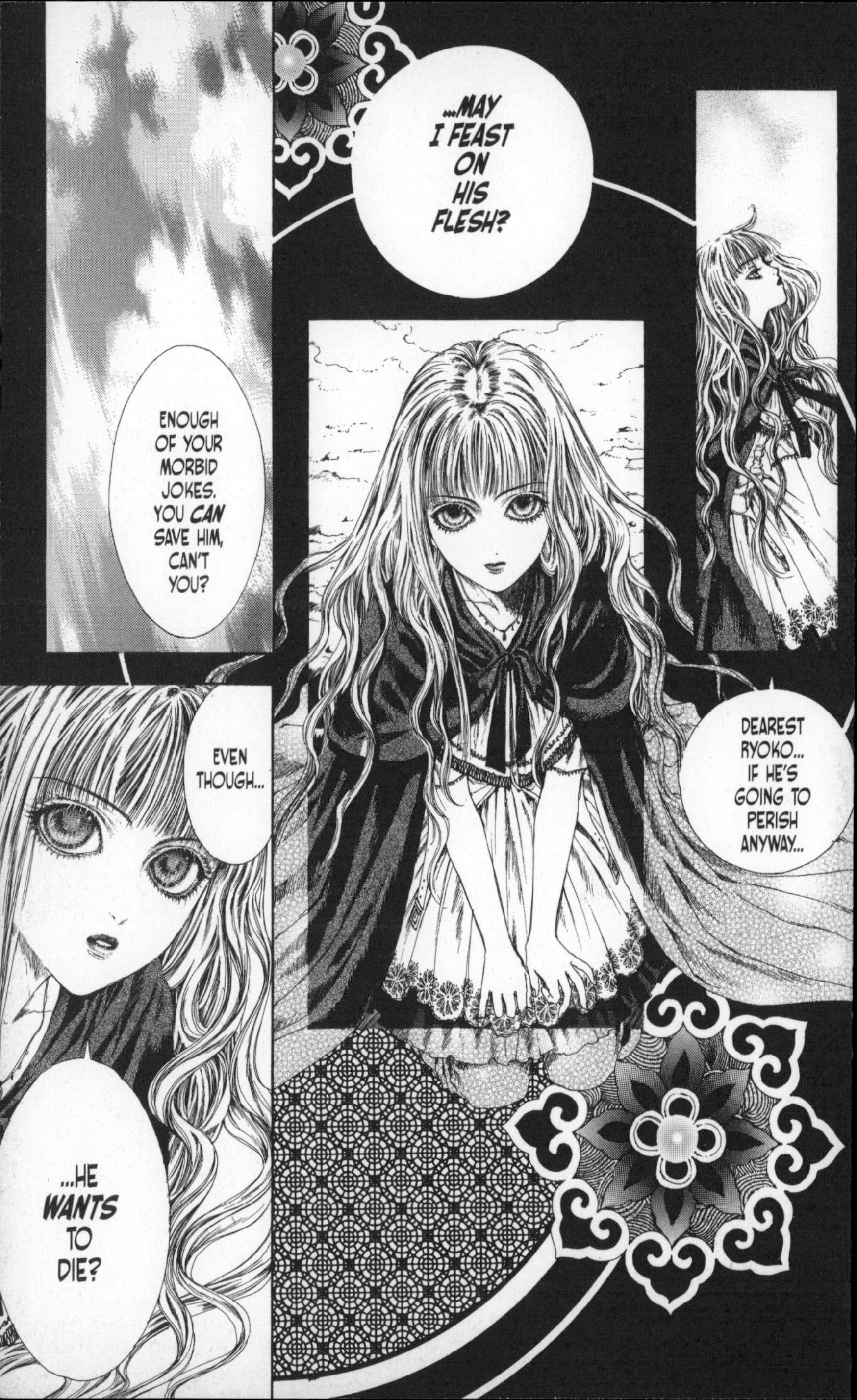
DEAREST RYOKO... IF HE'S GOING TO PERISH ANYWAY...
...MAY I FEAST ON HIS FLESH?
ENOUGH OF YOUR MORBID JOKES. YOU *CAN* SAVE HIM, CAN'T YOU?
EVEN THOUGH...
...HE *WANTS* TO DIE?

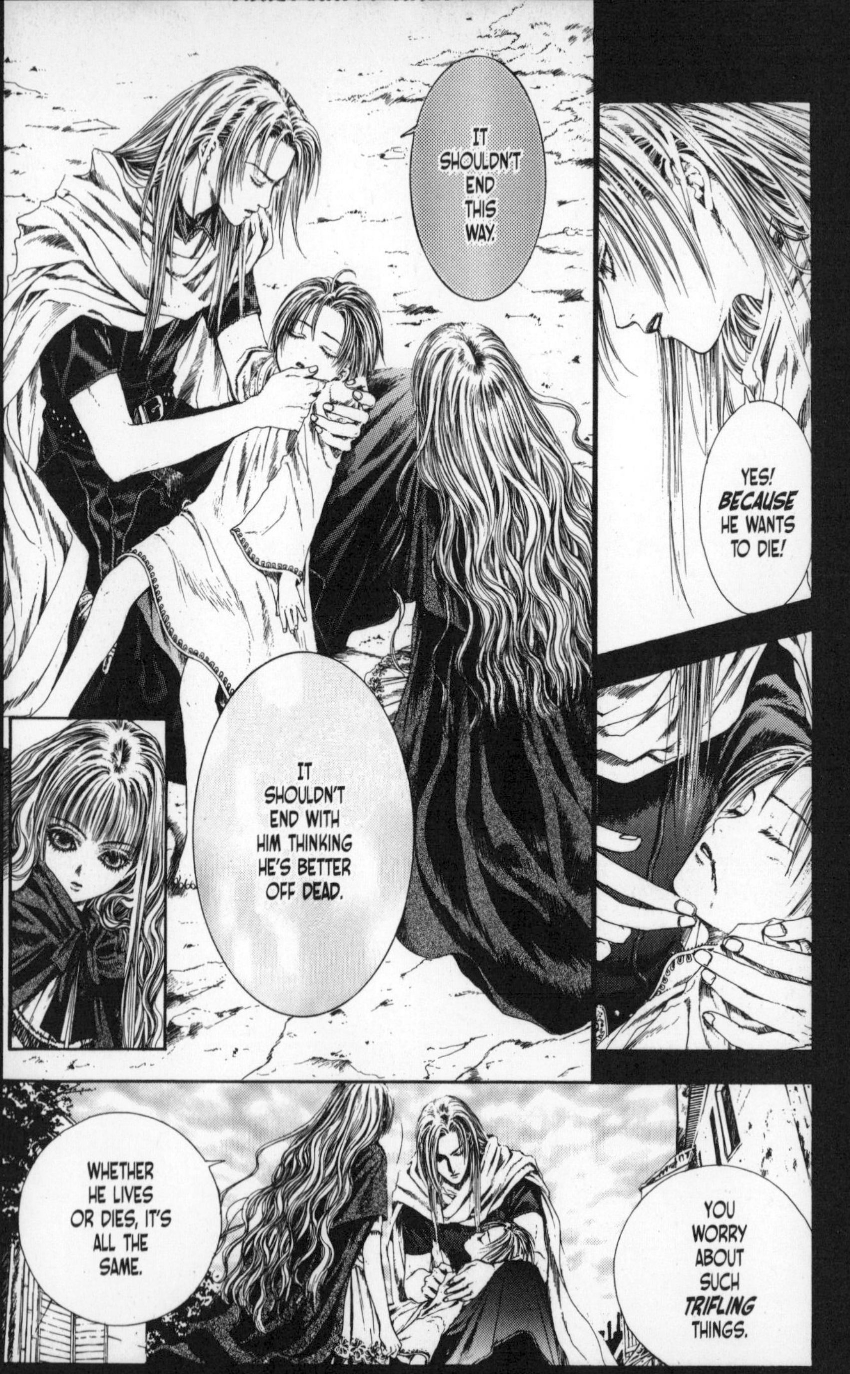
YES! *BECAUSE* HE WANTS TO DIE!
IT SHOULDN'T END THIS WAY.
IT SHOULDN'T END WITH HIM THINKING HE'S BETTER OFF DEAD.
YOU WORRY ABOUT SUCH *TRIFLING* THINGS.
WHETHER HE LIVES OR DIES, IT'S ALL THE SAME.

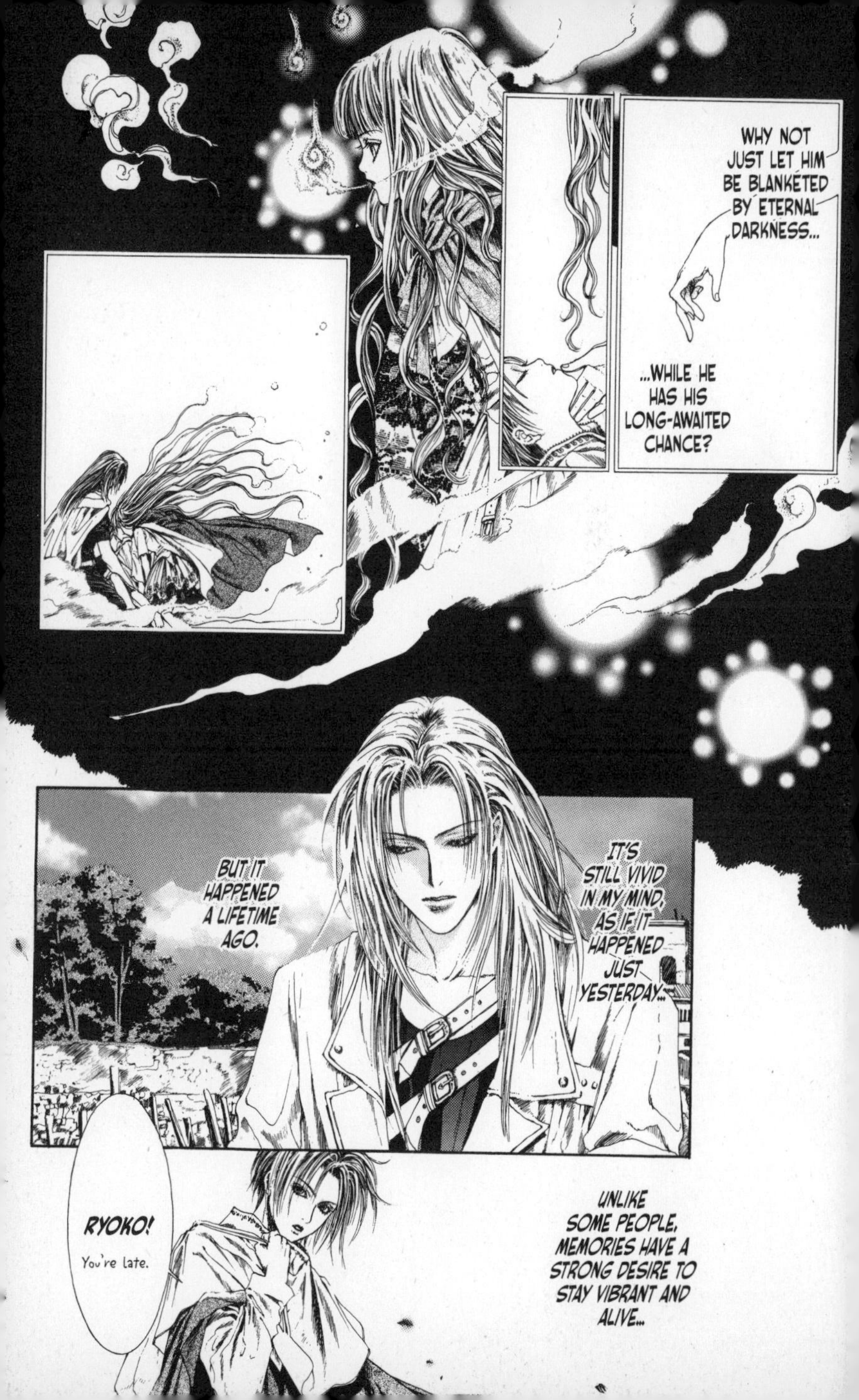
WHY NOT JUST LET HIM BE BLANKETED BY ETERNAL DARKNESS...
...WHILE HE HAS HIS LONG-AWAITED CHANCE?
IT'S STILL VIVID IN MY MIND, AS IF IT HAPPENED JUST YESTERDAY...
BUT IT HAPPENED A LIFETIME AGO.
UNLIKE SOME PEOPLE, MEMORIES HAVE A STRONG DESIRE TO STAY VIBRANT AND ALIVE...
RYOKO! You're late.

SKSSH

...ARE SO BEAUTIFUL IT DISGUSTS ME.

. . . .

IT'S A PERFECT BEAUTY... BUT AN UNNATURAL BEAUTY. THEY ARE PEACOCKISH AND ORNATE... AND I'VE HATED THAT KIND OF PAGEANTRY EVER SINCE I WAS A CHILD.

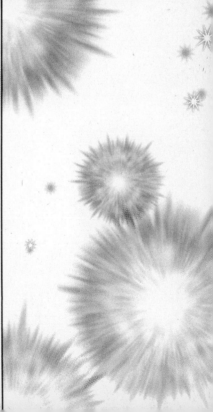

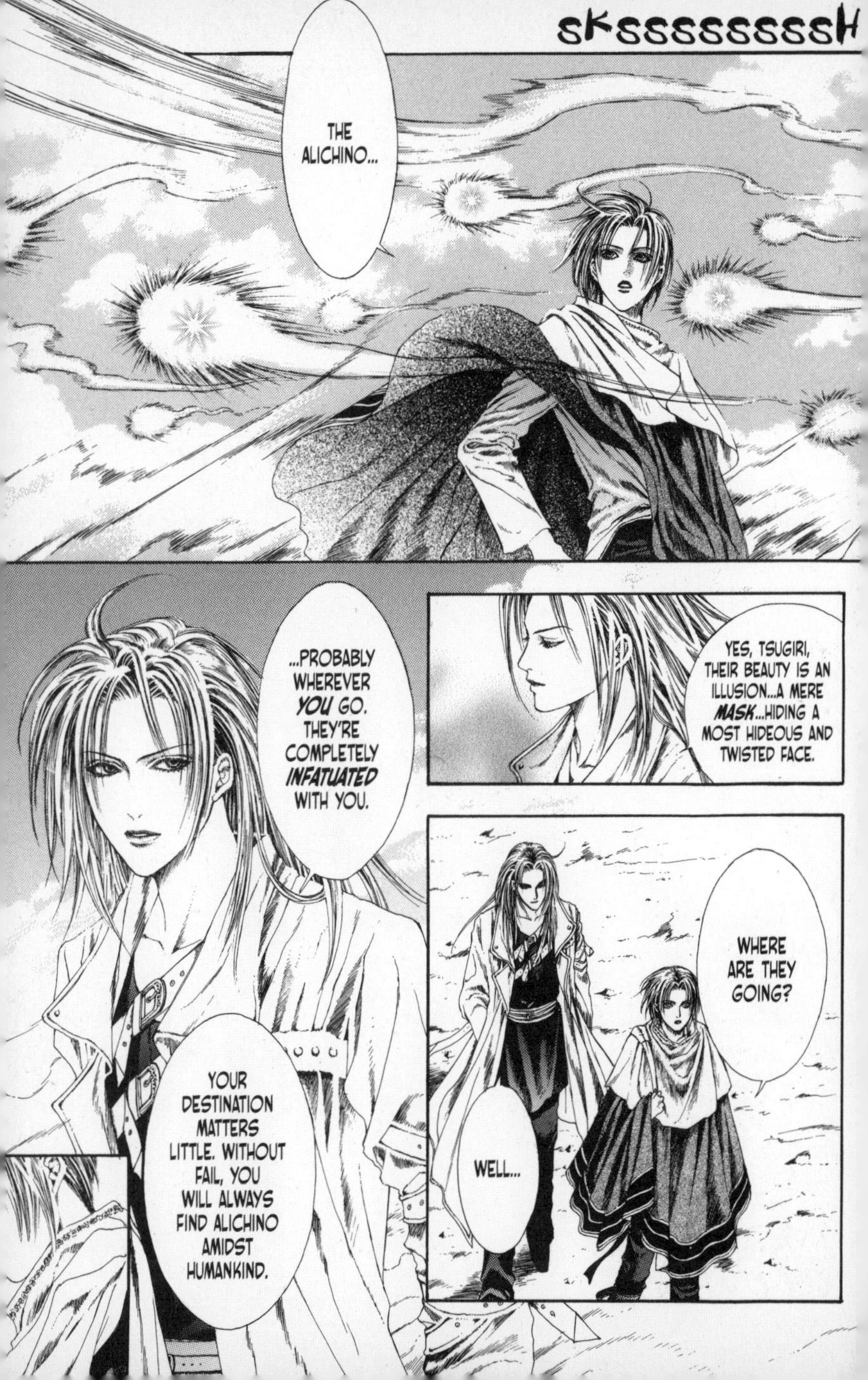
SKSSSSSSSSH
THE ALICHINO...
YES, TSUGIRI, THEIR BEAUTY IS AN ILLUSION...A MERE MASK...HIDING A MOST HIDEOUS AND TWISTED FACE.
WHERE ARE THEY GOING?
WELL...
...PROBABLY WHEREVER YOU GO. THEY'RE COMPLETELY INFATUATED WITH YOU.
YOUR DESTINATION MATTERS LITTLE. WITHOUT FAIL, YOU WILL ALWAYS FIND ALICHINO AMIDST HUMANKIND.

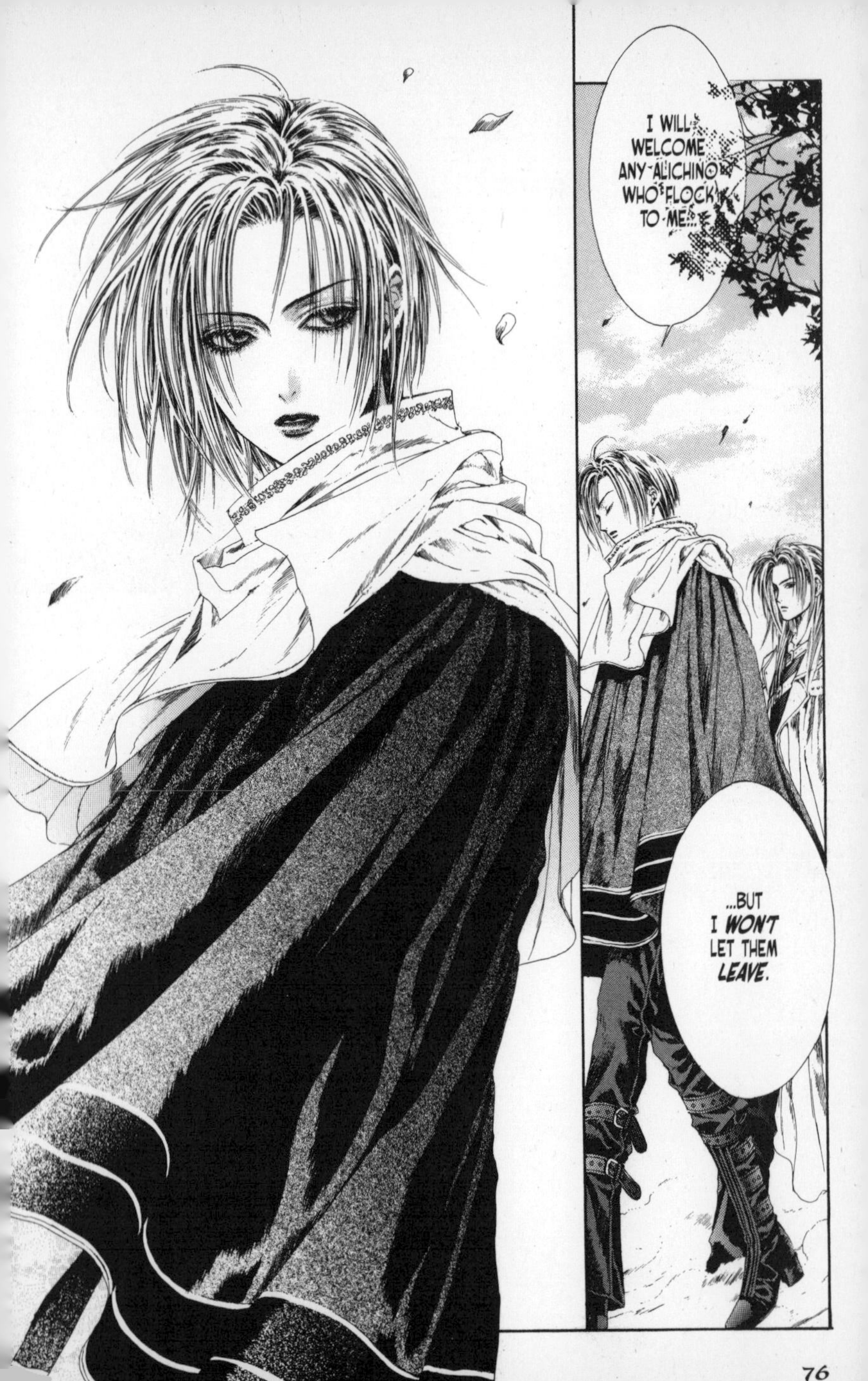
I WILL WELCOME ANY ALICHINO WHO FLOCK TO ME...
...BUT I *WON'T* LET THEM *LEAVE*.

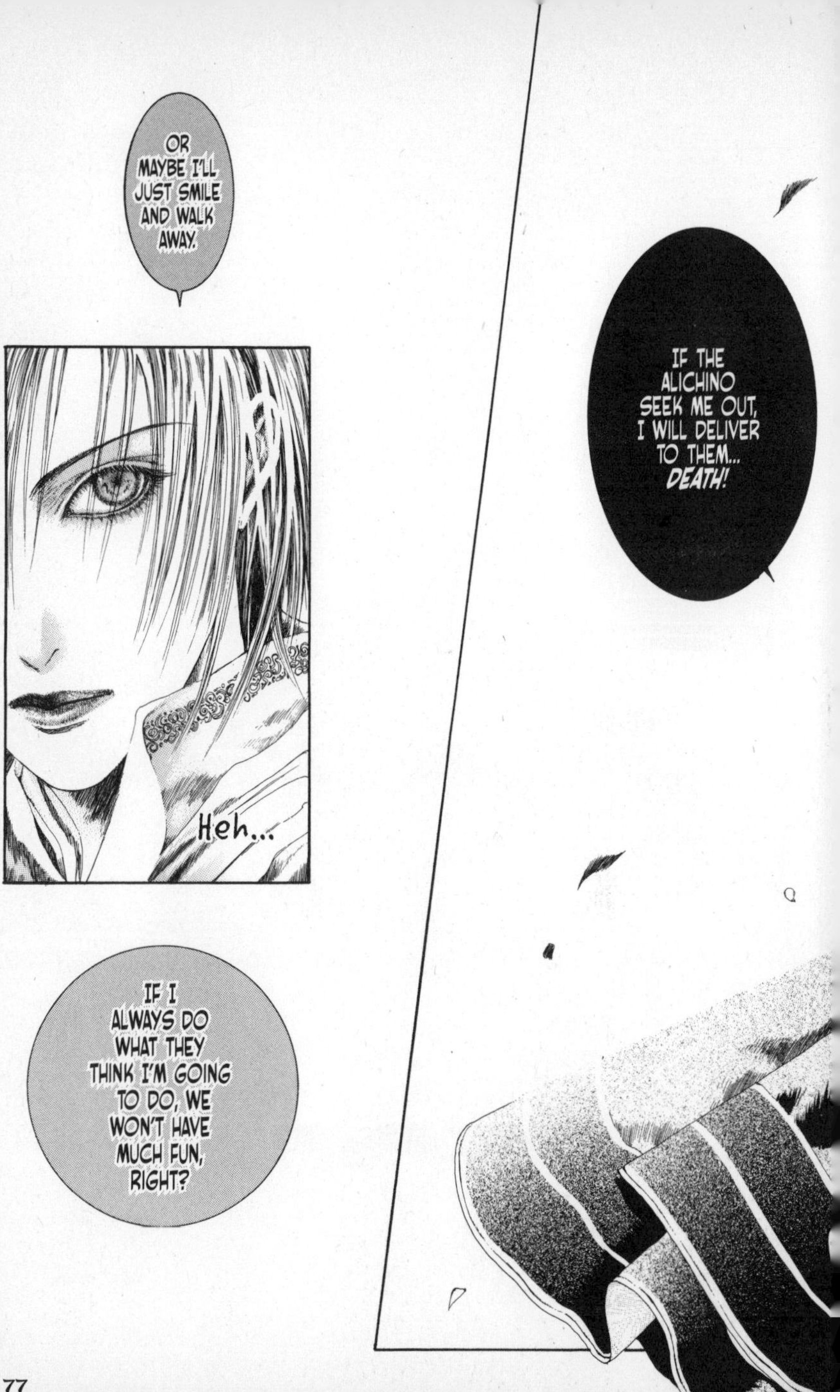
IF THE ALICHINO SEEK ME OUT, I WILL DELIVER TO THEM... DEATH!
OR MAYBE I'LL JUST SMILE AND WALK AWAY.
Heh...
IF I ALWAYS DO WHAT THEY THINK I'M GOING TO DO, WE WON'T HAVE MUCH FUN, RIGHT?

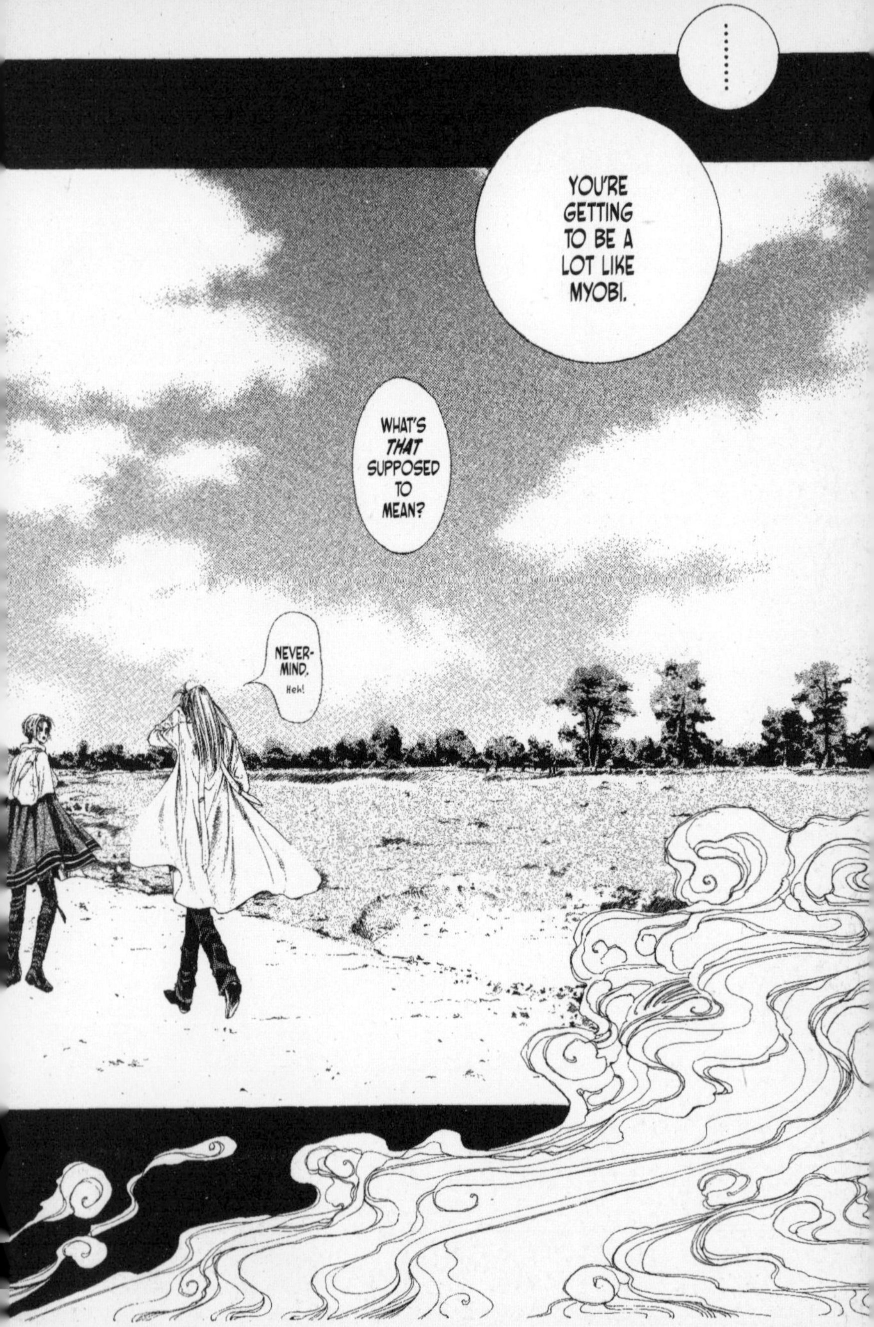
......
YOU'RE GETTING TO BE A LOT LIKE MYOBI.
WHAT'S *THAT* SUPPOSED TO MEAN?
NEVER-MIND.
Heh!

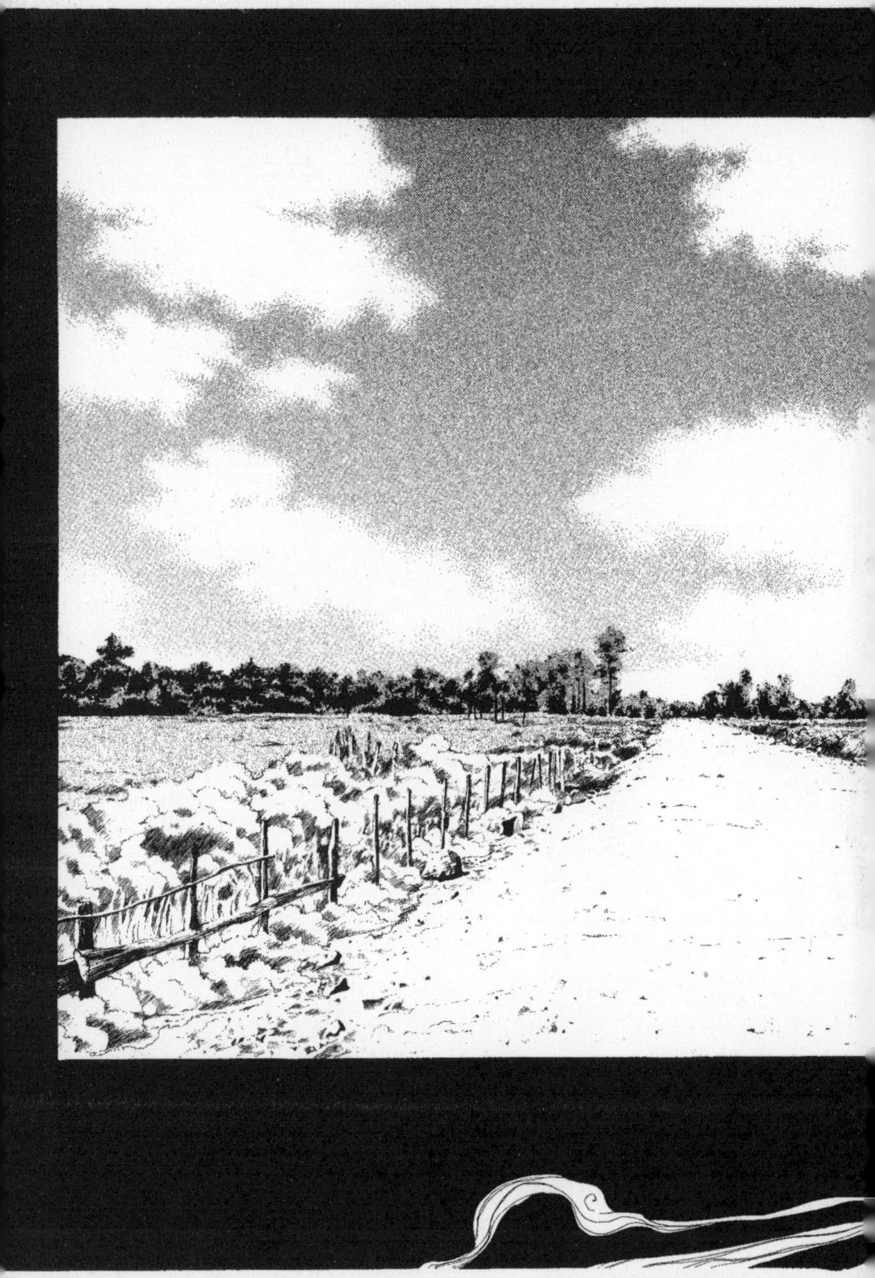

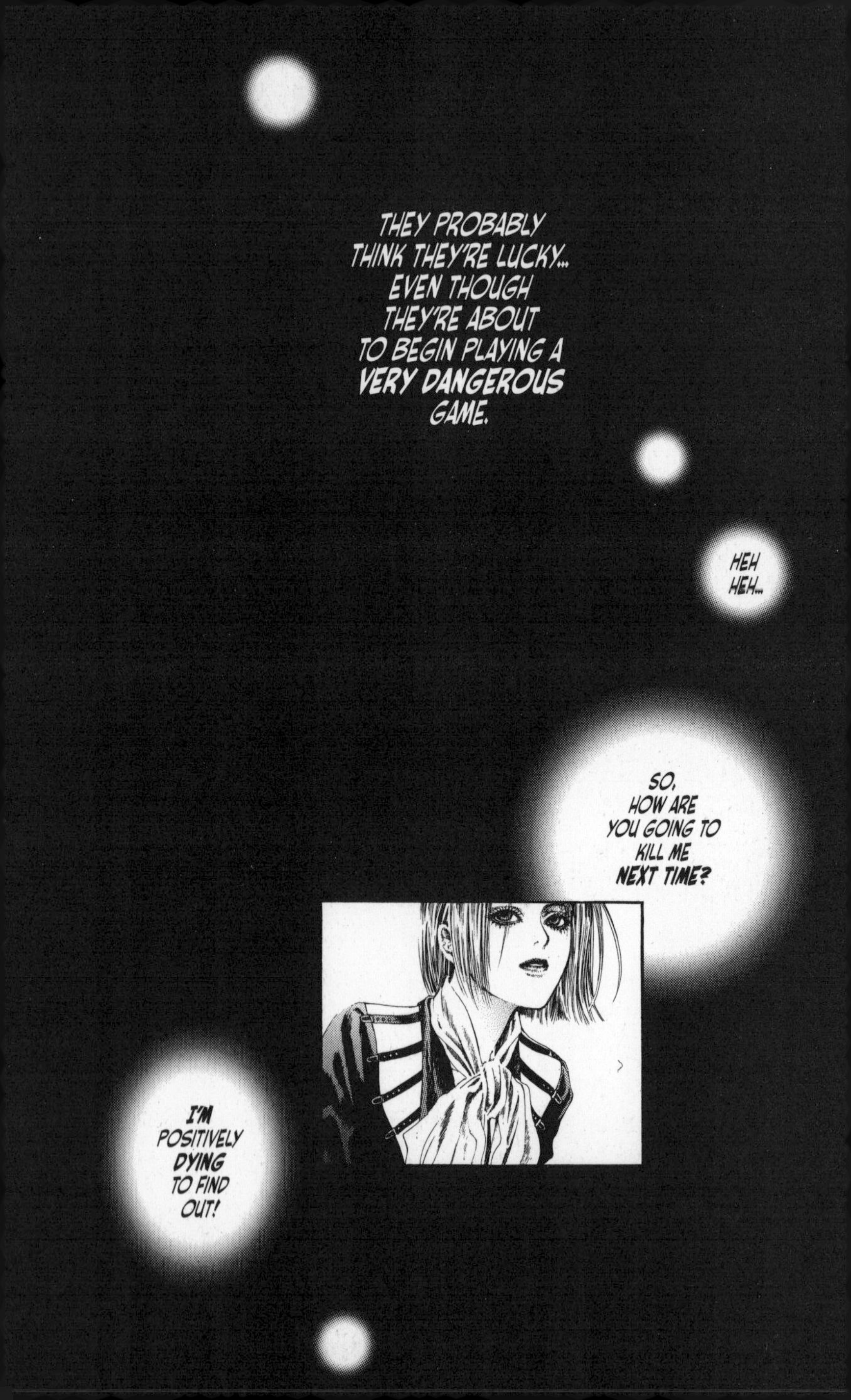
THEY PROBABLY THINK THEY'RE LUCKY... EVEN THOUGH THEY'RE ABOUT TO BEGIN PLAYING A VERY DANGEROUS GAME.
HEH HEH...
SO, HOW ARE YOU GOING TO KILL ME NEXT TIME?
I'M POSITIVELY DYING TO FIND OUT!

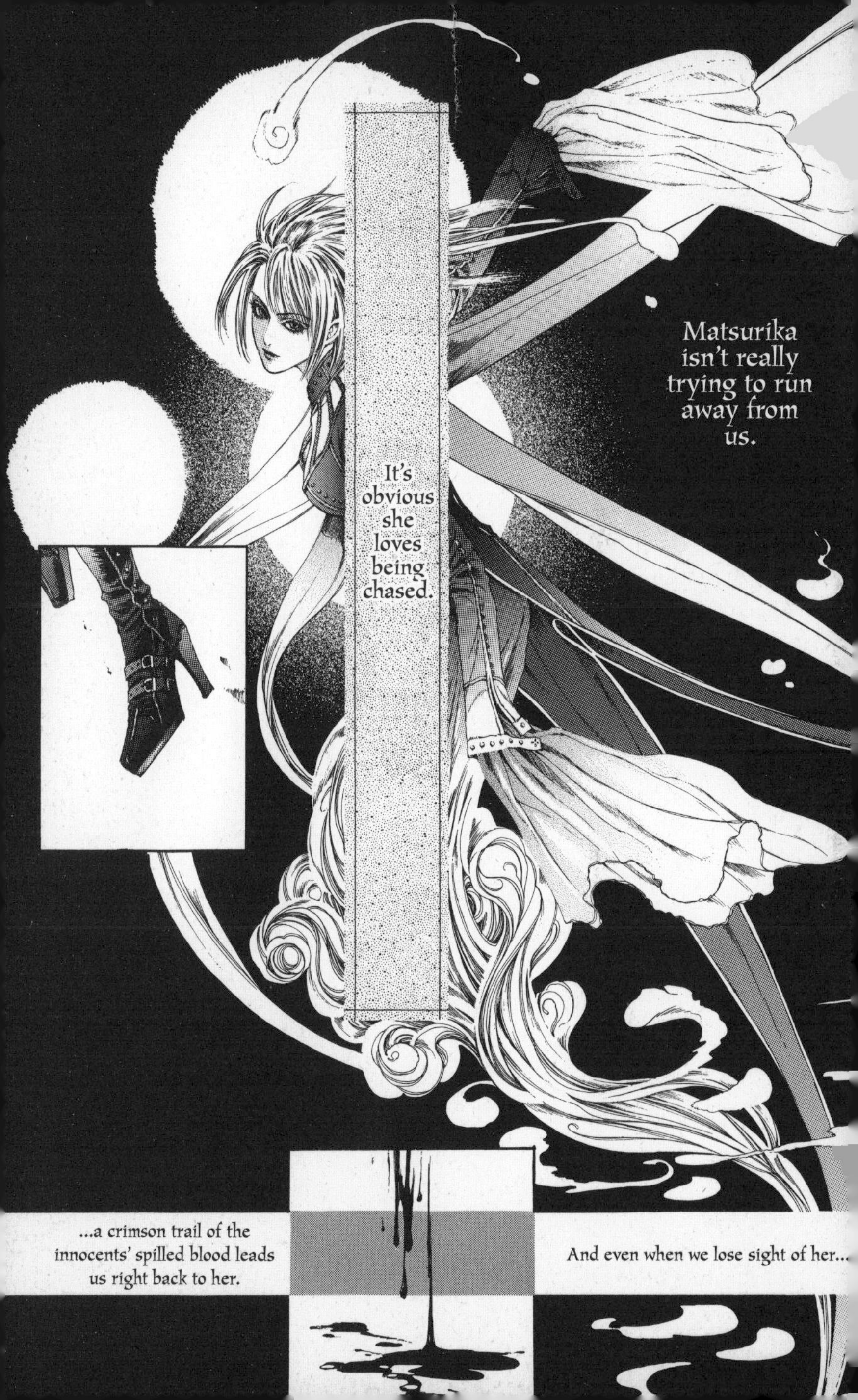
Matsurika isn't really trying to run away from us.
It's obvious she loves being chased.
And even when we lose sight of her...
...a crimson trail of the innocents' spilled blood leads us right back to her.

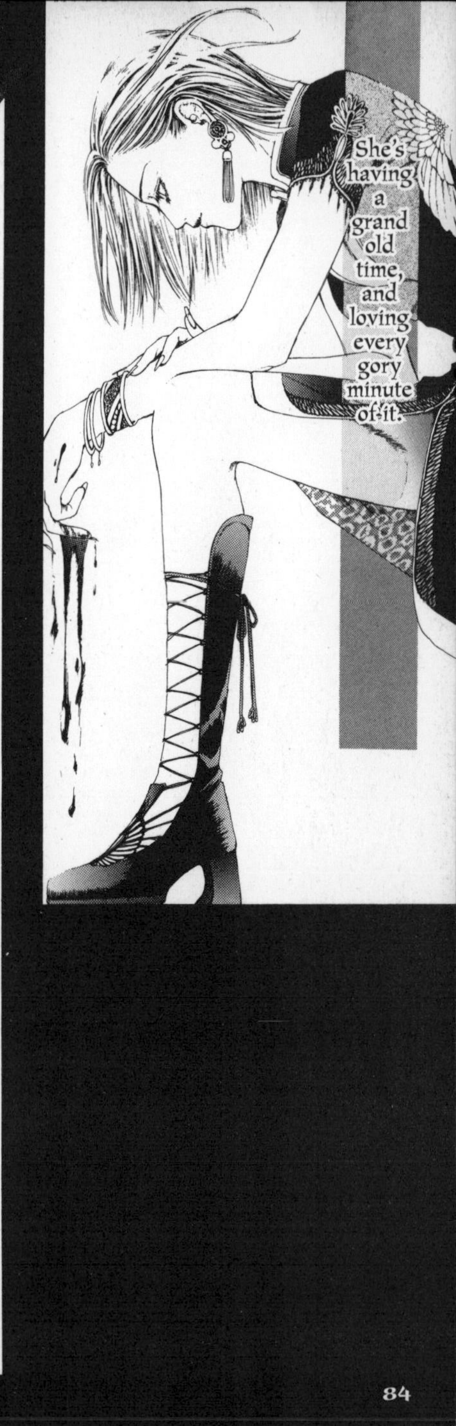
She's having a grand old time, and loving every gory minute of-it.
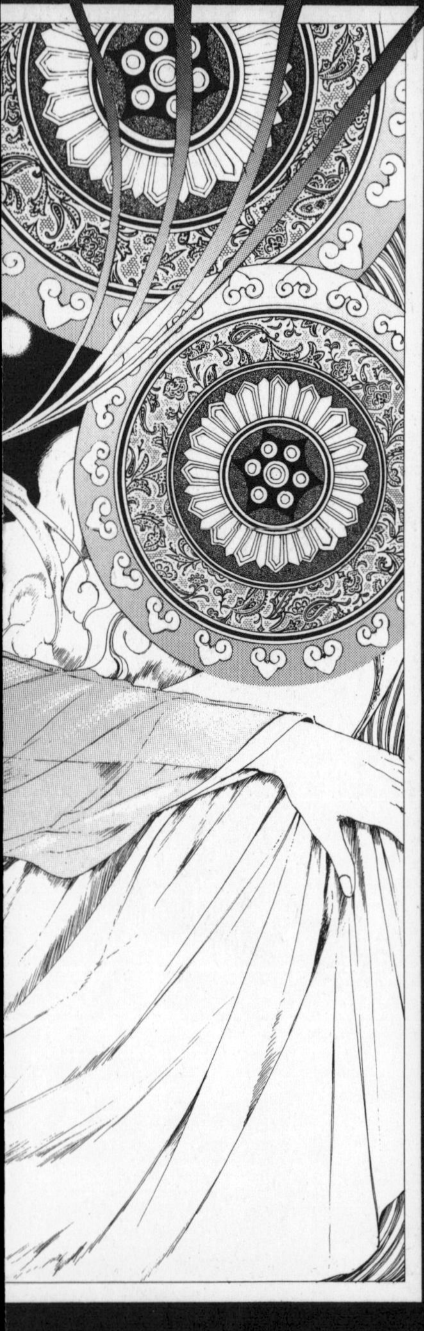

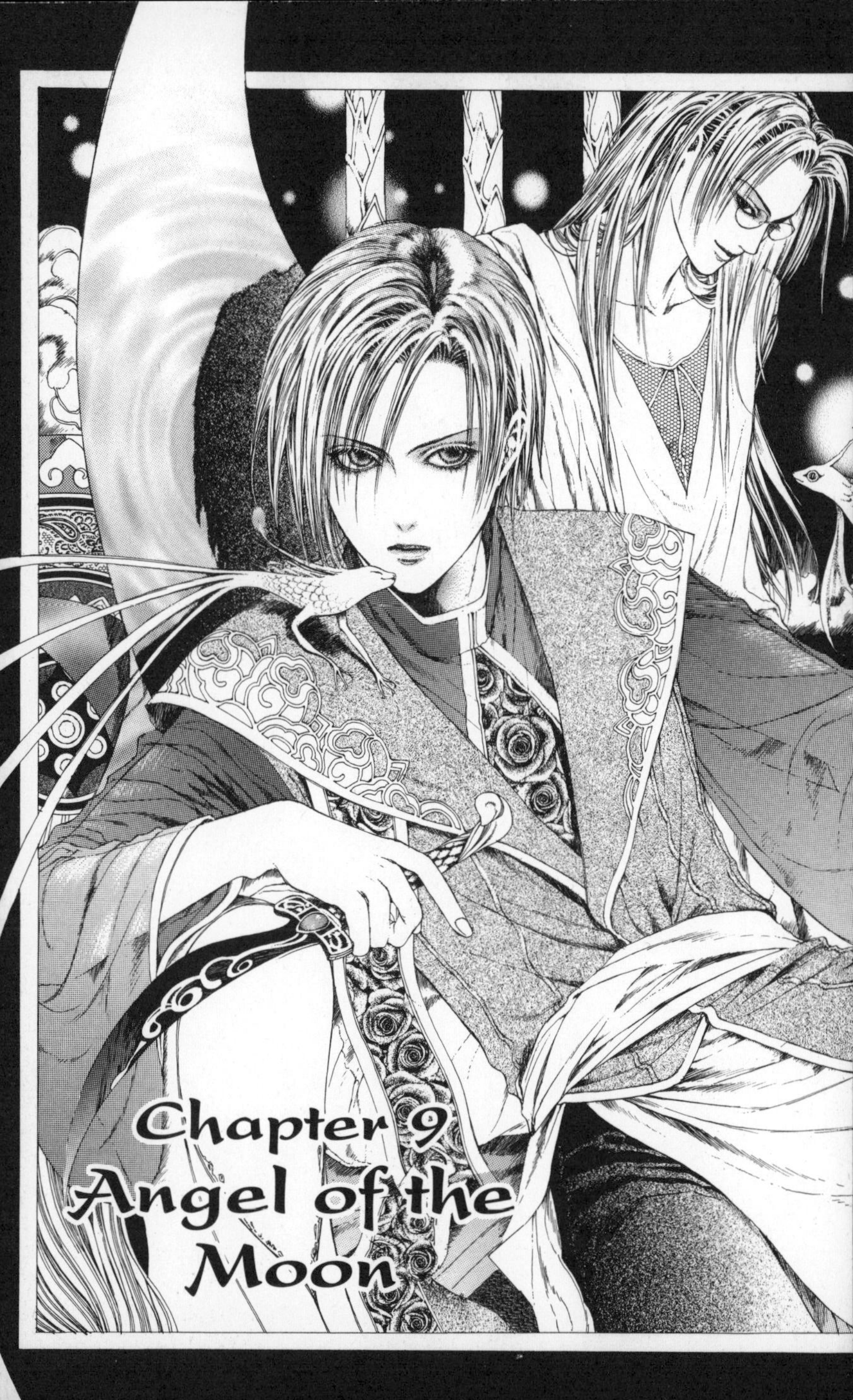
Chapter 9
Angel of the Moon

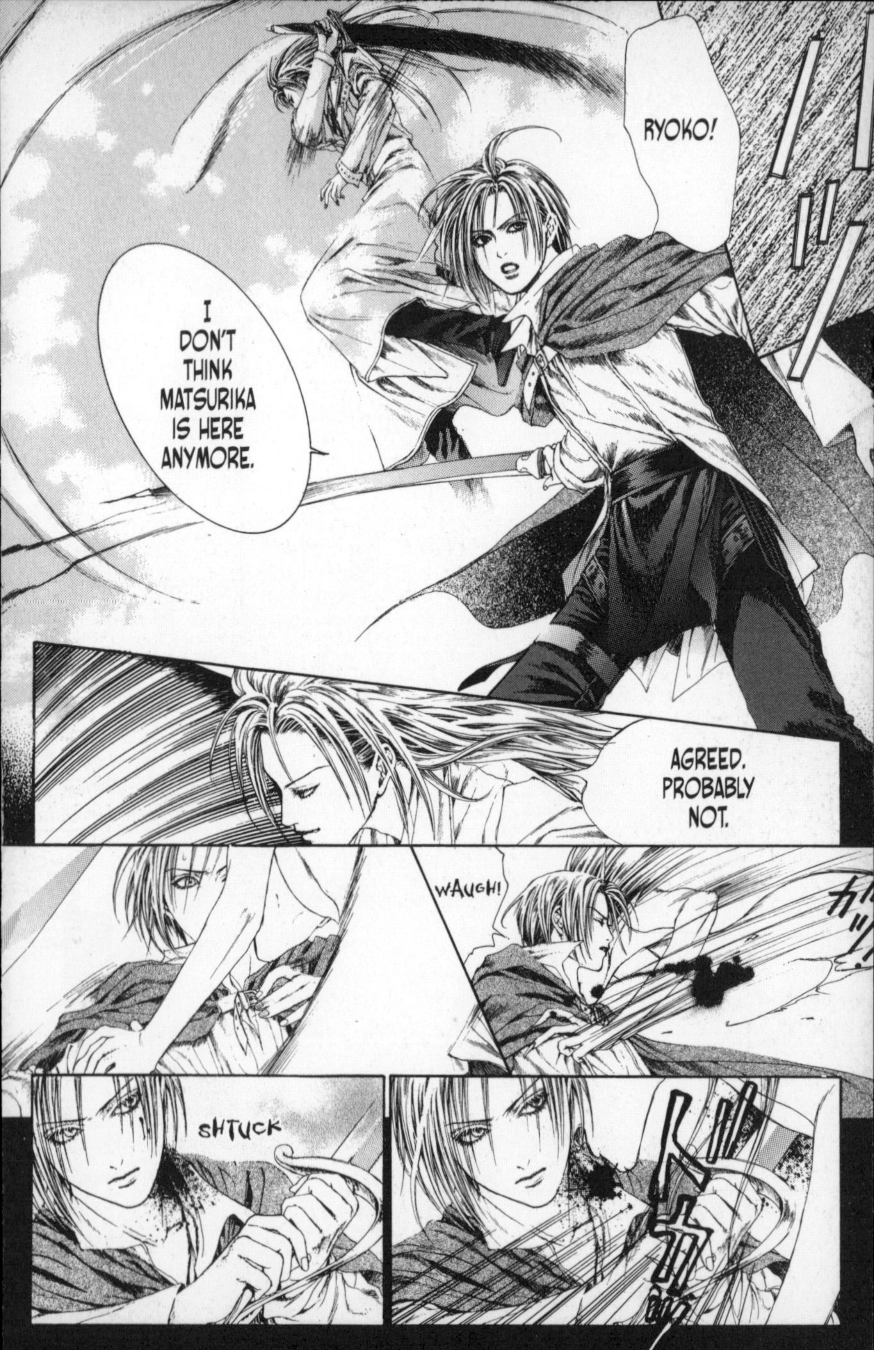
RYOKO!
I DON'T THINK MATSURIKA IS HERE ANYMORE.
AGREED. PROBABLY NOT.
WAUGH!
SHTUCK

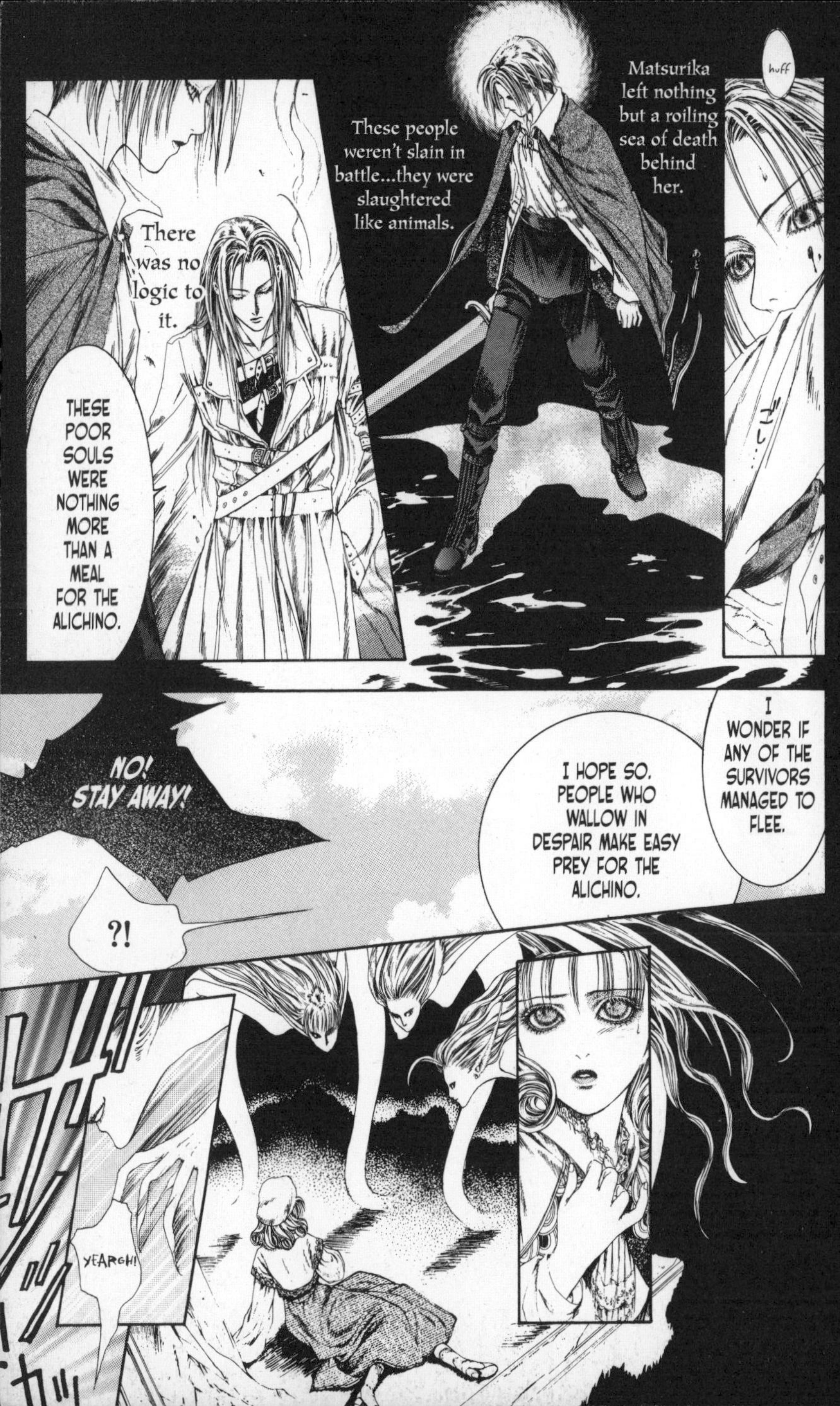
huff
Matsurika left nothing but a roiling sea of death behind her.
These people weren't slain in battle...they were slaughtered like animals.
There was no logic to it.
THESE POOR SOULS WERE NOTHING MORE THAN A MEAL FOR THE ALICHINO.
I WONDER IF ANY OF THE SURVIVORS MANAGED TO FLEE.
I HOPE SO. PEOPLE WHO WALLOW IN DESPAIR MAKE EASY PREY FOR THE ALICHINO.
NO! STAY AWAY!
?!
YEARGH!

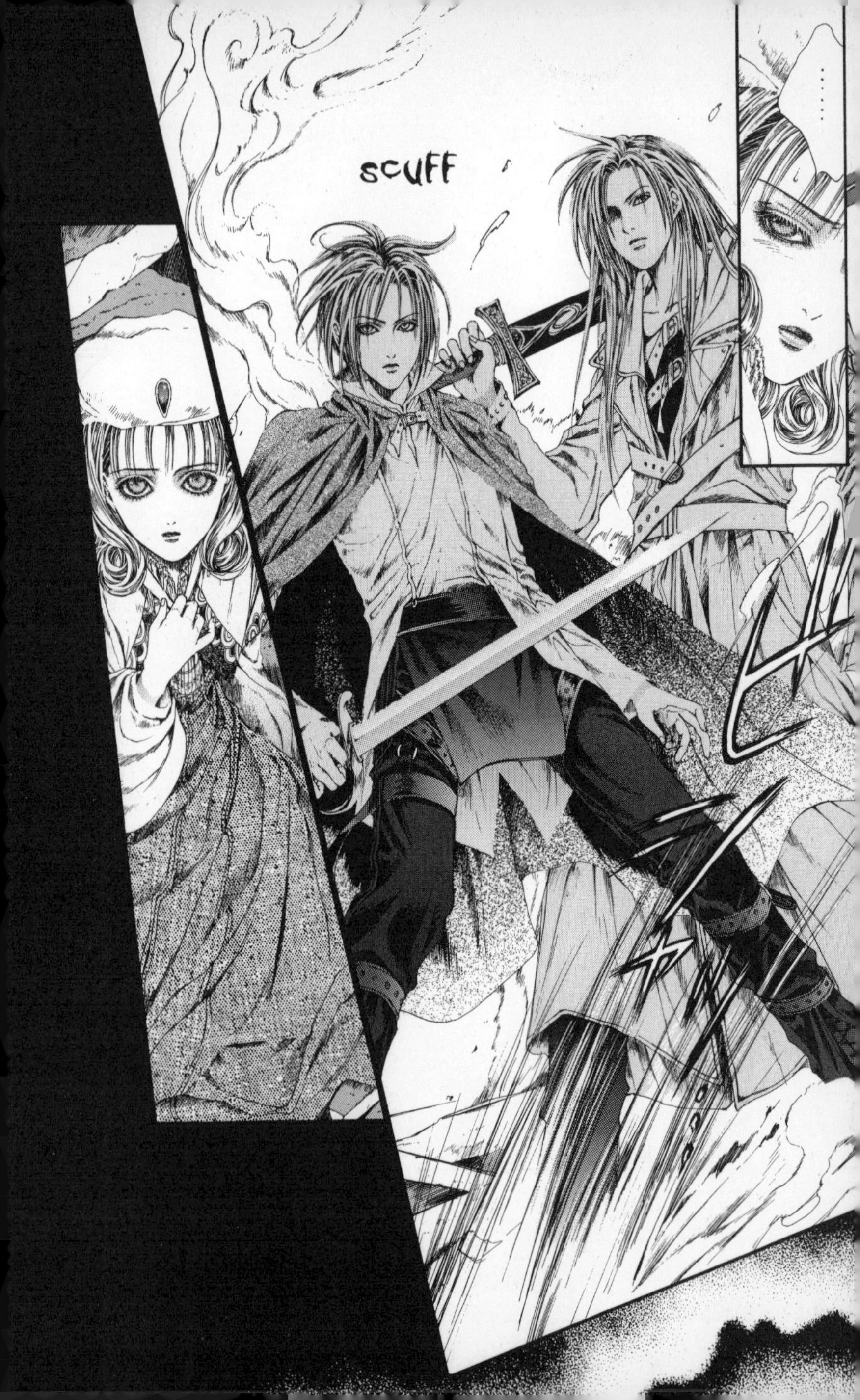
. . .
SCUFF

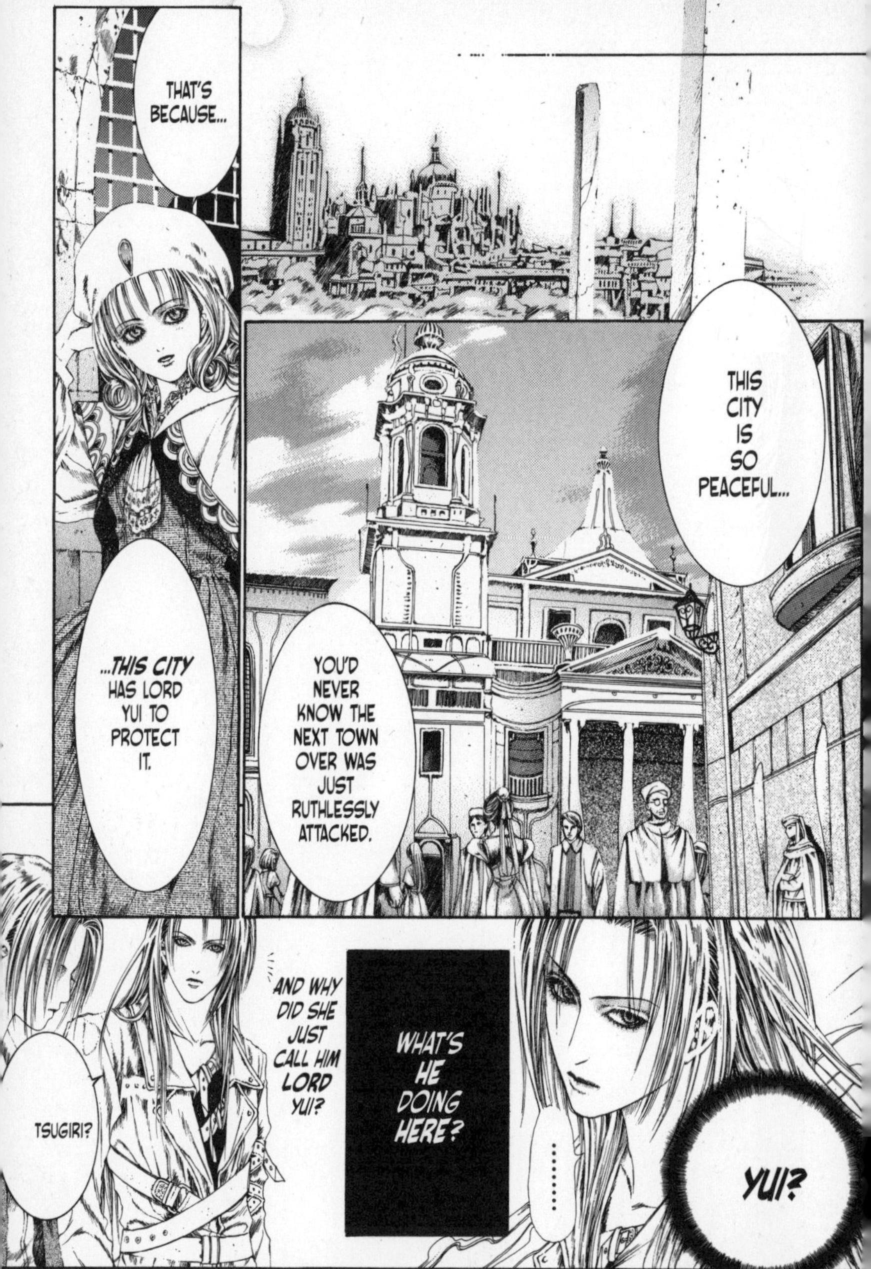
THIS CITY IS SO PEACEFUL...
YOU'D NEVER KNOW THE NEXT TOWN OVER WAS JUST RUTHLESSLY ATTACKED.
THAT'S BECAUSE...
...THIS CITY HAS LORD YUI TO PROTECT IT.
YUI?
......
WHAT'S HE DOING HERE?
AND WHY DID SHE JUST CALL HIM LORD YUI?
TSUGIRI?

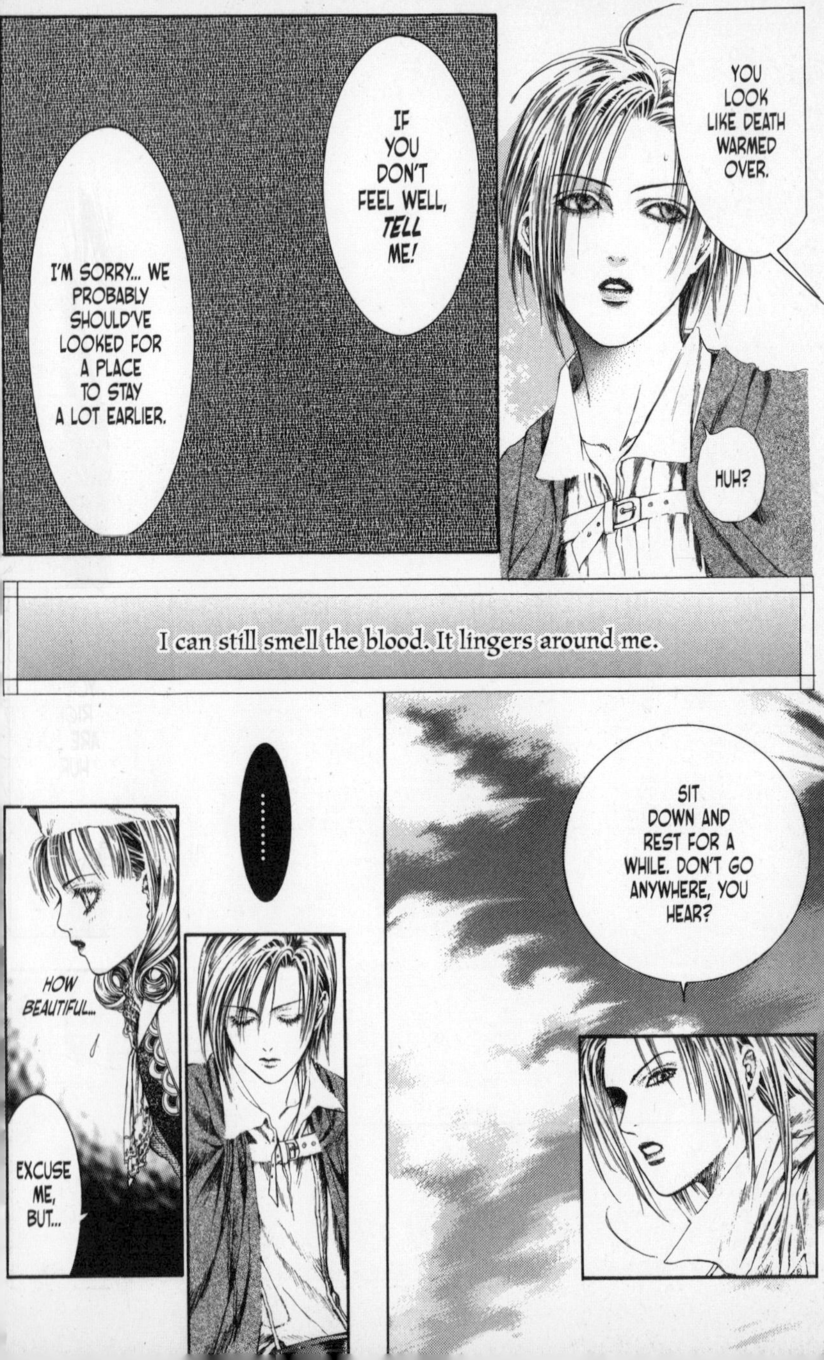
YOU LOOK LIKE DEATH WARMED OVER.
HUH?
IF YOU DON'T FEEL WELL, **TELL** ME!
I'M SORRY... WE PROBABLY SHOULD'VE LOOKED FOR A PLACE TO STAY A LOT EARLIER.
I can still smell the blood. It lingers around me.
SIT DOWN AND REST FOR A WHILE. DON'T GO ANYWHERE, YOU HEAR?
....
HOW BEAUTIFUL...
EXCUSE ME, BUT...

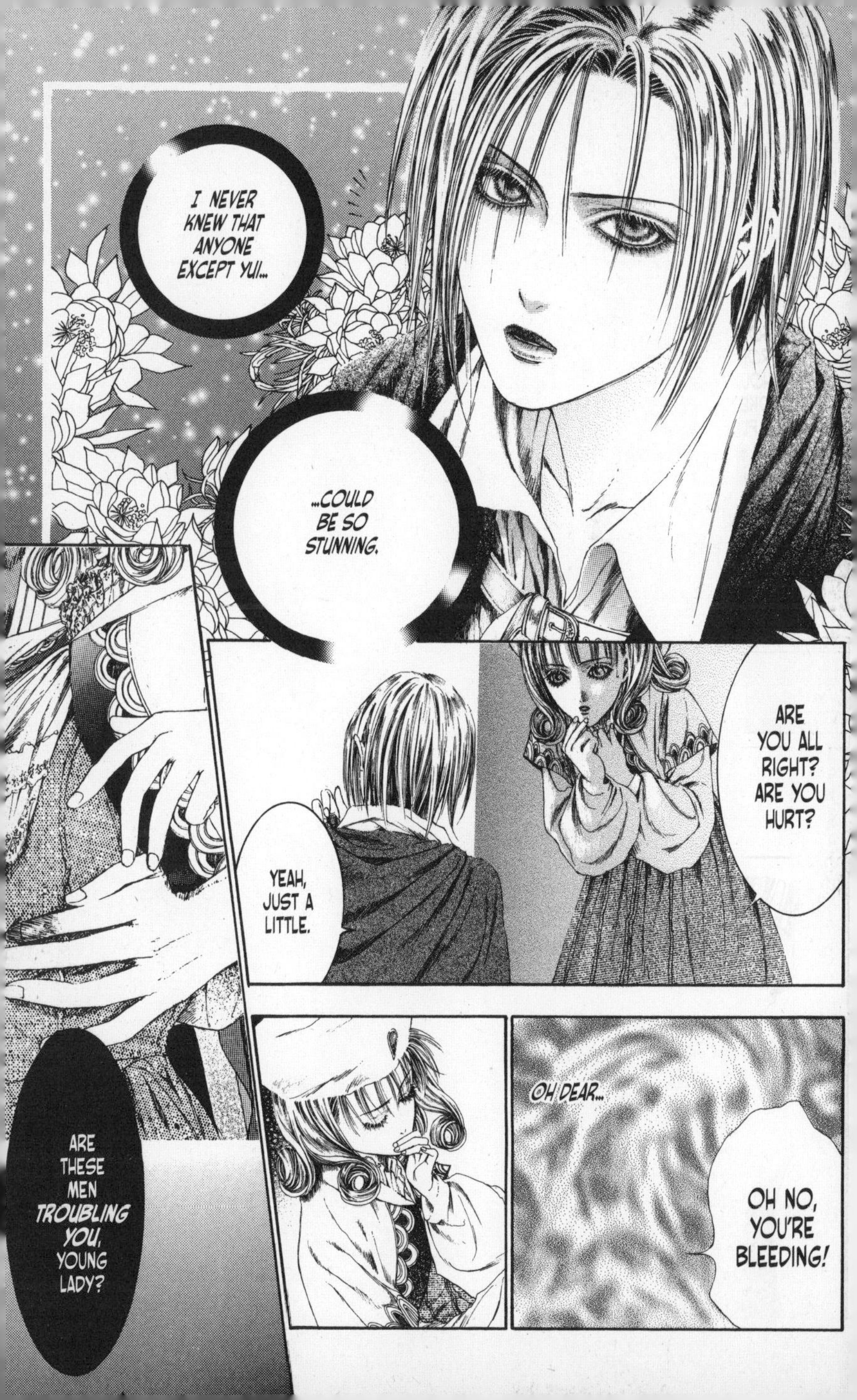
I NEVER KNEW THAT ANYONE EXCEPT YUI...
...COULD BE SO STUNNING.
ARE YOU ALL RIGHT? ARE YOU HURT?
YEAH, JUST A LITTLE.
OH DEAR...
OH NO, YOU'RE BLEEDING!
ARE THESE MEN TROUBLING YOU, YOUNG LADY?

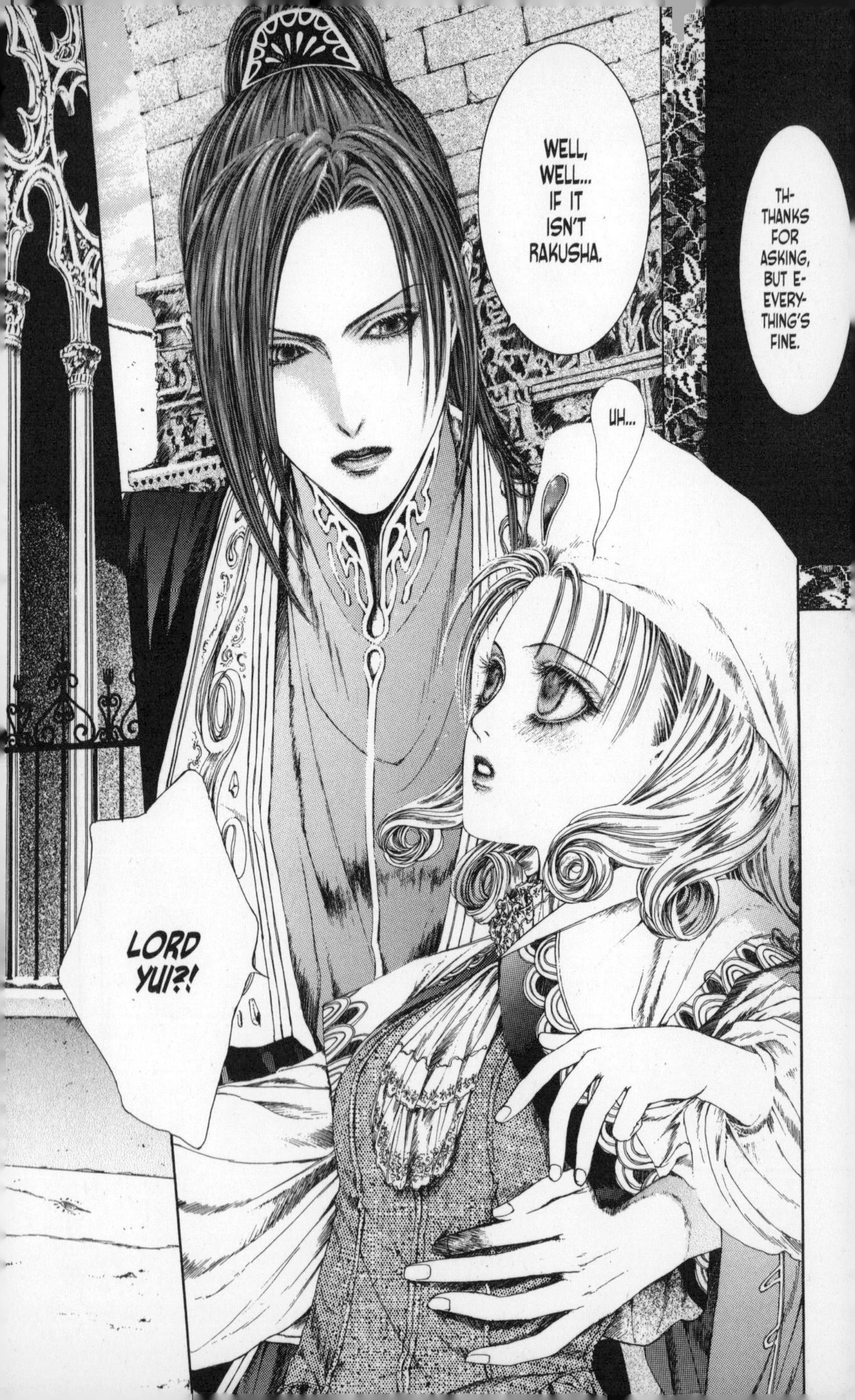
TH-THANKS FOR ASKING, BUT E-EVERYTHING'S FINE.
WELL, WELL... IF IT ISN'T RAKUSHA.
UH...
LORD YUI?!

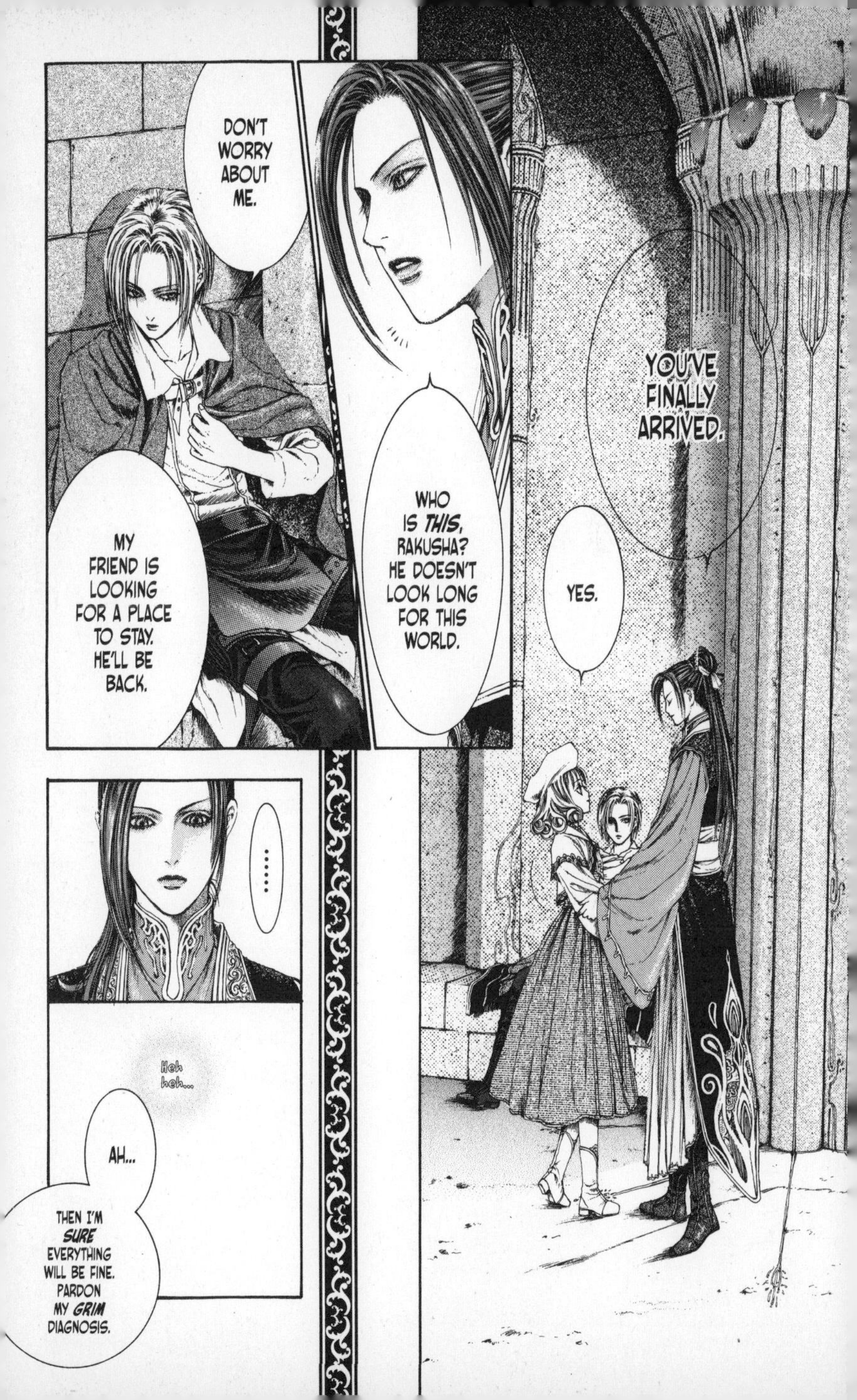

YOU'VE FINALLY ARRIVED.
YES.
WHO IS *THIS*, RAKUSHA? HE DOESN'T LOOK LONG FOR THIS WORLD.
DON'T WORRY ABOUT ME.
MY FRIEND IS LOOKING FOR A PLACE TO STAY. HE'LL BE BACK.
......
Heh heh...
AH...
THEN I'M *SURE* EVERYTHING WILL BE FINE. PARDON MY *GRIM* DIAGNOSIS.

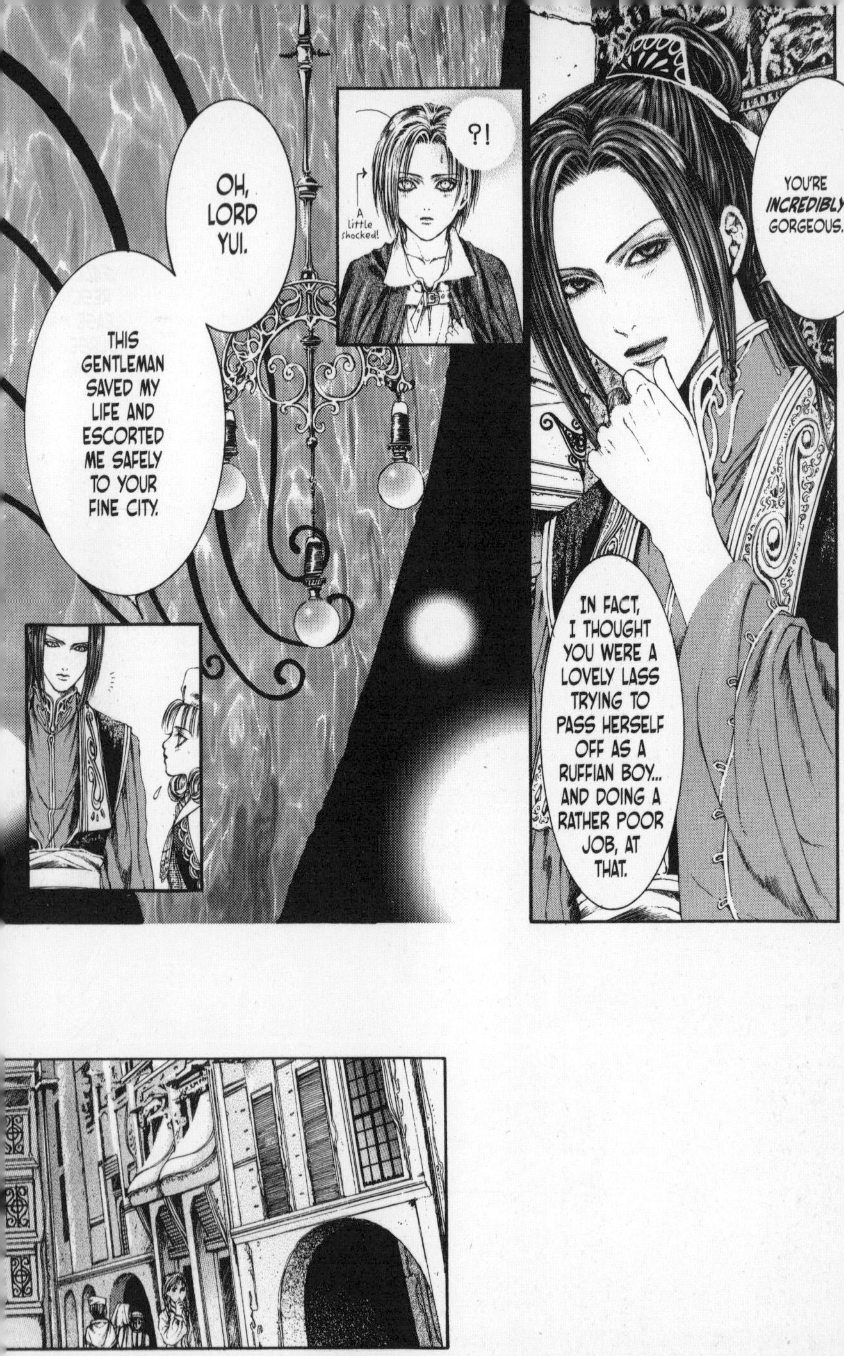
YOU'RE INCREDIBLY GORGEOUS.
IN FACT, I THOUGHT YOU WERE A LOVELY LASS TRYING TO PASS HERSELF OFF AS A RUFFIAN BOY... AND DOING A RATHER POOR JOB, AT THAT.
?!
A little shocked!
OH, LORD YUI.
THIS GENTLEMAN SAVED MY LIFE AND ESCORTED ME SAFELY TO YOUR FINE CITY.

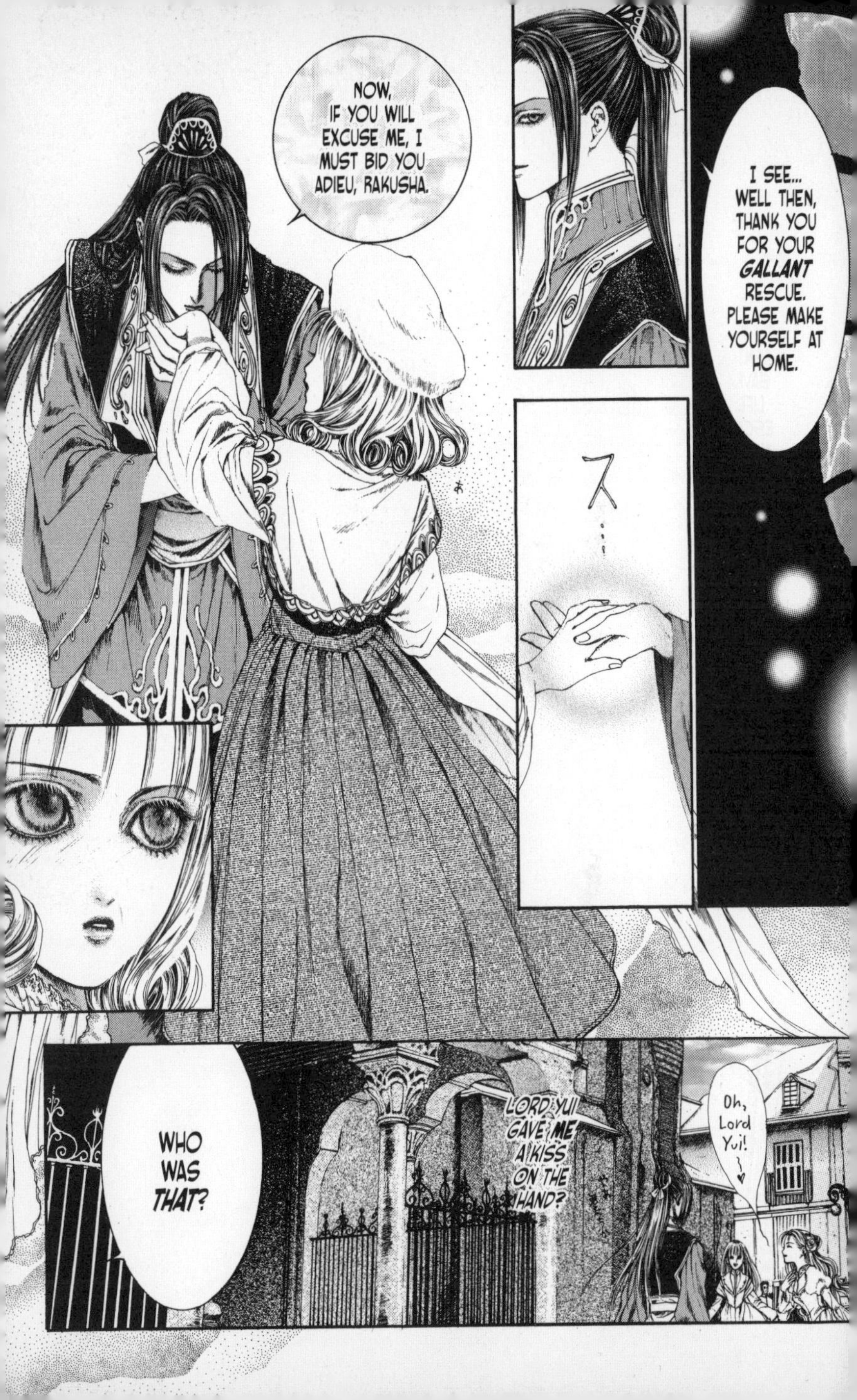
I SEE... WELL THEN, THANK YOU FOR YOUR *GALLANT* RESCUE. PLEASE MAKE YOURSELF AT HOME.
NOW, IF YOU WILL EXCUSE ME, I MUST BID YOU ADIEU, RAKUSHA.
ス...
Oh, Lord Yui!
LORD YUI GAVE ME A KISS ON THE HAND?
WHO WAS *THAT*?

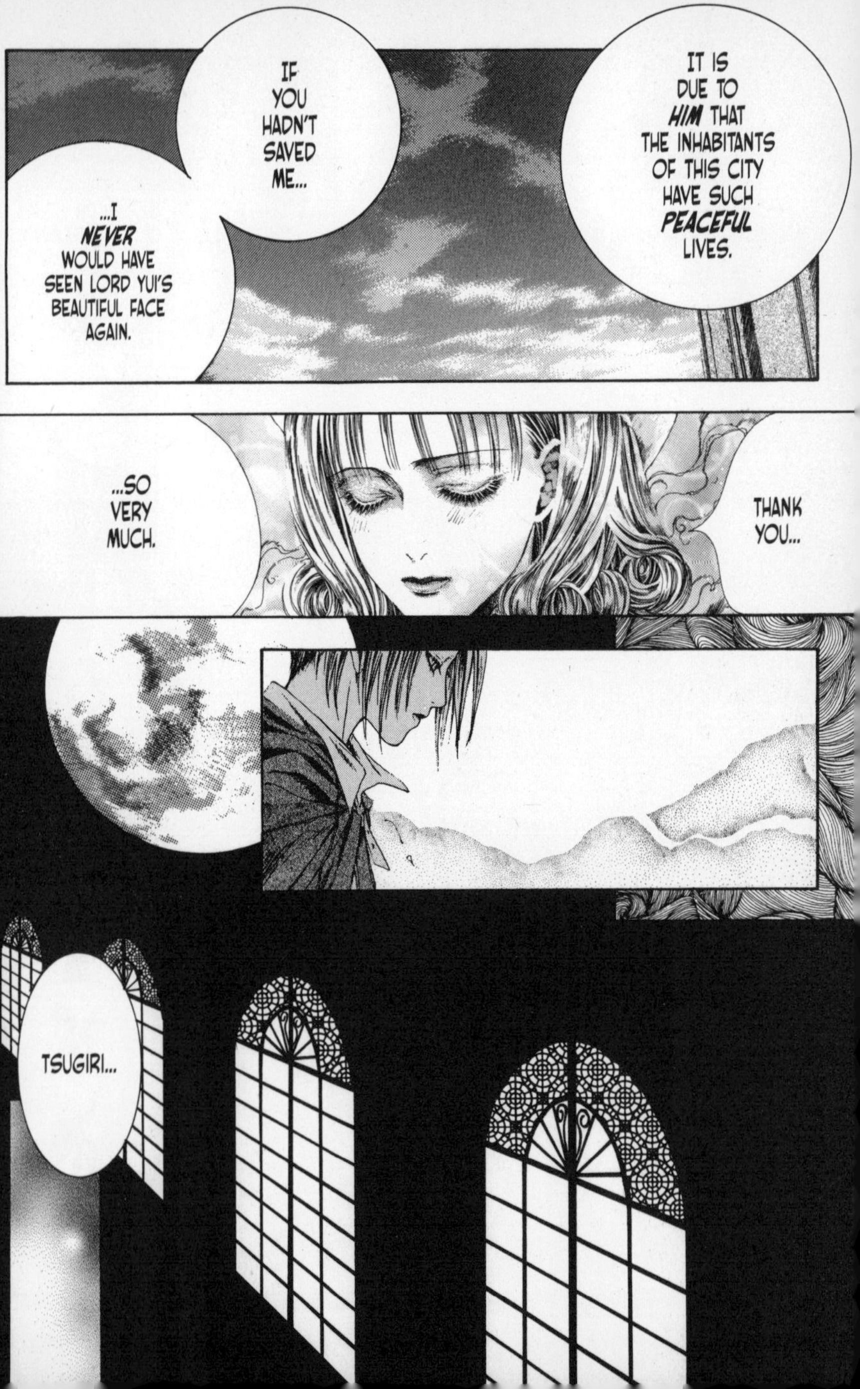
IT IS DUE TO *HIM* THAT THE INHABITANTS OF THIS CITY HAVE SUCH *PEACEFUL* LIVES.
IF YOU HADN'T SAVED ME...
...I *NEVER* WOULD HAVE SEEN LORD YUI'S BEAUTIFUL FACE AGAIN.
THANK YOU...
...SO VERY MUCH.
TSUGIRI...

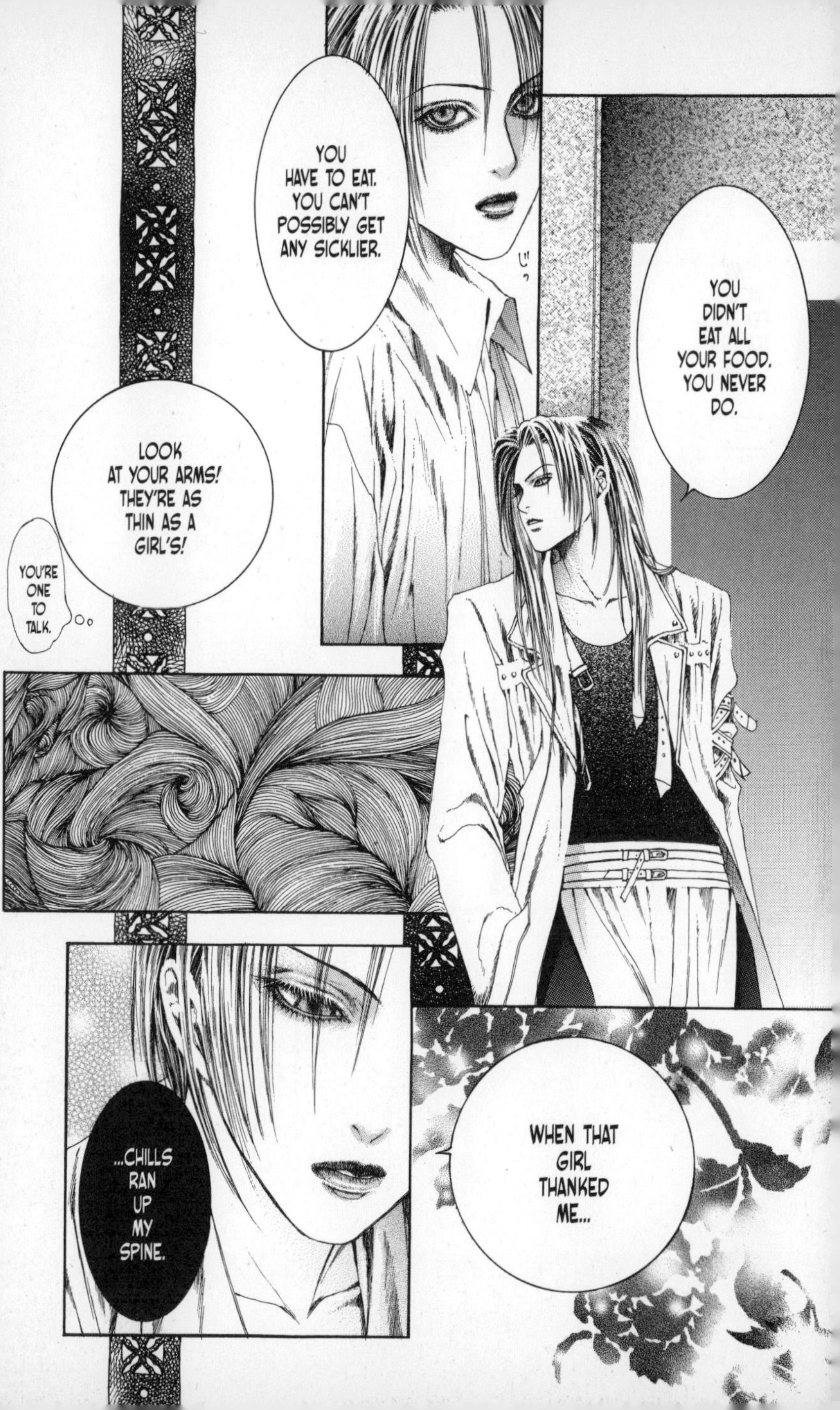
YOU DIDN'T EAT ALL YOUR FOOD. YOU NEVER DO.
YOU HAVE TO EAT. YOU CAN'T POSSIBLY GET ANY SICKLIER.
LOOK AT YOUR ARMS! THEY'RE AS THIN AS A GIRL'S!
YOU'RE ONE TO TALK.
WHEN THAT GIRL THANKED ME...
...CHILLS RAN UP MY SPINE.

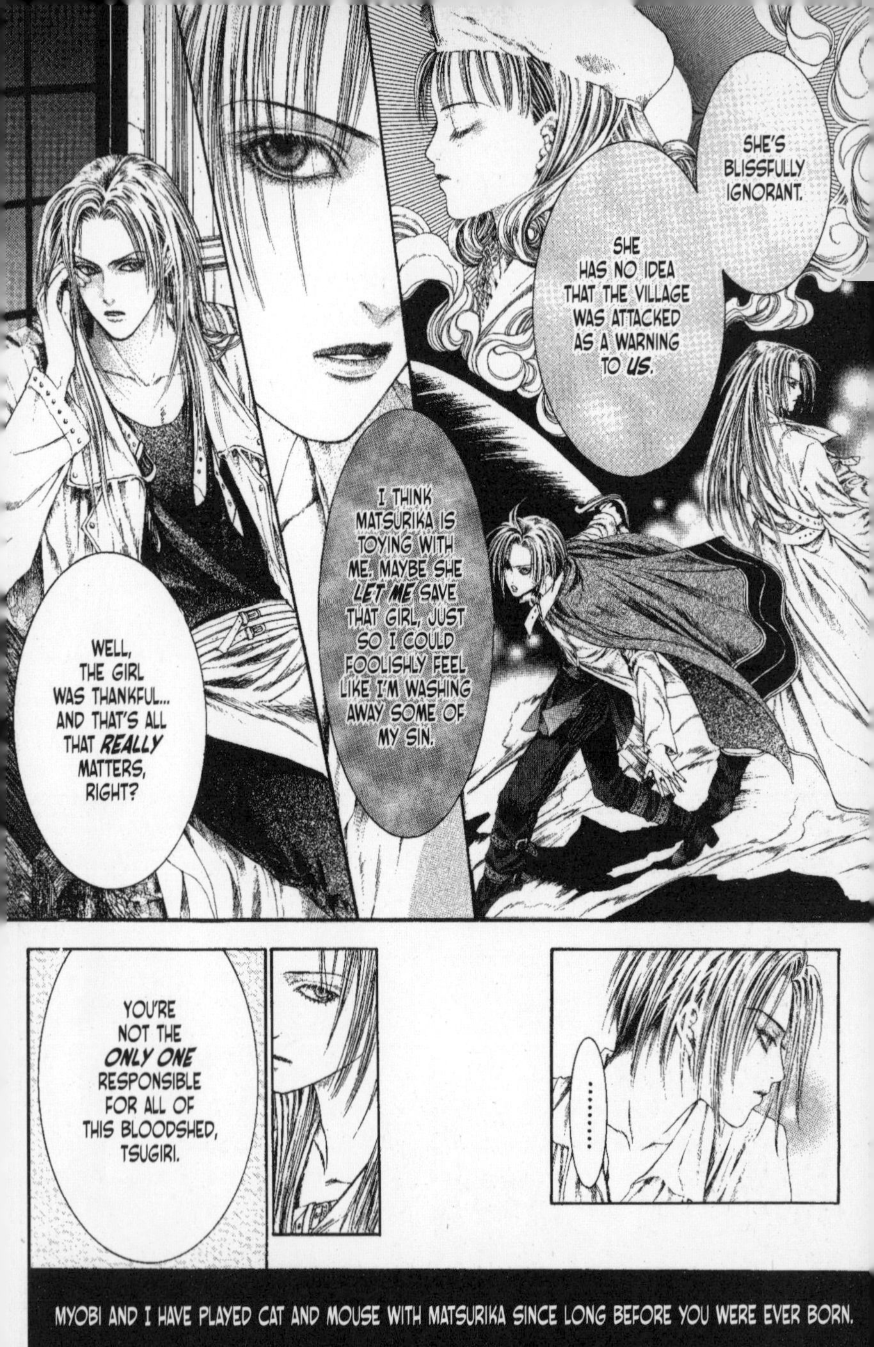
SHE'S BLISSFULLY IGNORANT.
SHE HAS NO IDEA THAT THE VILLAGE WAS ATTACKED AS A WARNING TO *US*.
I THINK MATSURIKA IS TOYING WITH ME. MAYBE SHE *LET ME* SAVE THAT GIRL, JUST SO I COULD FOOLISHLY FEEL LIKE I'M WASHING AWAY SOME OF MY SIN.
WELL, THE GIRL WAS THANKFUL... AND THAT'S ALL THAT *REALLY* MATTERS, RIGHT?
......
YOU'RE NOT THE *ONLY ONE* RESPONSIBLE FOR ALL OF THIS BLOODSHED, TSUGIRI.
MYOBI AND I HAVE PLAYED CAT AND MOUSE WITH MATSURIKA SINCE LONG BEFORE YOU WERE EVER BORN.

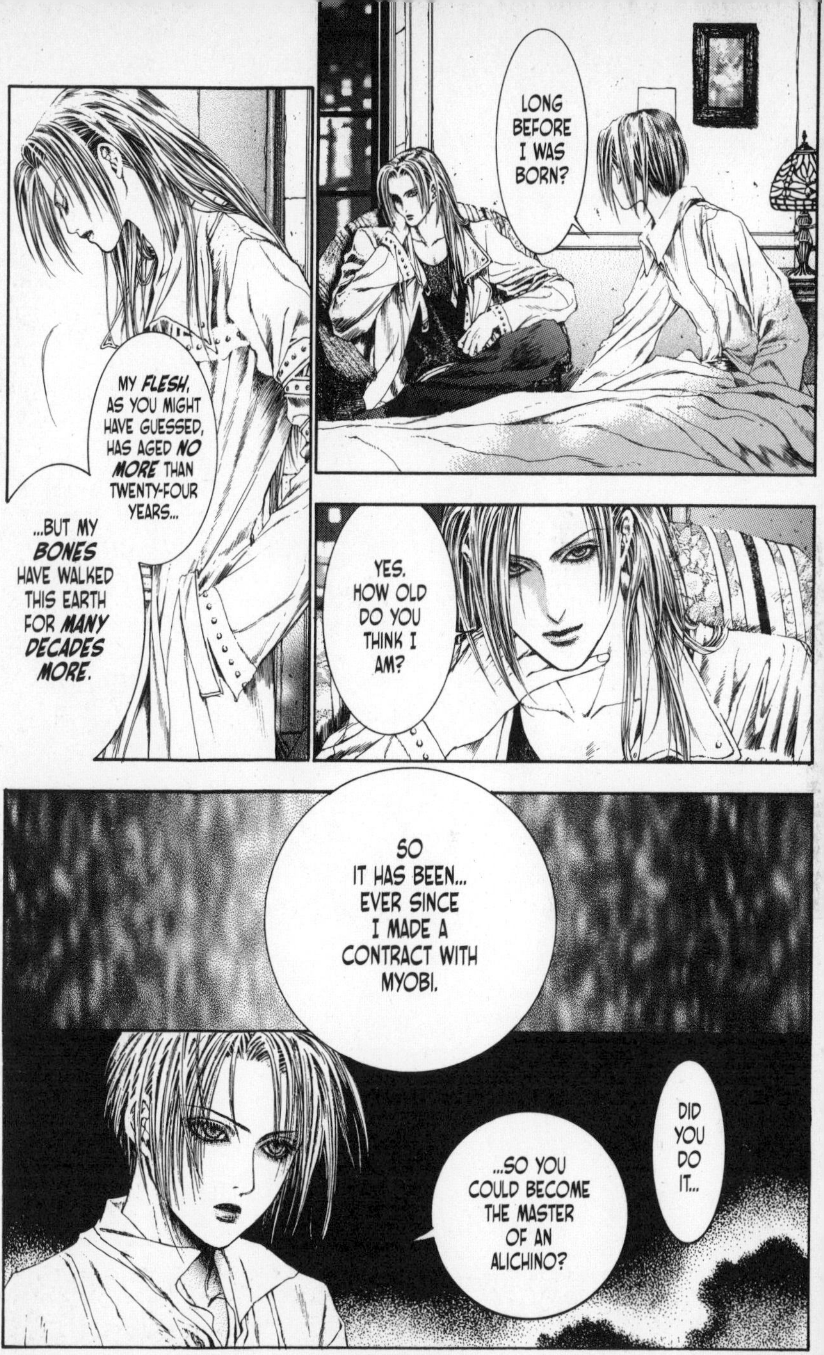
LONG BEFORE I WAS BORN?
YES. HOW OLD DO YOU THINK I AM?
MY FLESH, AS YOU MIGHT HAVE GUESSED, HAS AGED NO MORE THAN TWENTY-FOUR YEARS...
...BUT MY BONES HAVE WALKED THIS EARTH FOR MANY DECADES MORE.
SO IT HAS BEEN... EVER SINCE I MADE A CONTRACT WITH MYOBI.
DID YOU DO IT...
...SO YOU COULD BECOME THE MASTER OF AN ALICHINO?

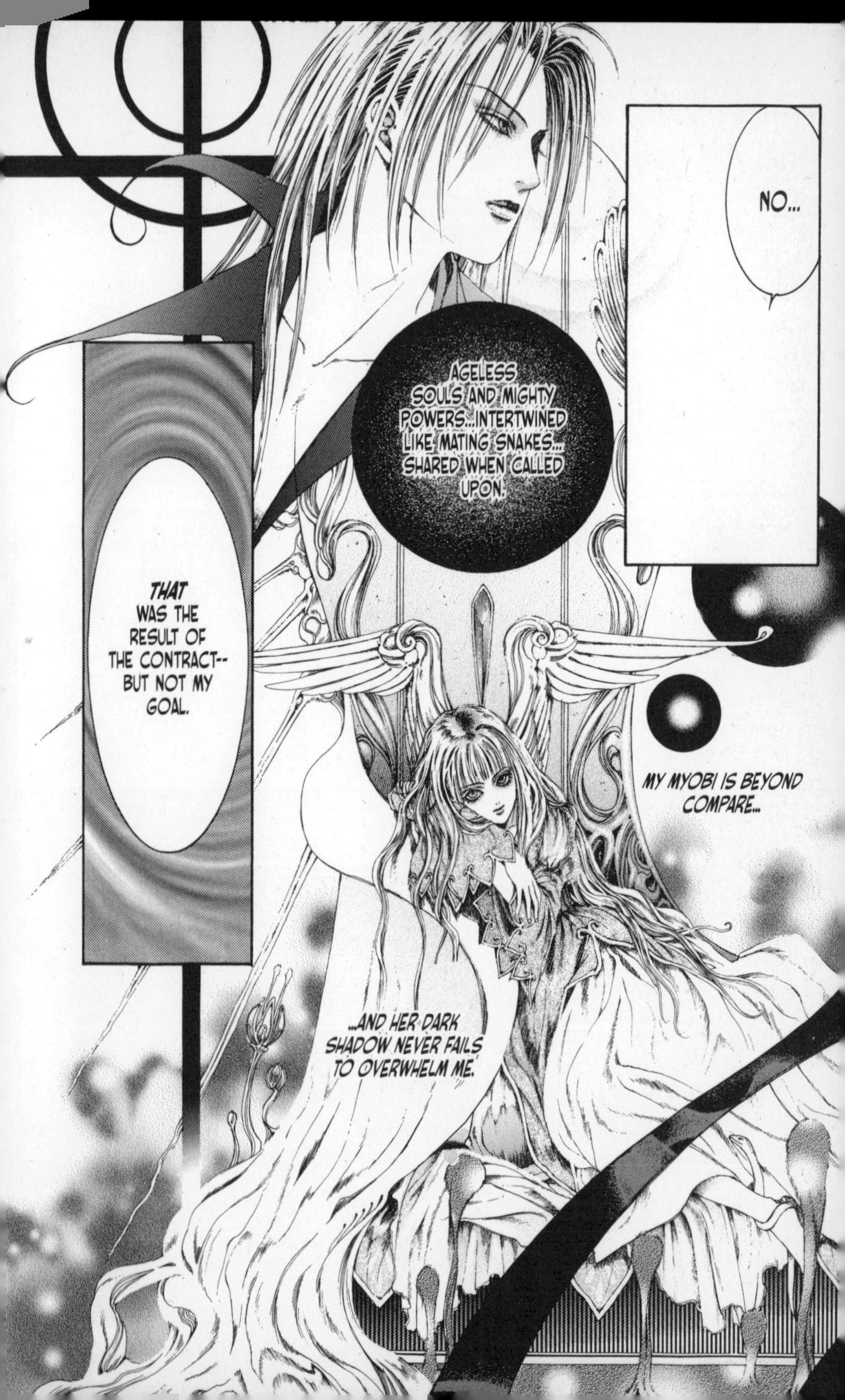
NO...
AGELESS SOULS AND MIGHTY POWERS...INTERTWINED LIKE MATING SNAKES... SHARED WHEN CALLED UPON.
THAT WAS THE RESULT OF THE CONTRACT-- BUT NOT MY GOAL.
MY MYOBI IS BEYOND COMPARE...
...AND HER DARK SHADOW NEVER FAILS TO OVERWHELM ME.

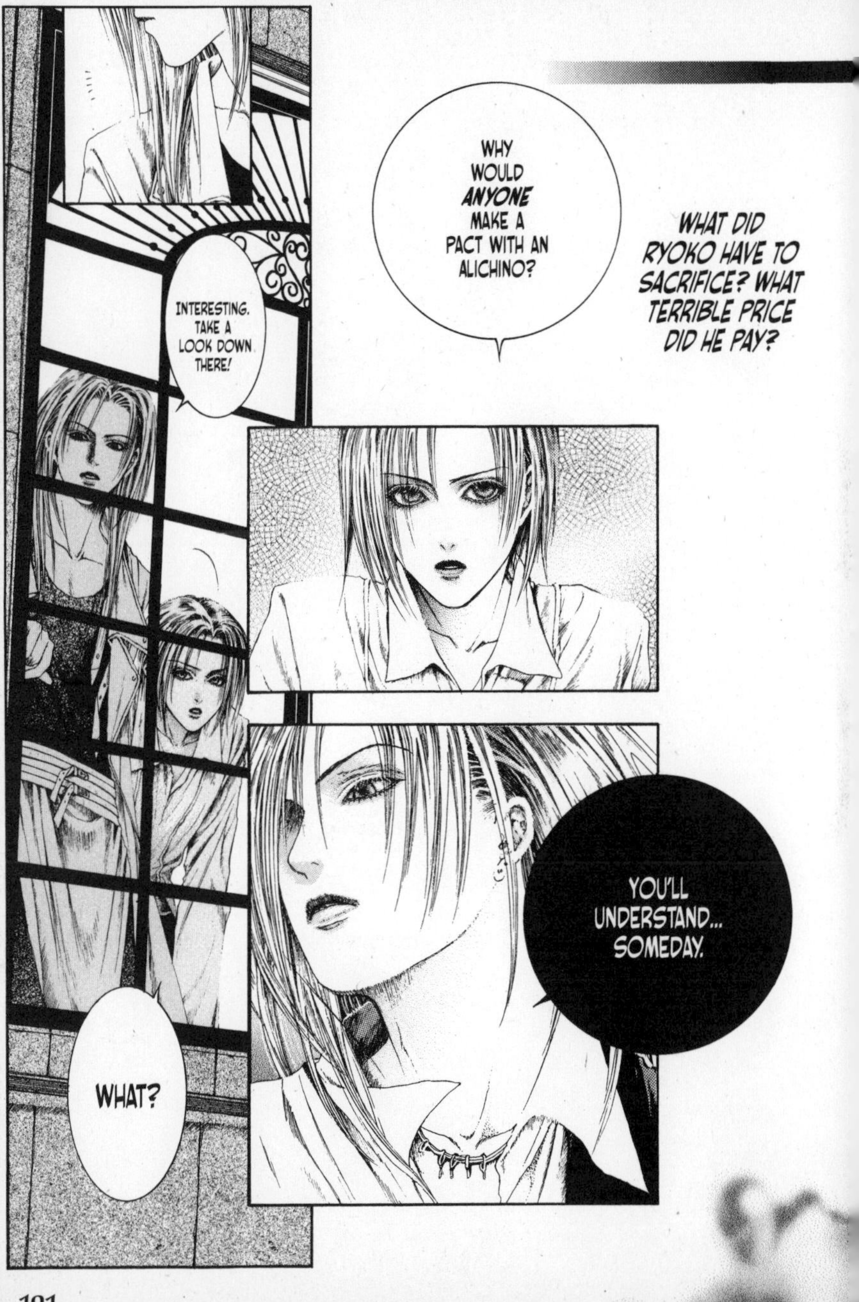
WHAT DID RYOKO HAVE TO SACRIFICE? WHAT TERRIBLE PRICE DID HE PAY?
WHY WOULD ANYONE MAKE A PACT WITH AN ALICHINO?
YOU'LL UNDERSTAND... SOMEDAY.
INTERESTING. TAKE A LOOK DOWN THERE!
WHAT?

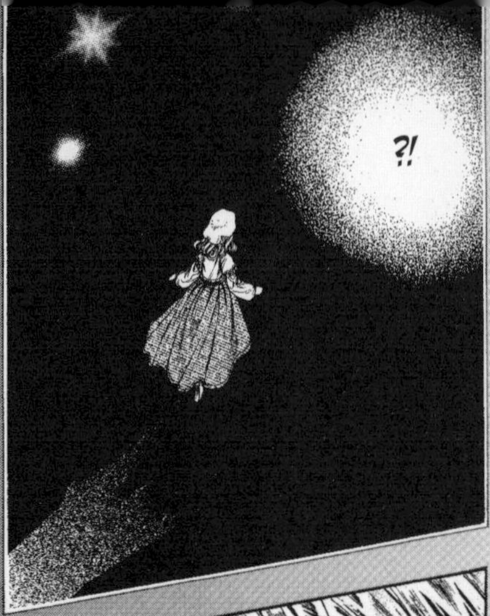
?!

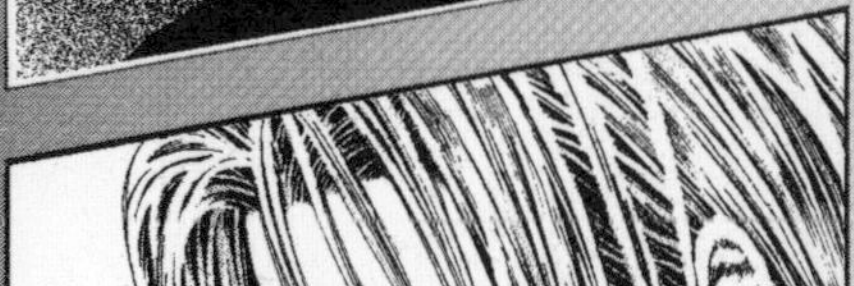
WHERE IS SHE GOING AT THIS TIME OF NIGHT?

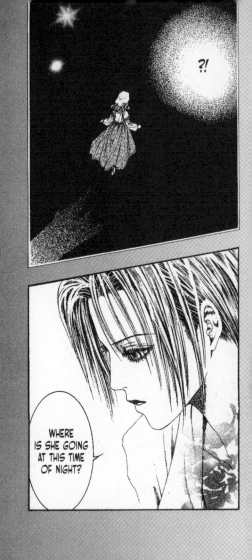

Chapter 10
Charisma

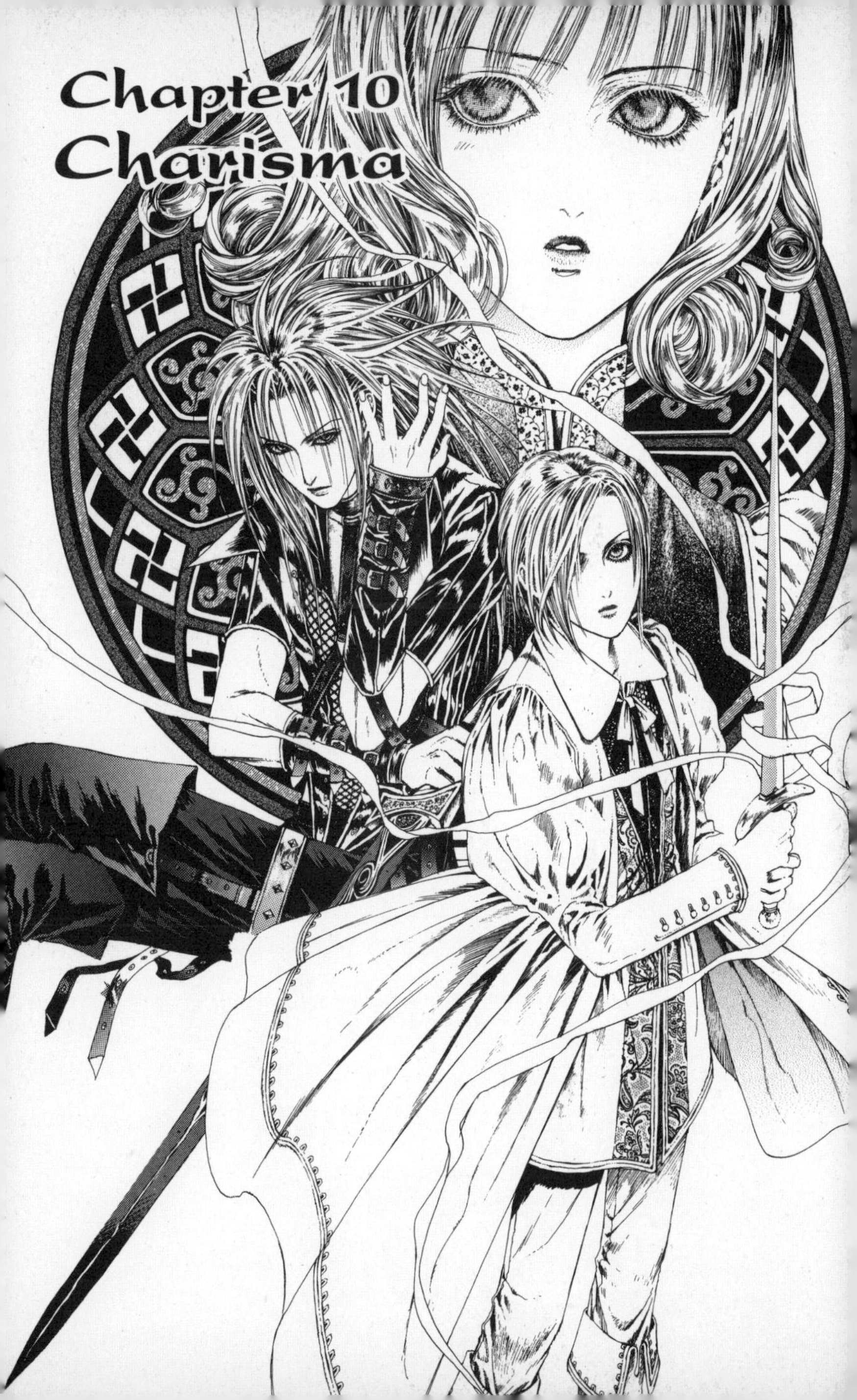

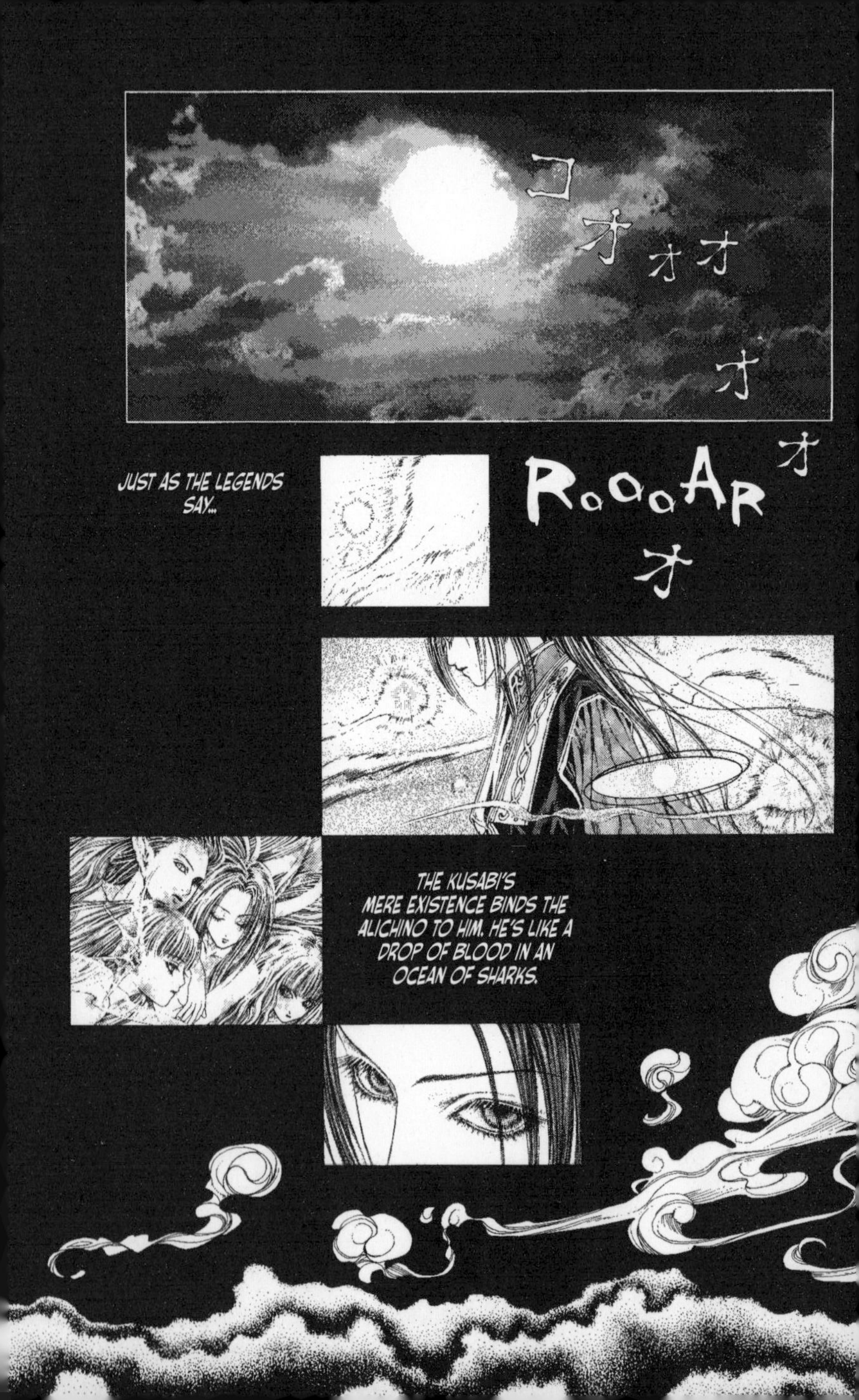
コオォオオ
RoooAR
オオ
JUST AS THE LEGENDS SAY...
THE KUSABI'S MERE EXISTENCE BINDS THE ALICHINO TO HIM. HE'S LIKE A DROP OF BLOOD IN AN OCEAN OF SHARKS.

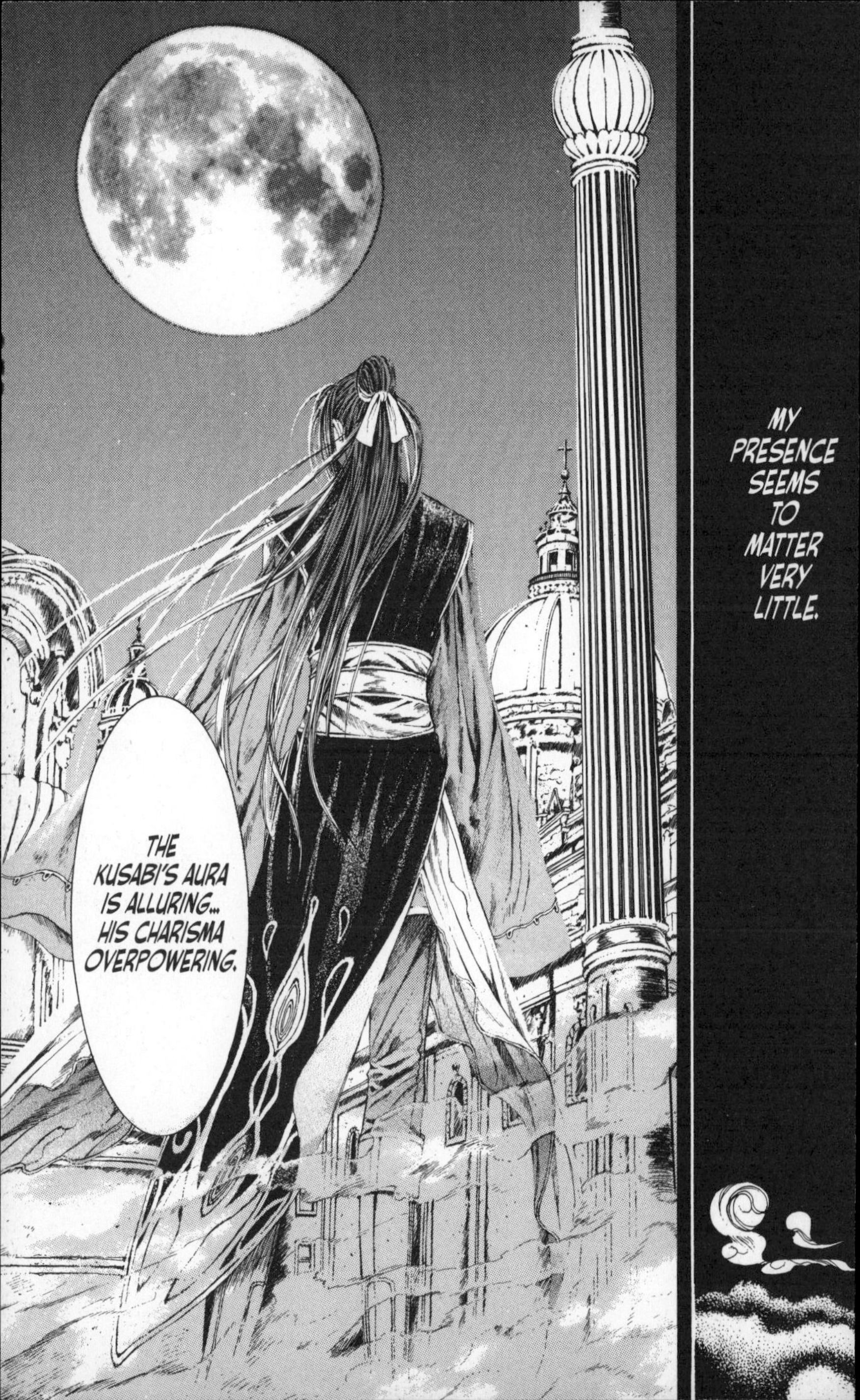
MY PRESENCE SEEMS TO MATTER VERY LITTLE.
THE KUSABI'S AURA IS ALLURING... HIS CHARISMA OVERPOWERING.

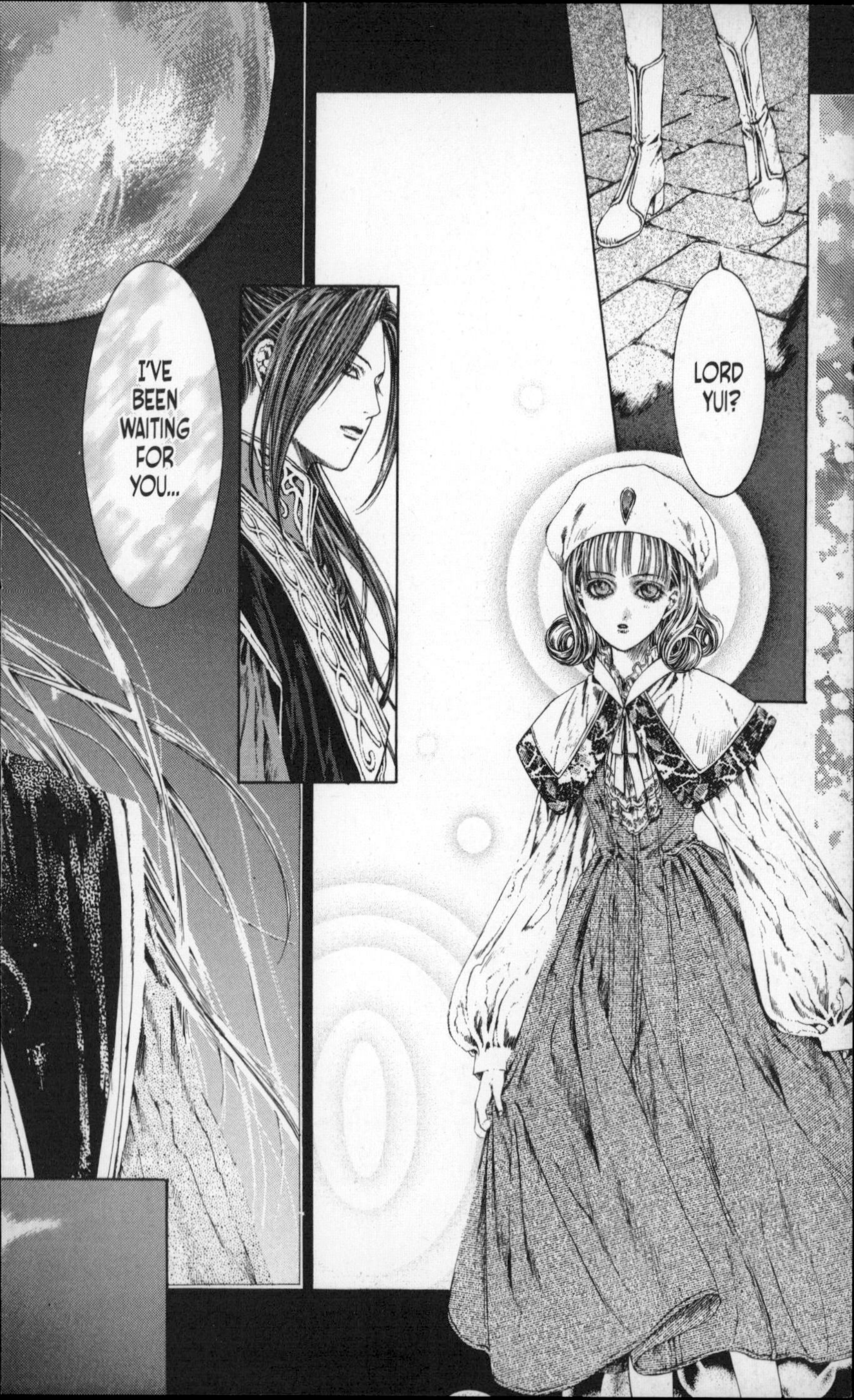
LORD YUI?
I'VE BEEN WAITING FOR YOU...

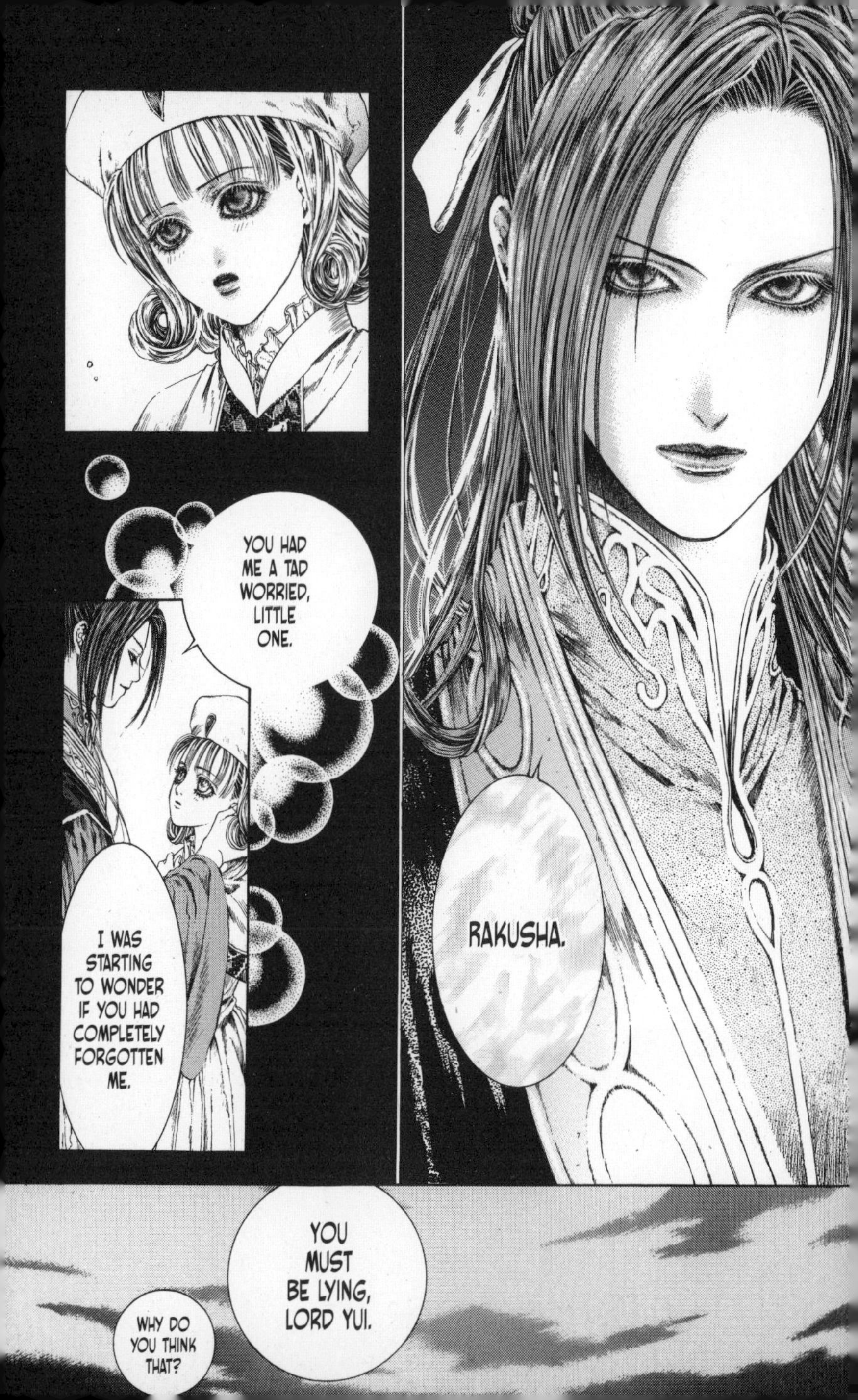
RAKUSHA.
YOU HAD ME A TAD WORRIED, LITTLE ONE.
I WAS STARTING TO WONDER IF YOU HAD COMPLETELY FORGOTTEN ME.
YOU MUST BE LYING, LORD YUI.
WHY DO YOU THINK THAT?

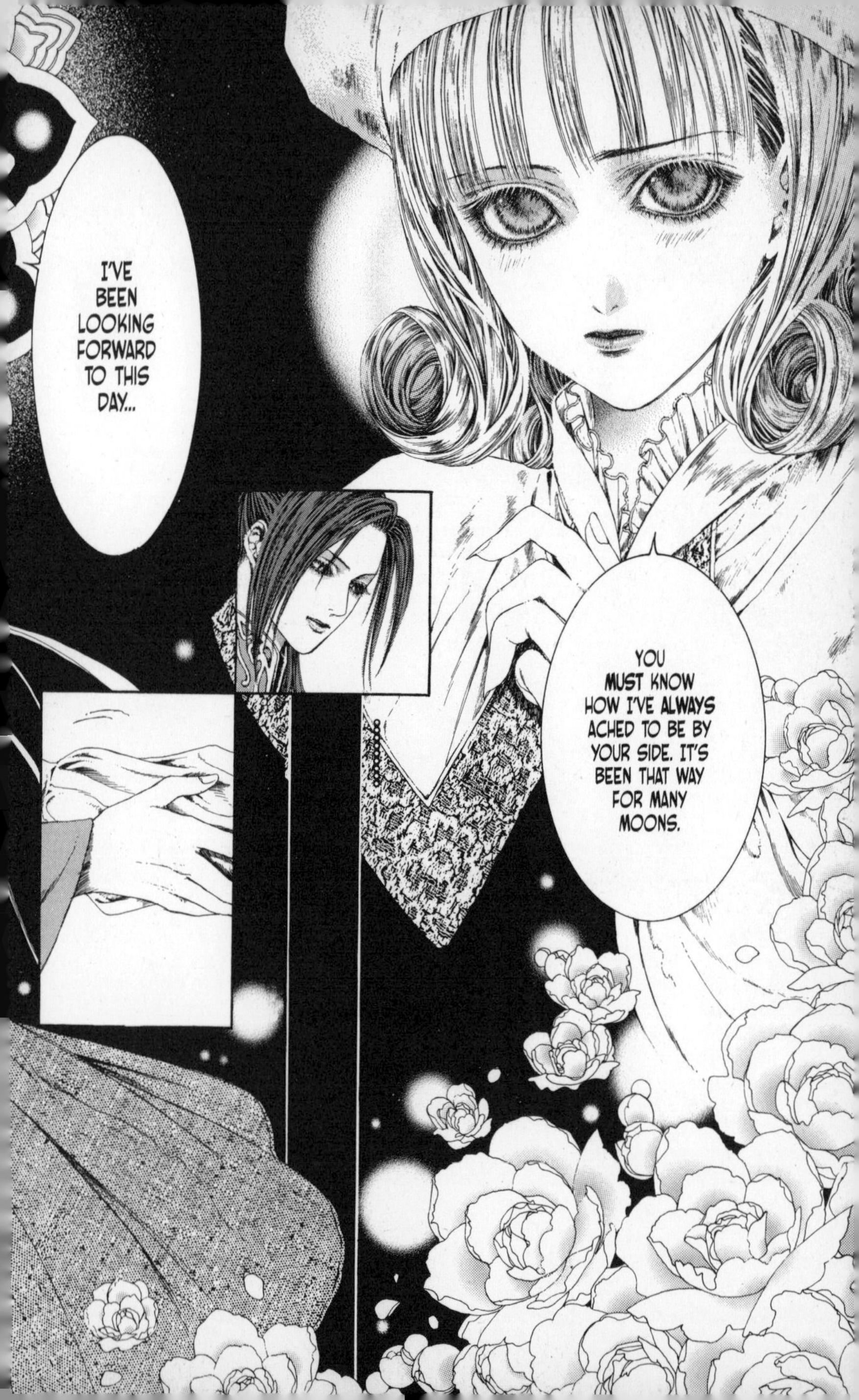
YOU MUST KNOW HOW I'VE ALWAYS ACHED TO BE BY YOUR SIDE. IT'S BEEN THAT WAY FOR MANY MOONS.
I'VE BEEN LOOKING FORWARD TO THIS DAY...

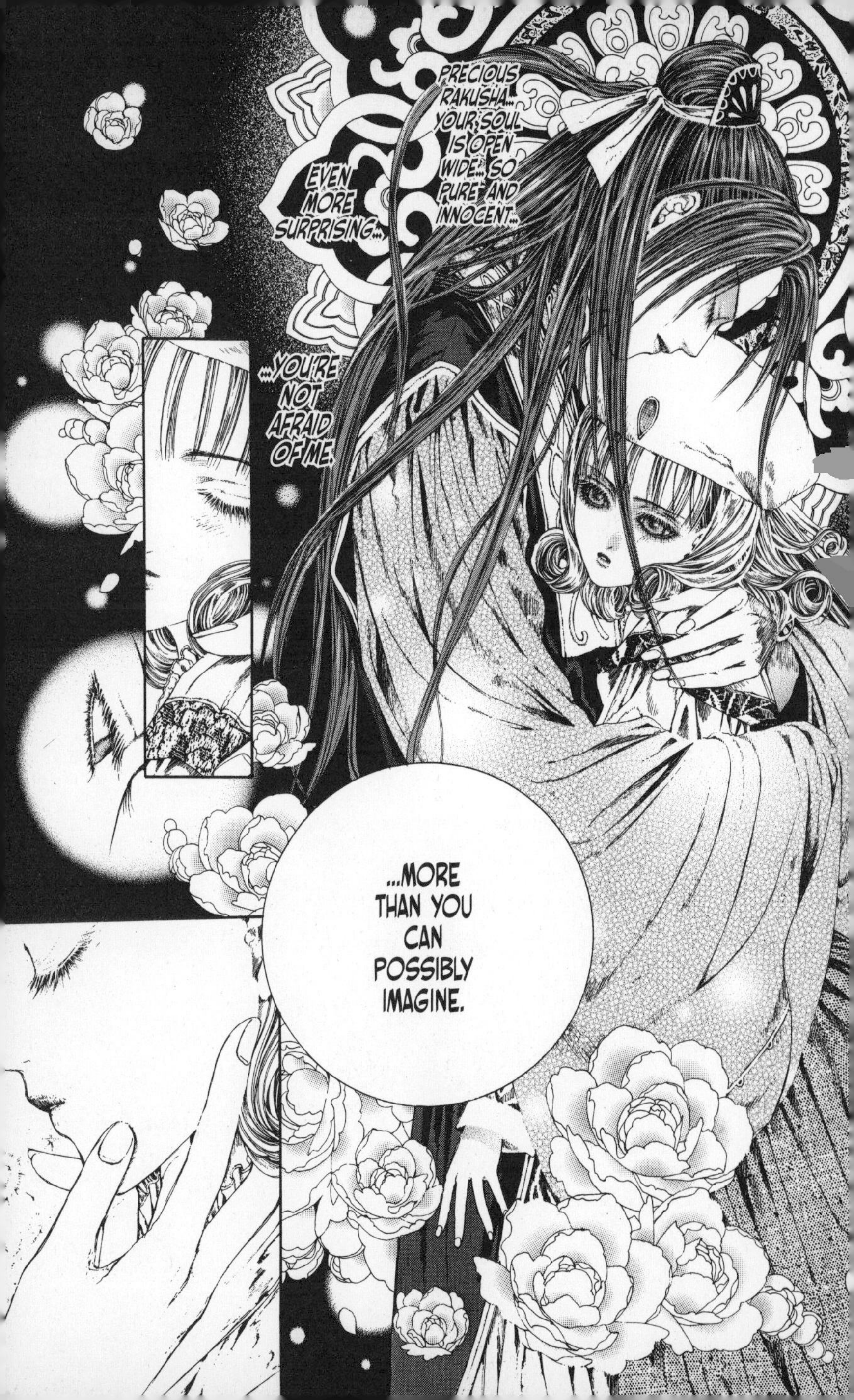
PRECIOUS RAKUSHA... YOUR SOUL IS OPEN WIDE... SO PURE AND INNOCENT...
EVEN MORE SURPRISING...
...YOU'RE NOT AFRAID OF ME.
...MORE THAN YOU CAN POSSIBLY IMAGINE.

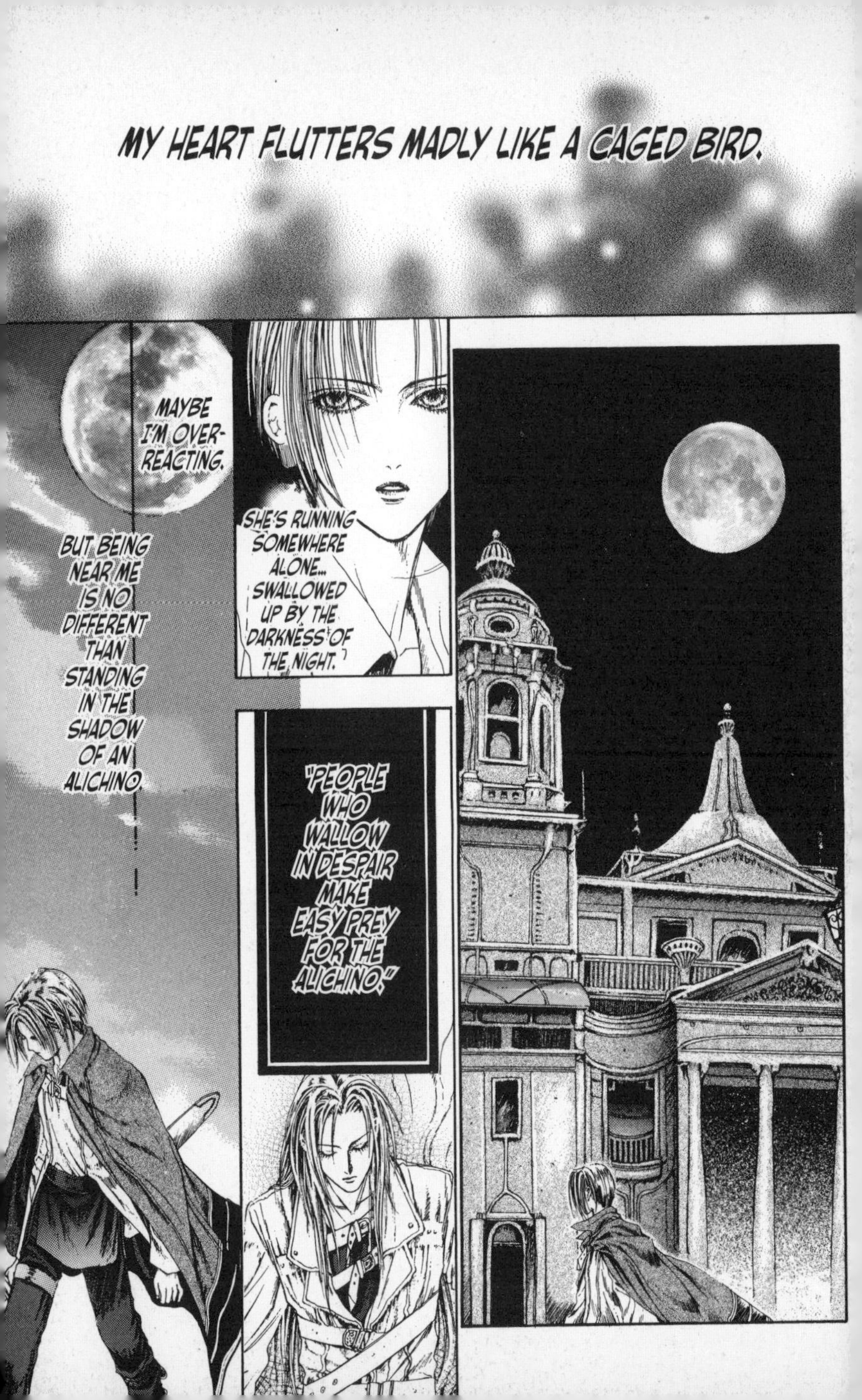
MY HEART FLUTTERS MADLY LIKE A CAGED BIRD.
SHE'S RUNNING SOMEWHERE ALONE... SWALLOWED UP BY THE DARKNESS OF THE NIGHT.
"PEOPLE WHO WALLOW IN DESPAIR MAKE EASY PREY FOR THE ALICHINO."
MAYBE I'M OVER-REACTING.
BUT BEING NEAR ME IS NO DIFFERENT THAN STANDING IN THE SHADOW OF AN ALICHINO.

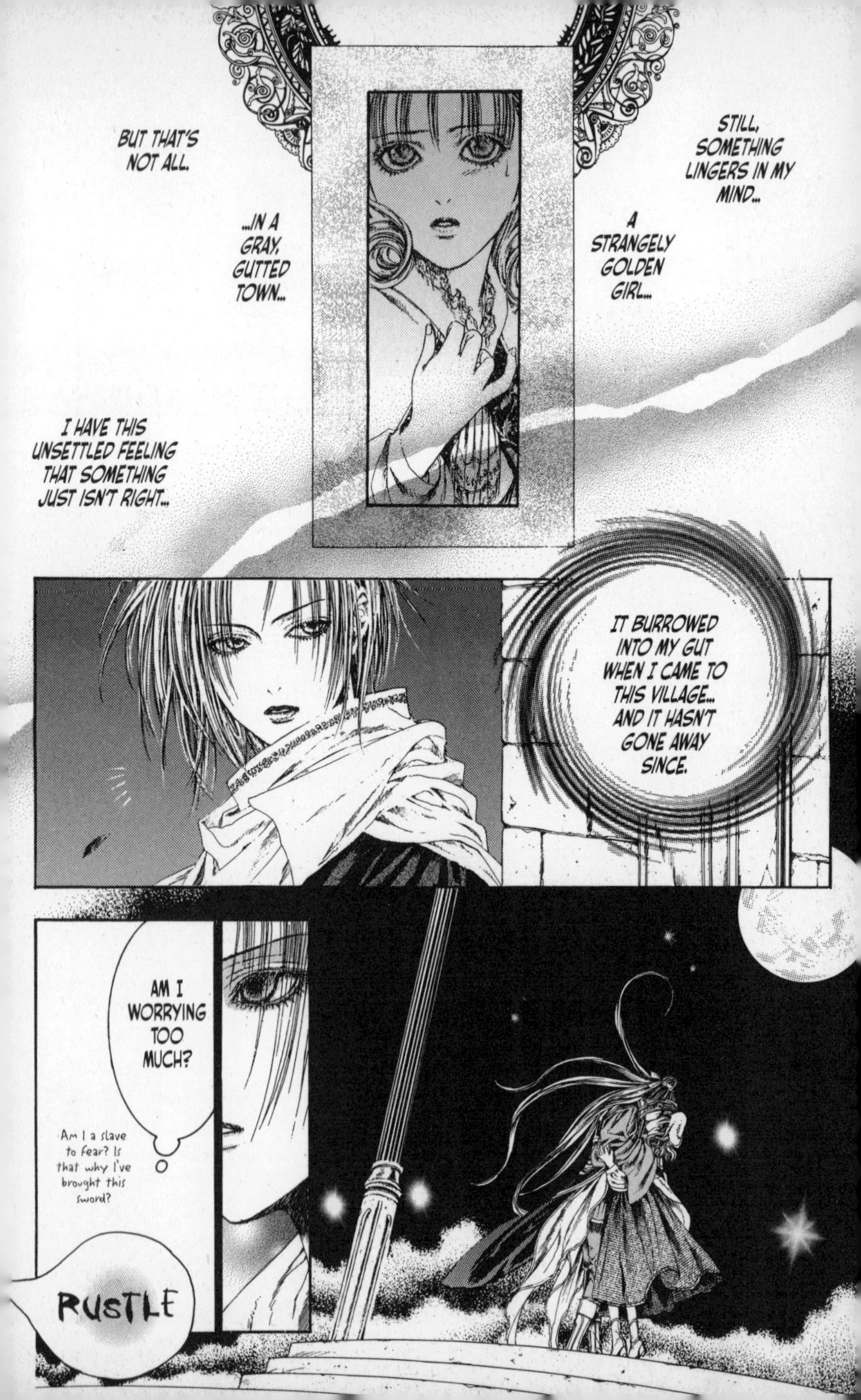
STILL, SOMETHING LINGERS IN MY MIND...
A STRANGELY GOLDEN GIRL...
...IN A GRAY, GUTTED TOWN...
BUT THAT'S NOT ALL.
I HAVE THIS UNSETTLED FEELING THAT SOMETHING JUST ISN'T RIGHT...
IT BURROWED INTO MY GUT WHEN I CAME TO THIS VILLAGE... AND IT HASN'T GONE AWAY SINCE.
AM I WORRYING TOO MUCH?
Am I a slave to fear? Is that why I've brought this sword?
RUSTLE

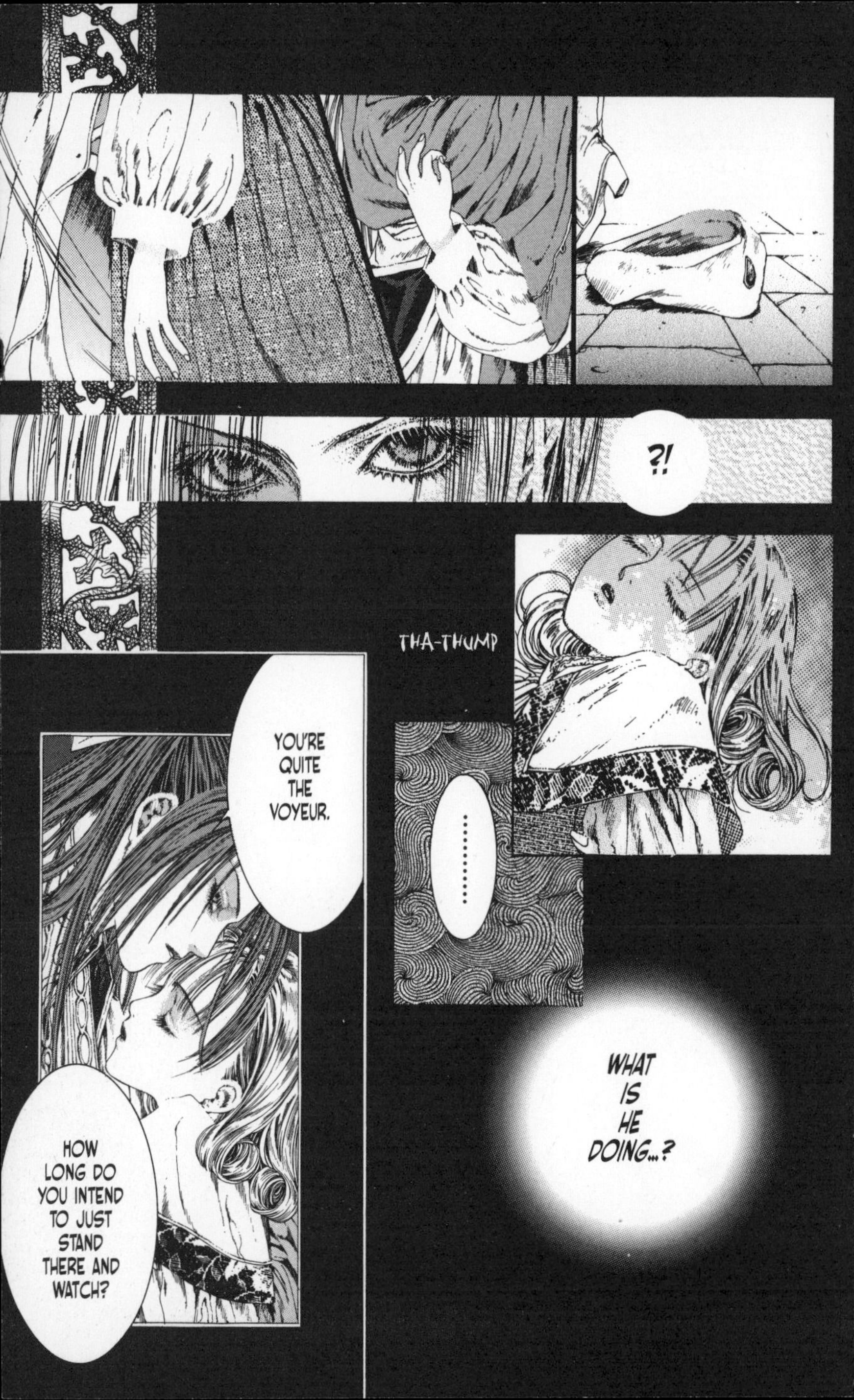
?!
THA-THUMP
......
WHAT IS HE DOING...?
YOU'RE QUITE THE VOYEUR.
HOW LONG DO YOU INTEND TO JUST STAND THERE AND WATCH?

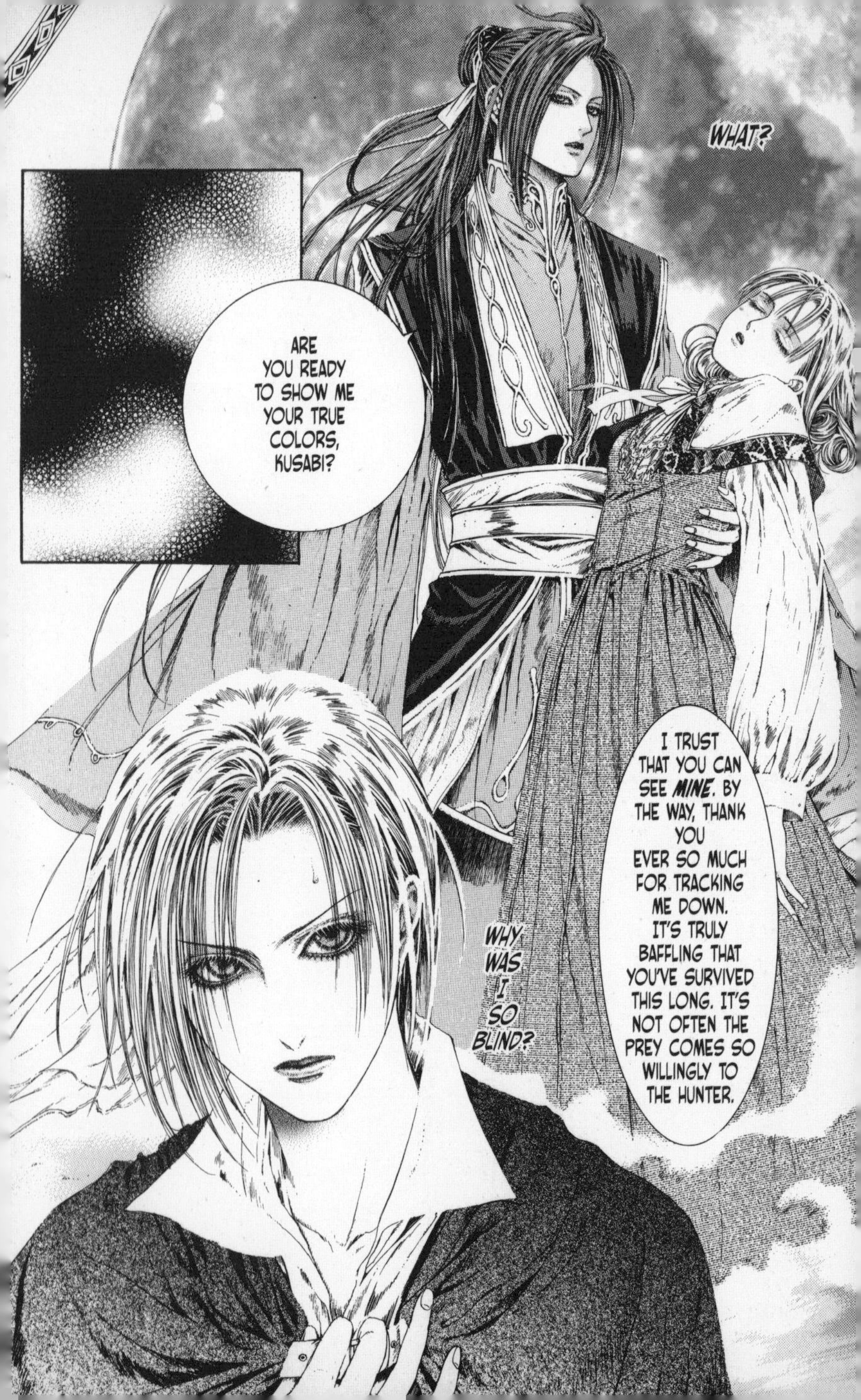
WHAT?
ARE YOU READY TO SHOW ME YOUR TRUE COLORS, KUSABI?
I TRUST THAT YOU CAN SEE *MINE*. BY THE WAY, THANK YOU EVER SO MUCH FOR TRACKING ME DOWN. IT'S TRULY BAFFLING THAT YOU'VE SURVIVED THIS LONG. IT'S NOT OFTEN THE PREY COMES SO WILLINGLY TO THE HUNTER.
WHY WAS I SO BLIND?

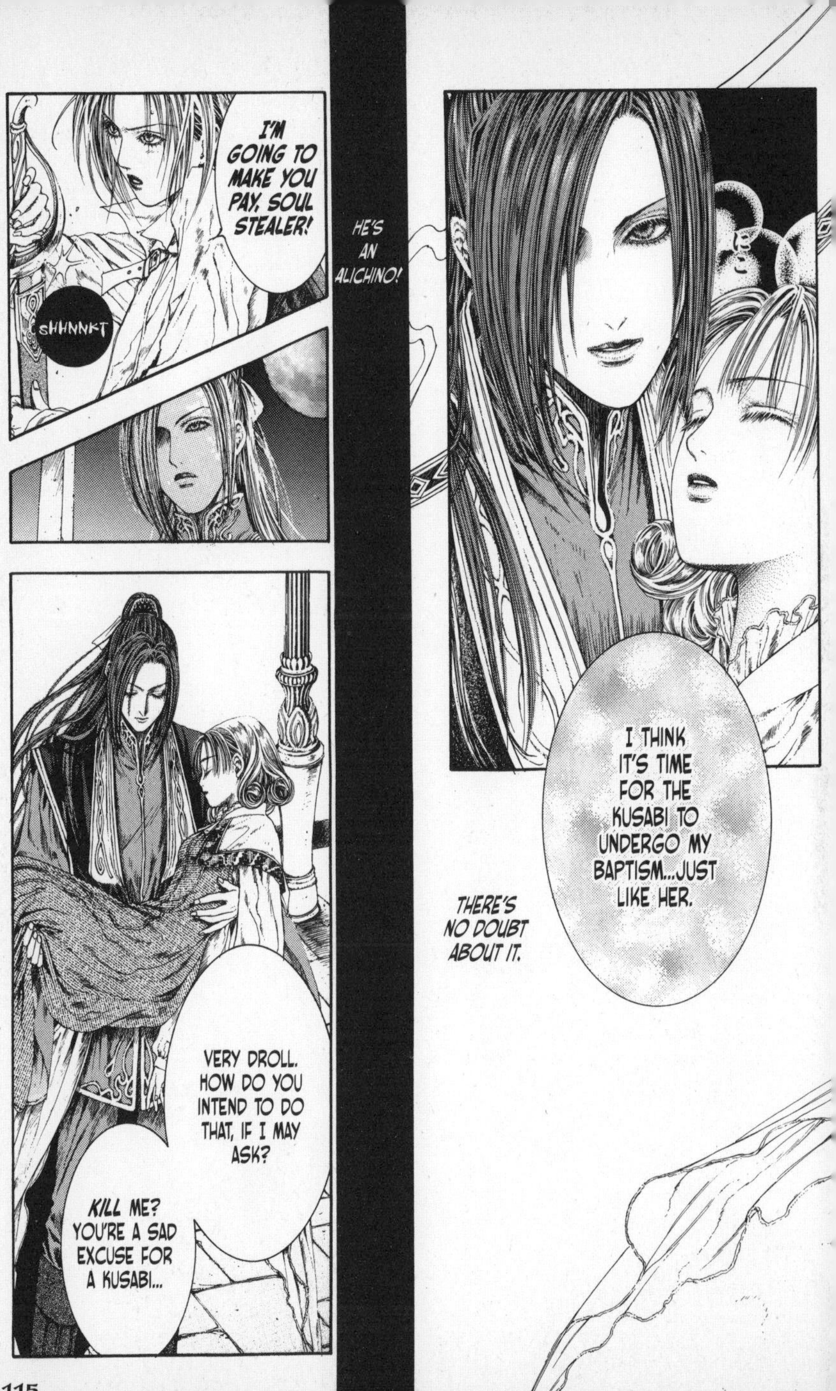
I THINK IT'S TIME FOR THE KUSABI TO UNDERGO MY BAPTISM...JUST LIKE HER.
HE'S AN ALICHINO!
THERE'S NO DOUBT ABOUT IT.
I'M GOING TO MAKE YOU PAY, SOUL STEALER!
SHHNNKT
VERY DROLL. HOW DO YOU INTEND TO DO THAT, IF I MAY ASK?
KILL ME? YOU'RE A SAD EXCUSE FOR A KUSABI...

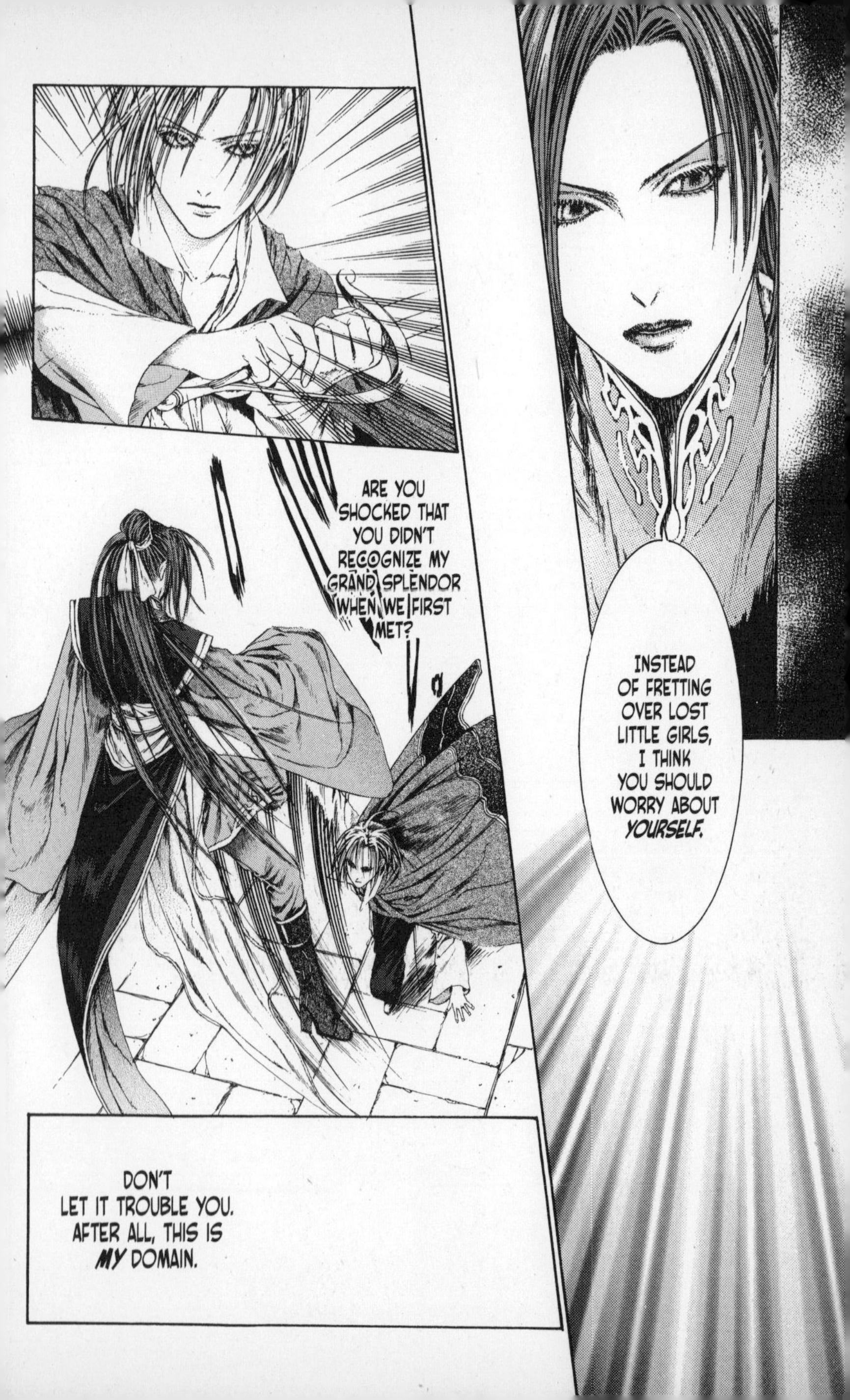
INSTEAD OF FRETTING OVER LOST LITTLE GIRLS, I THINK YOU SHOULD WORRY ABOUT *YOURSELF.*
ARE YOU SHOCKED THAT YOU DIDN'T RECOGNIZE MY GRAND SPLENDOR WHEN WE FIRST MET?
DON'T LET IT TROUBLE YOU. AFTER ALL, THIS IS *MY* DOMAIN.

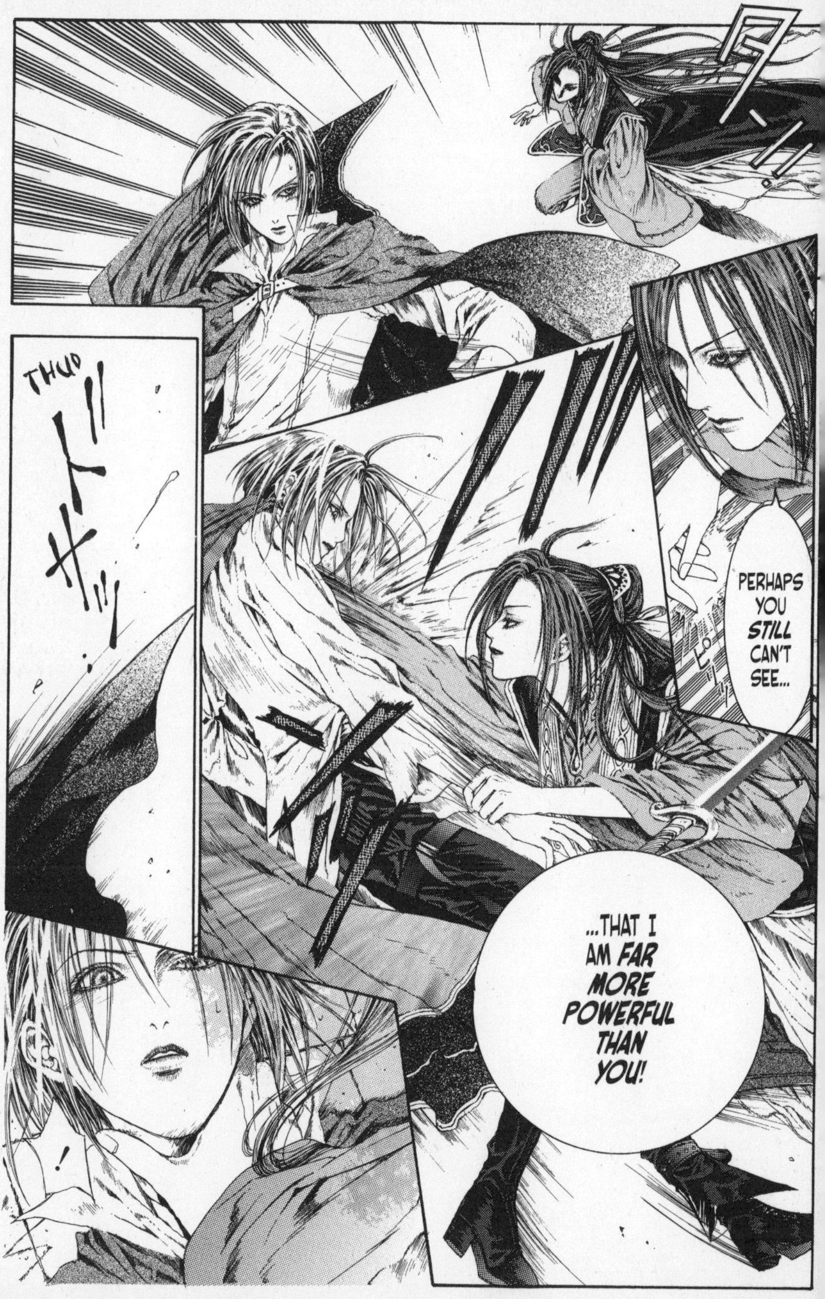
PERHAPS YOU STILL CAN'T SEE...
THUD
...THAT I AM FAR MORE POWERFUL THAN YOU!
!

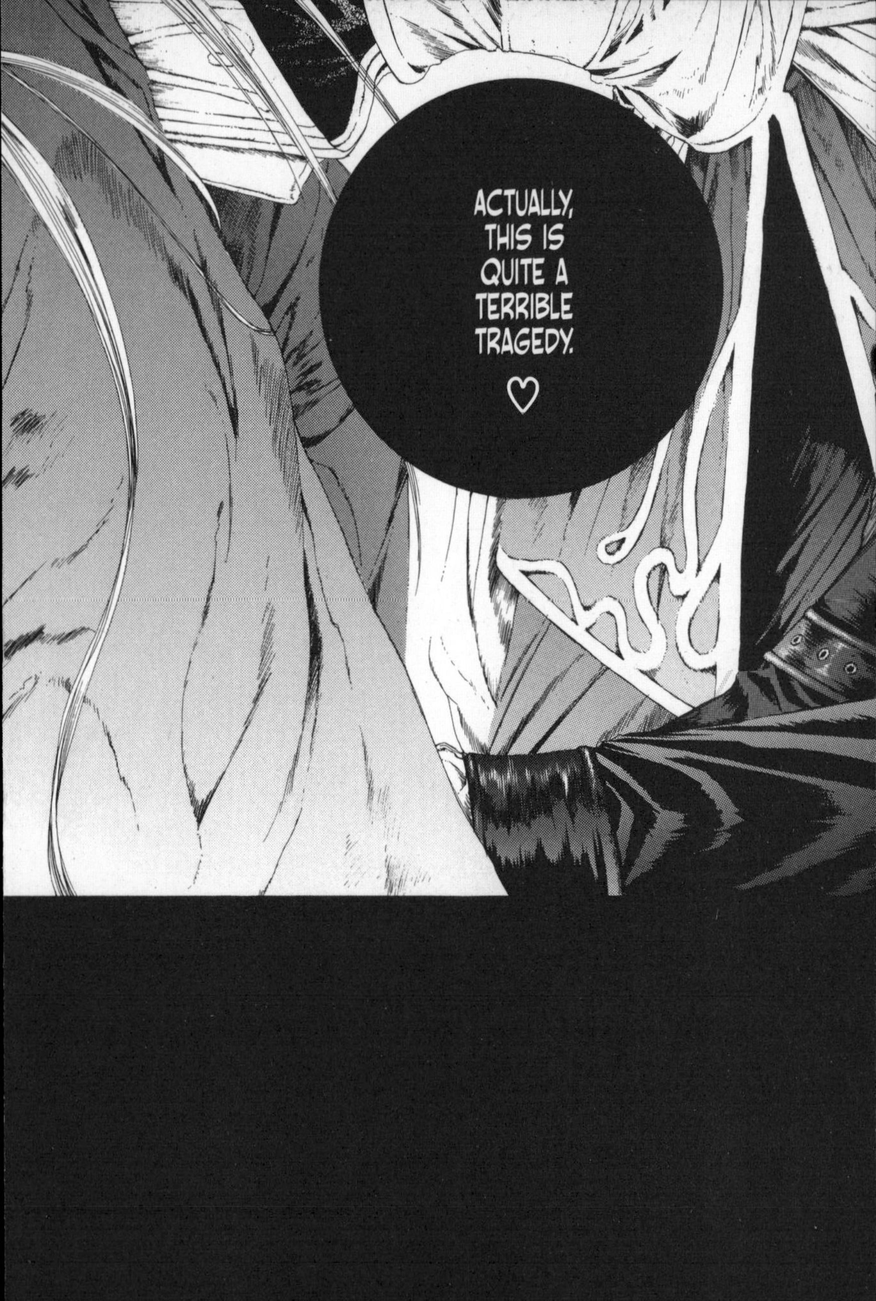
ACTUALLY, THIS IS QUITE A TERRIBLE TRAGEDY. ♡

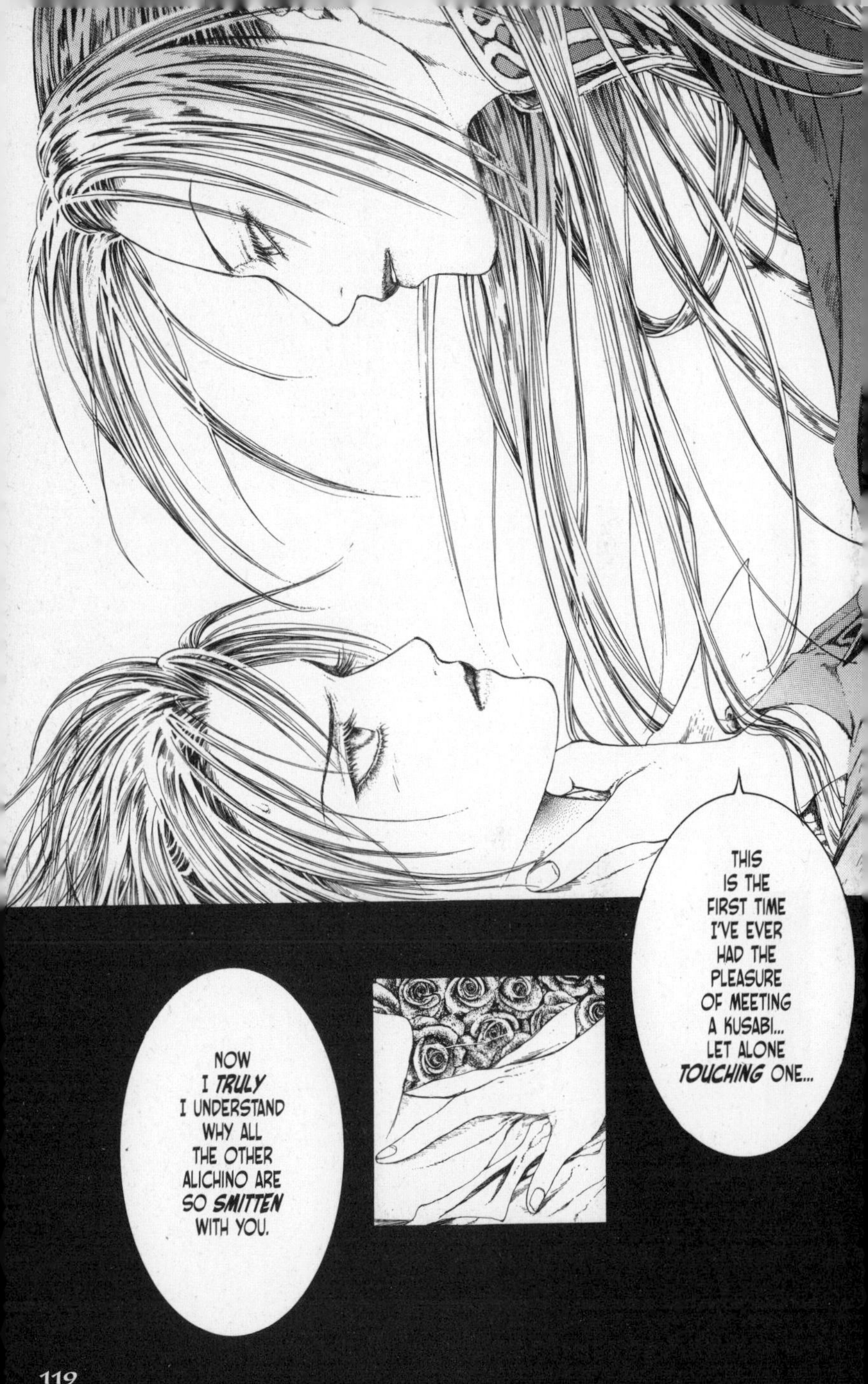
THIS IS THE FIRST TIME I'VE EVER HAD THE PLEASURE OF MEETING A KUSABI... LET ALONE *TOUCHING* ONE...
NOW I *TRULY* I UNDERSTAND WHY ALL THE OTHER ALICHINO ARE SO *SMITTEN* WITH YOU.

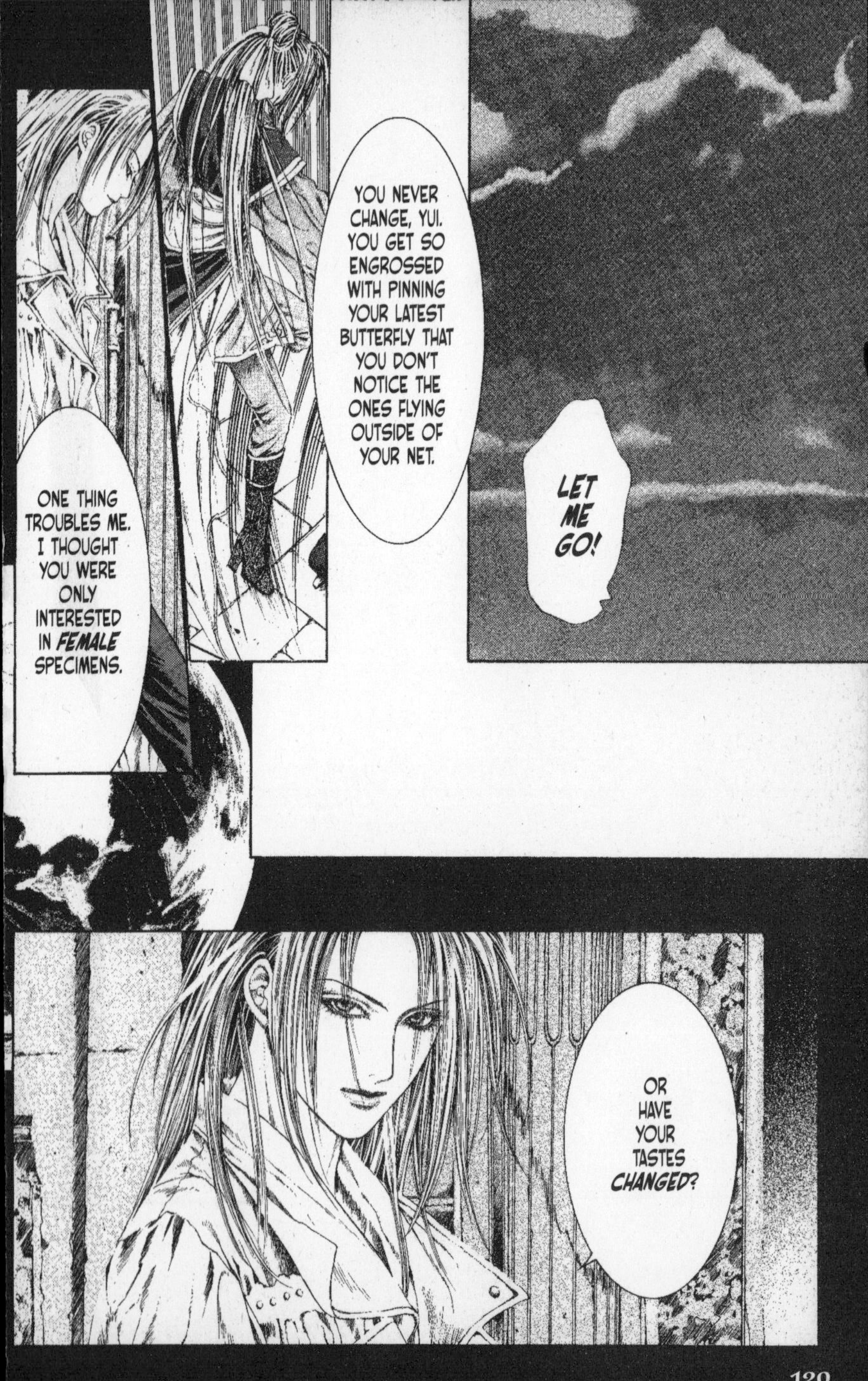
LET ME GO!
YOU NEVER CHANGE, YUI. YOU GET SO ENGROSSED WITH PINNING YOUR LATEST BUTTERFLY THAT YOU DON'T NOTICE THE ONES FLYING OUTSIDE OF YOUR NET.
ONE THING TROUBLES ME. I THOUGHT YOU WERE ONLY INTERESTED IN *FEMALE* SPECIMENS.
OR HAVE YOUR TASTES *CHANGED*?

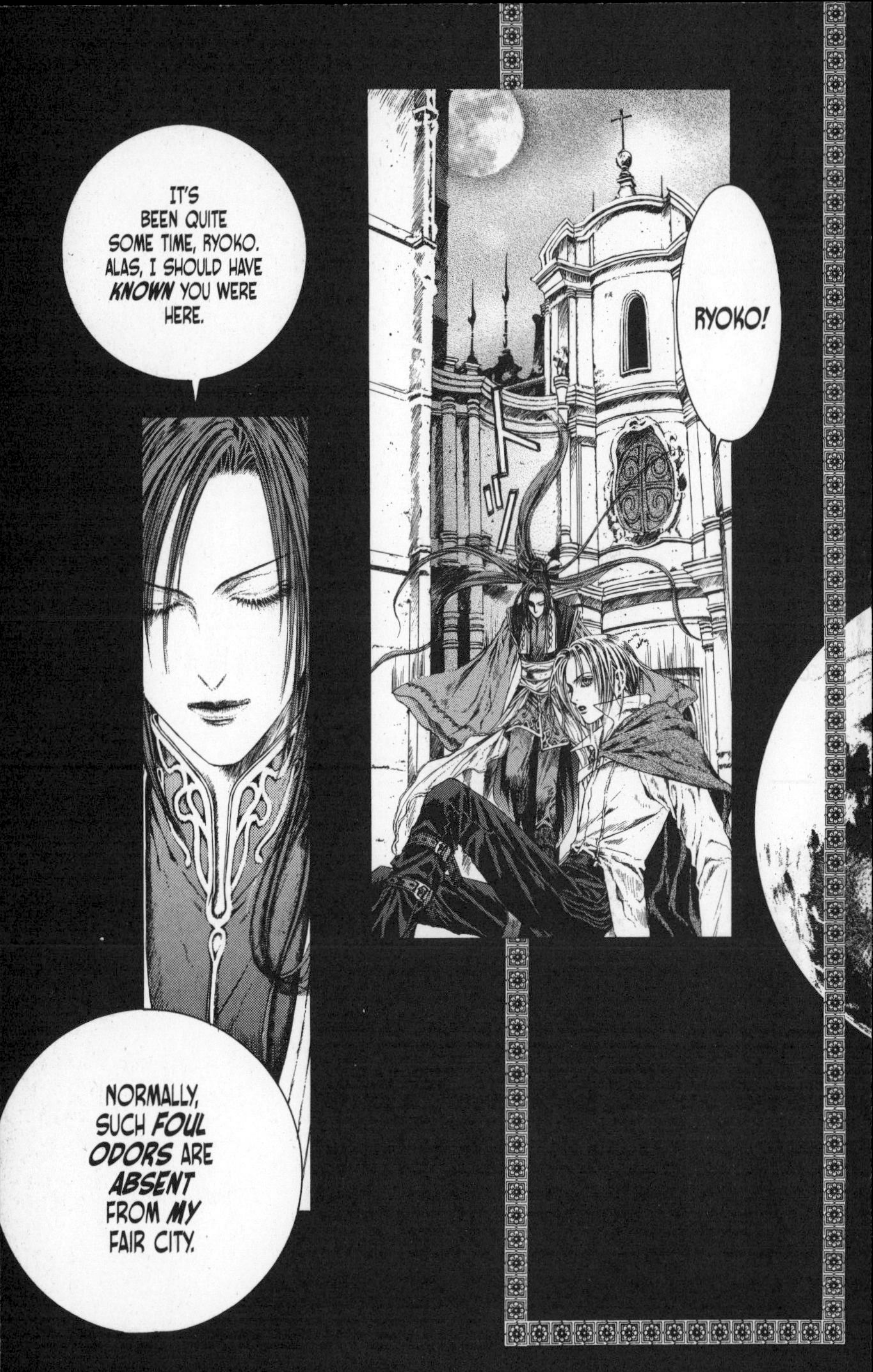
RYOKO!
IT'S BEEN QUITE SOME TIME, RYOKO. ALAS, I SHOULD HAVE KNOWN YOU WERE HERE.
NORMALLY, SUCH FOUL ODORS ARE ABSENT FROM MY FAIR CITY.

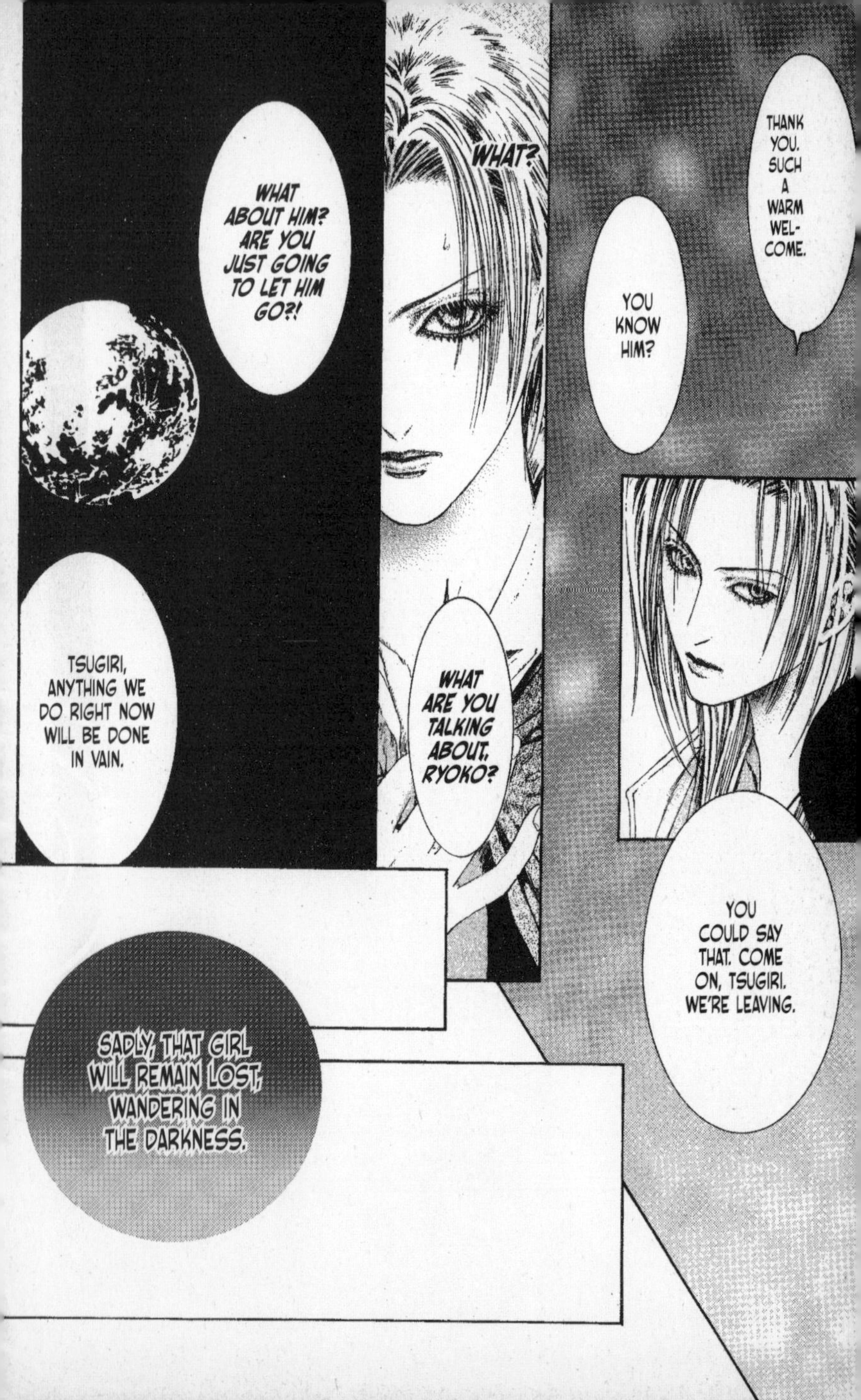
THANK YOU. SUCH A WARM WEL-COME.
YOU KNOW HIM?
YOU COULD SAY THAT. COME ON, TSUGIRI. WE'RE LEAVING.
WHAT?
WHAT ARE YOU TALKING ABOUT, RYOKO?
WHAT ABOUT HIM? ARE YOU JUST GOING TO LET HIM GO?!
TSUGIRI, ANYTHING WE DO RIGHT NOW WILL BE DONE IN VAIN.
SADLY, THAT GIRL WILL REMAIN LOST, WANDERING IN THE DARKNESS.

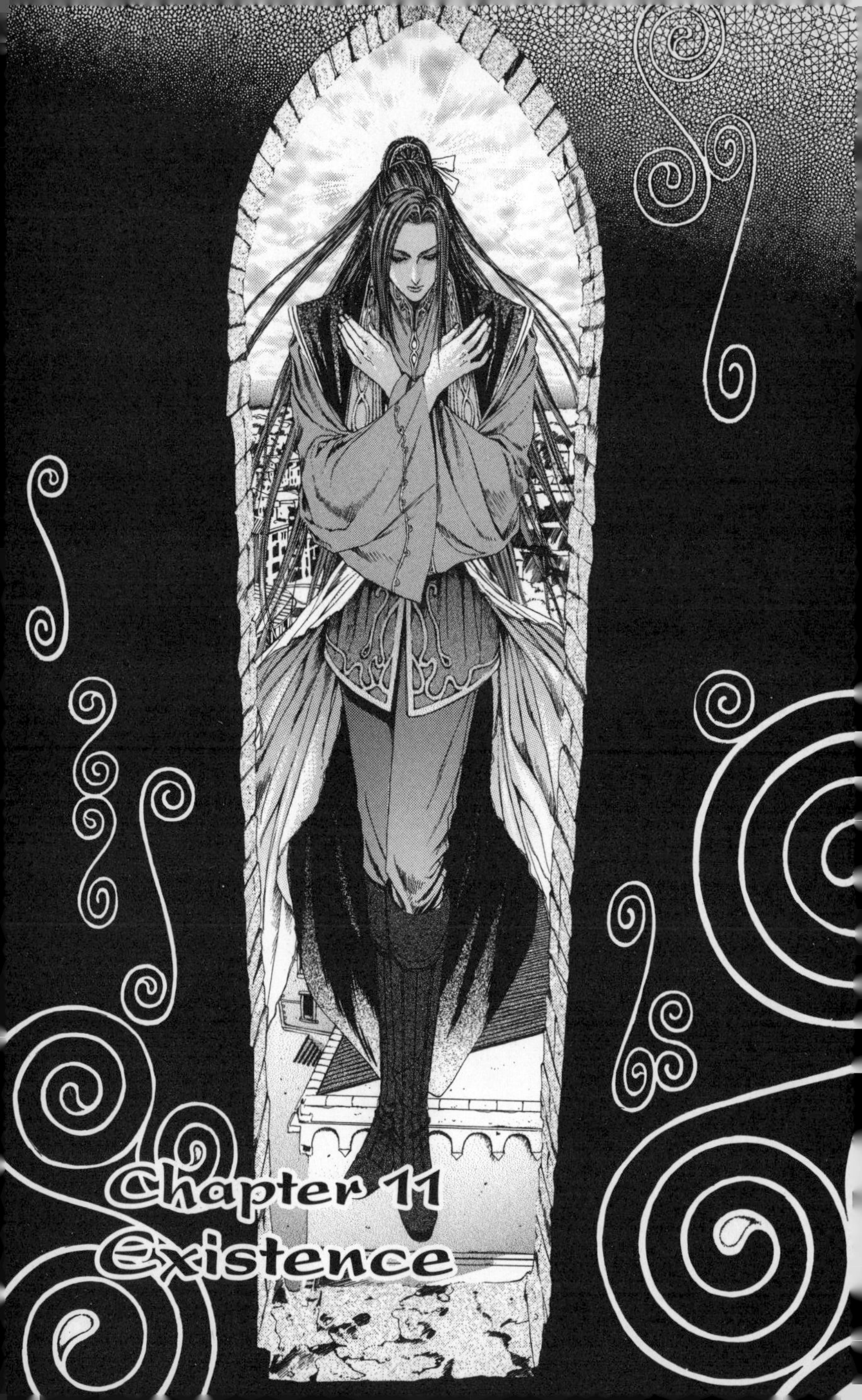
Chapter 11
Existence

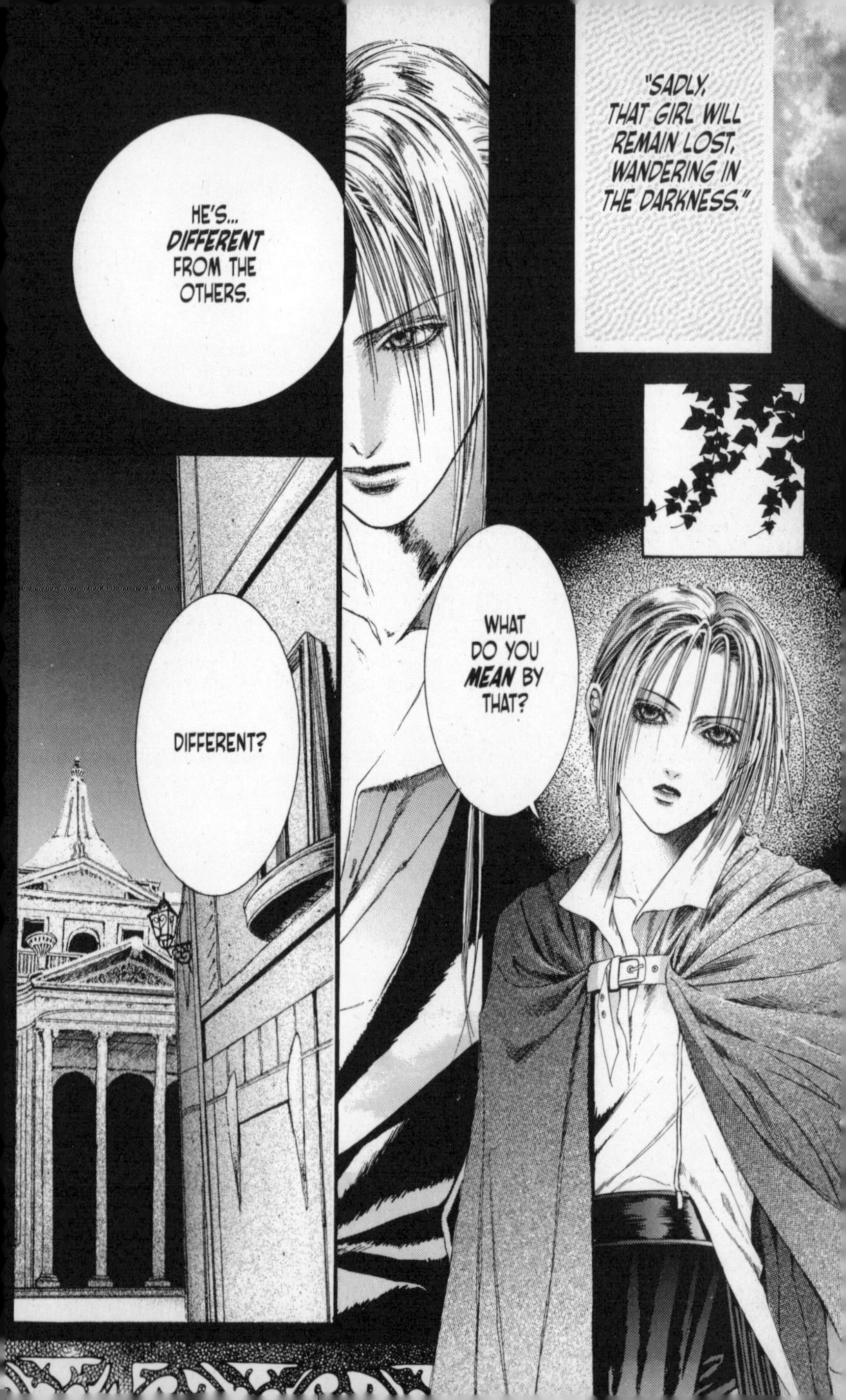
"SADLY, THAT GIRL WILL REMAIN LOST, WANDERING IN THE DARKNESS."
HE'S... **DIFFERENT** FROM THE OTHERS.
WHAT DO YOU **MEAN** BY THAT?
DIFFERENT?

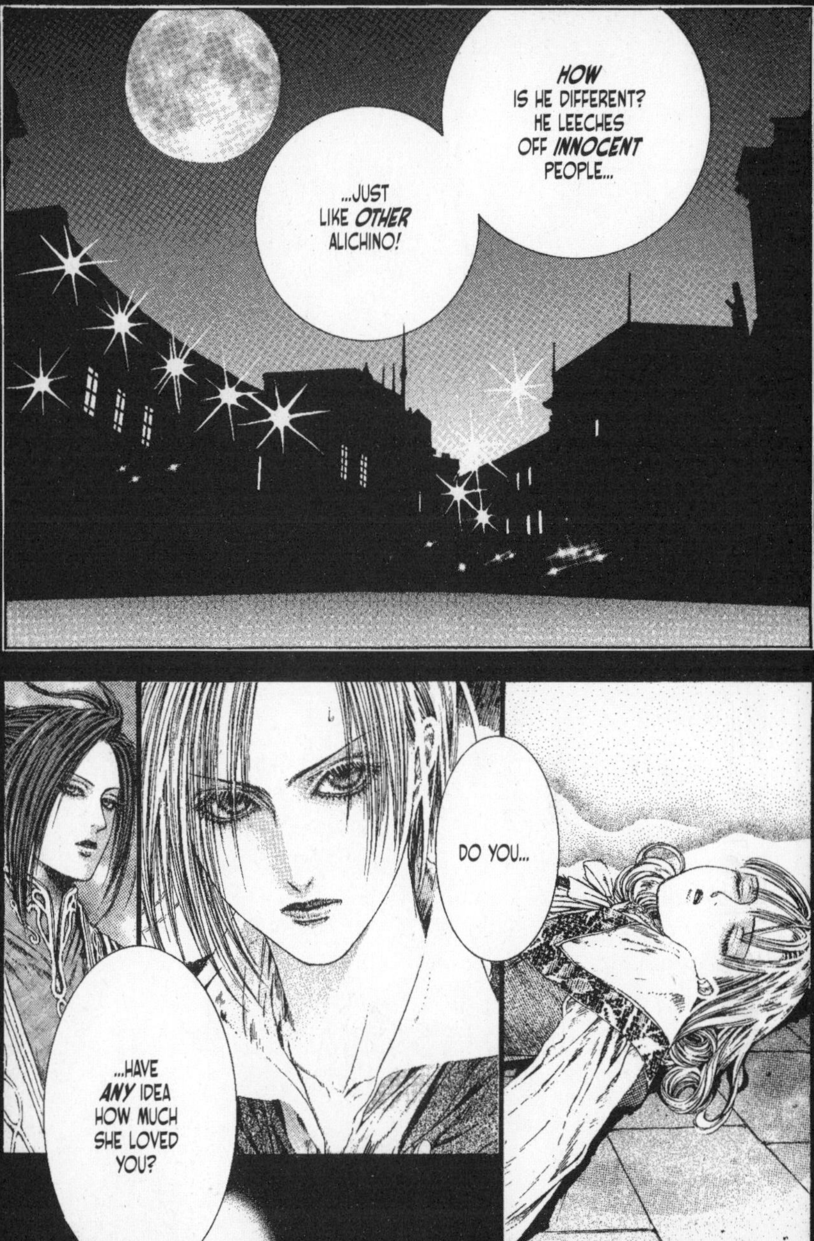
HOW IS HE DIFFERENT? HE LEECHES OFF INNOCENT PEOPLE...
...JUST LIKE OTHER ALICHINO!
DO YOU...
...HAVE ANY IDEA HOW MUCH SHE LOVED YOU?

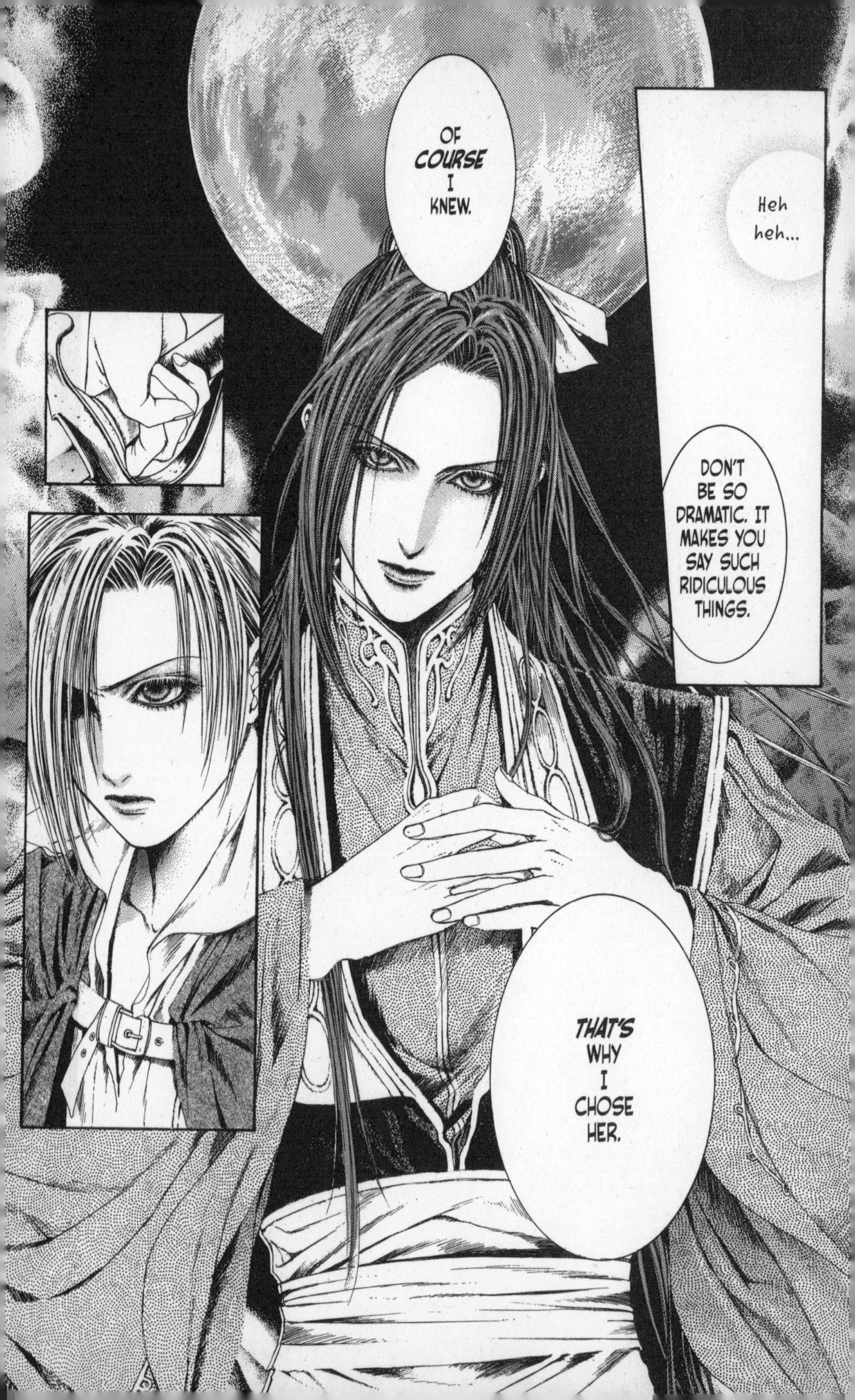

Heh heh...
OF COURSE I KNEW.
DON'T BE SO DRAMATIC. IT MAKES YOU SAY SUCH RIDICULOUS THINGS.
THAT'S WHY I CHOSE HER.

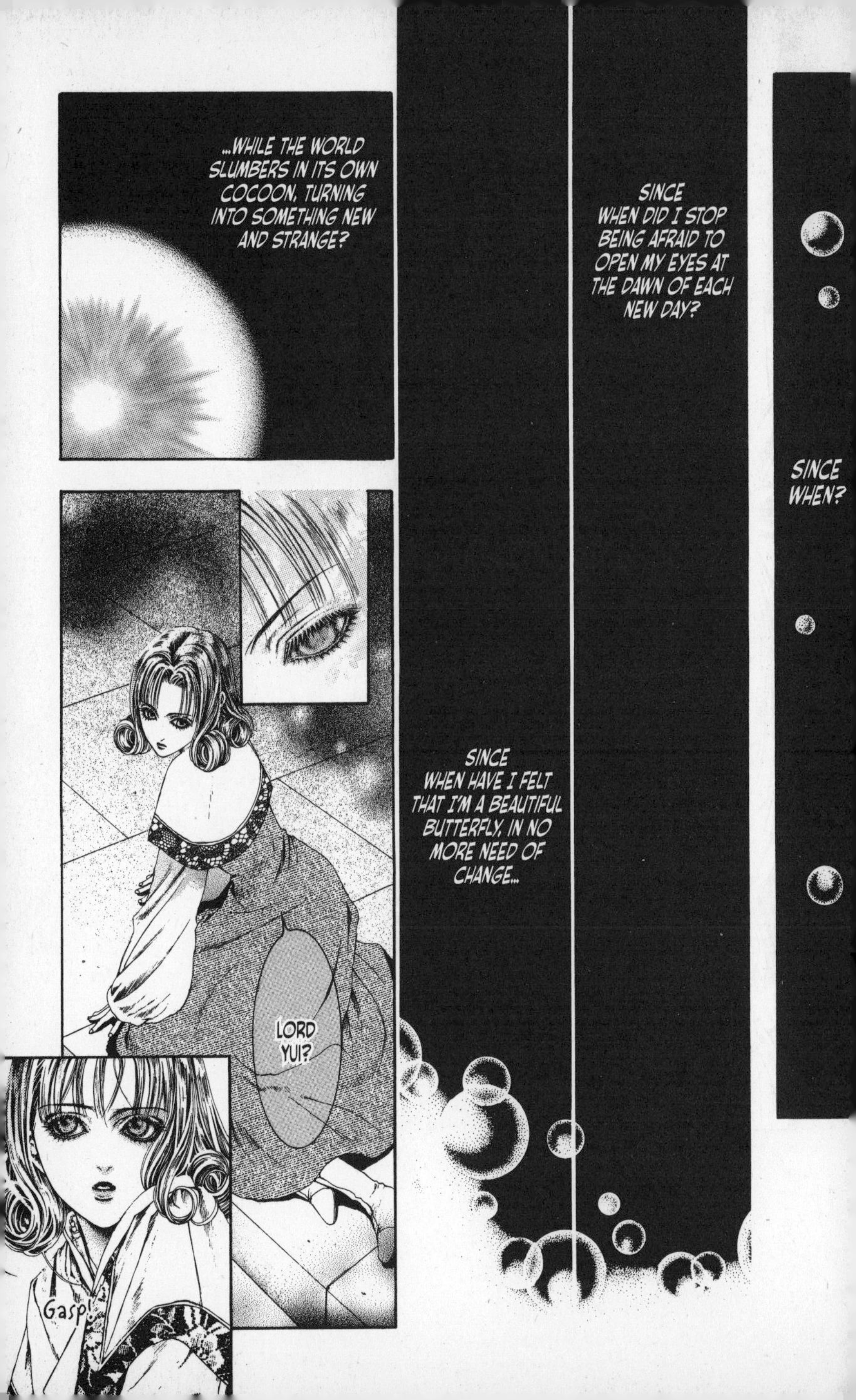
SINCE WHEN?
SINCE WHEN DID I STOP BEING AFRAID TO OPEN MY EYES AT THE DAWN OF EACH NEW DAY?
SINCE WHEN HAVE I FELT THAT I'M A BEAUTIFUL BUTTERFLY, IN NO MORE NEED OF CHANGE...
...WHILE THE WORLD SLUMBERS IN ITS OWN COCOON, TURNING INTO SOMETHING NEW AND STRANGE?
LORD YUI?
Gasp!

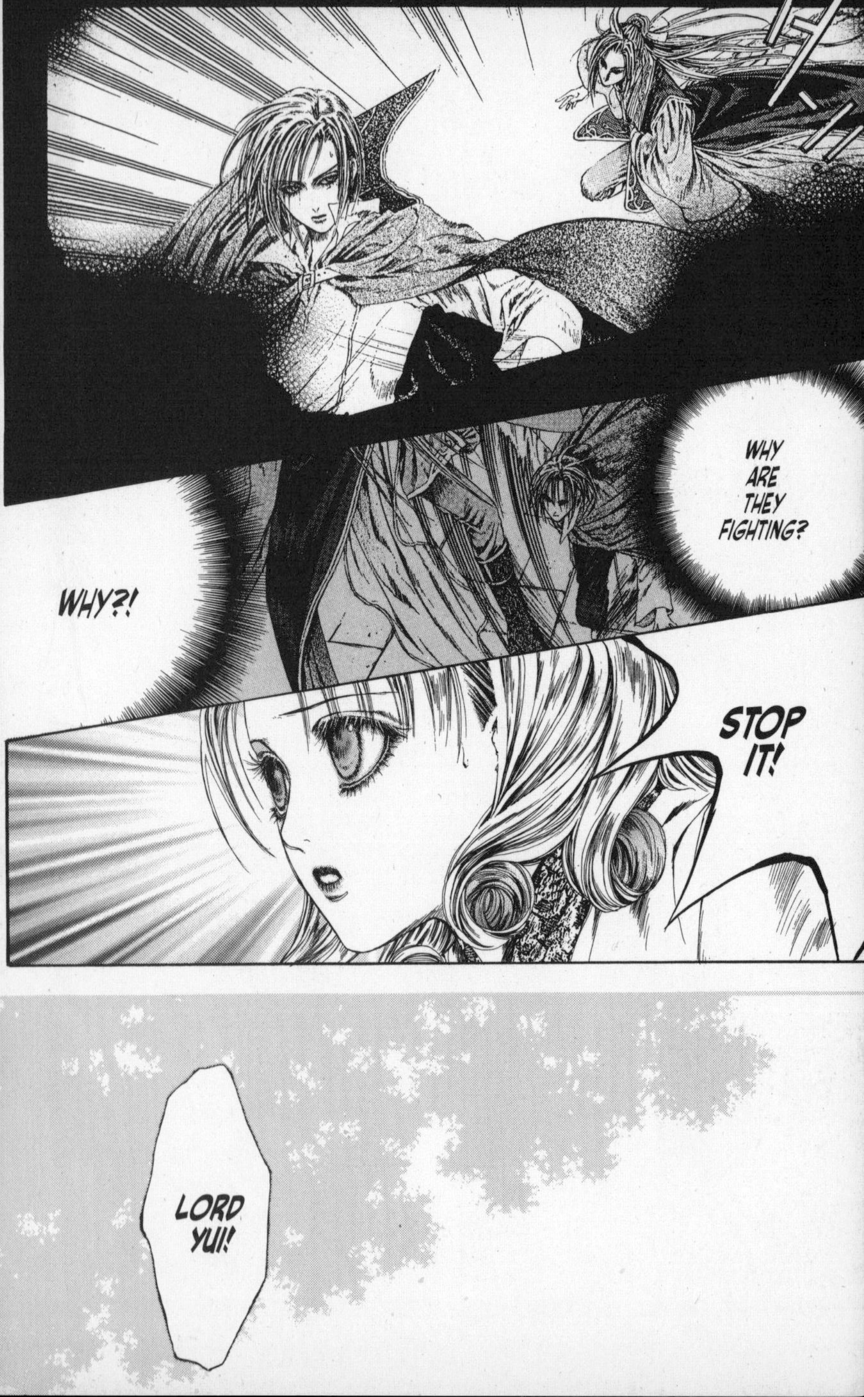
WHY ARE THEY FIGHTING?
WHY?!
STOP IT!
LORD YUI!

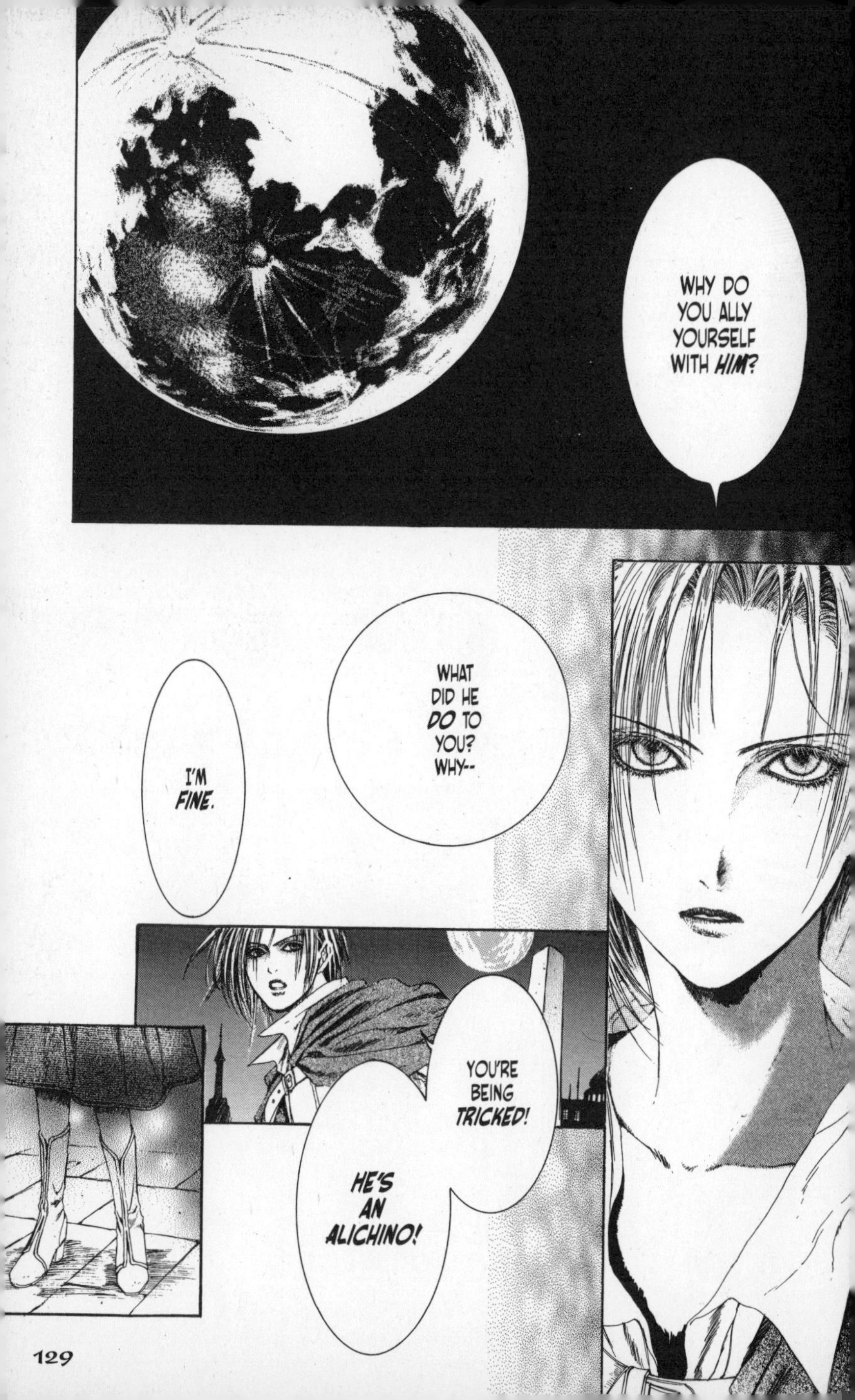

WHY DO YOU ALLY YOURSELF WITH HIM?
WHAT DID HE DO TO YOU? WHY--
I'M FINE.
YOU'RE BEING TRICKED!
HE'S AN ALICHINO!

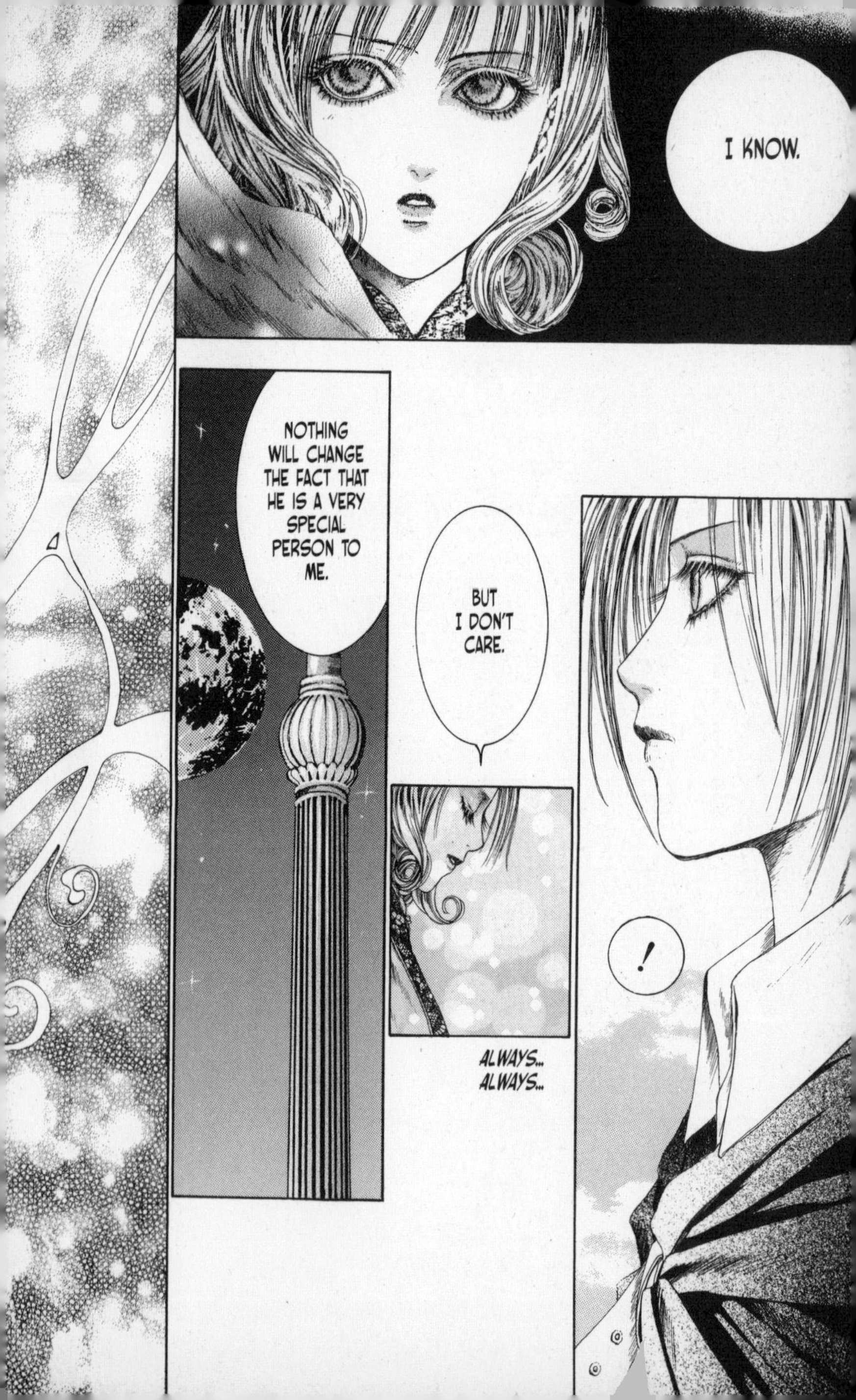
I KNOW.
NOTHING WILL CHANGE THE FACT THAT HE IS A VERY SPECIAL PERSON TO ME.
BUT I DON'T CARE.
!
ALWAYS... ALWAYS...

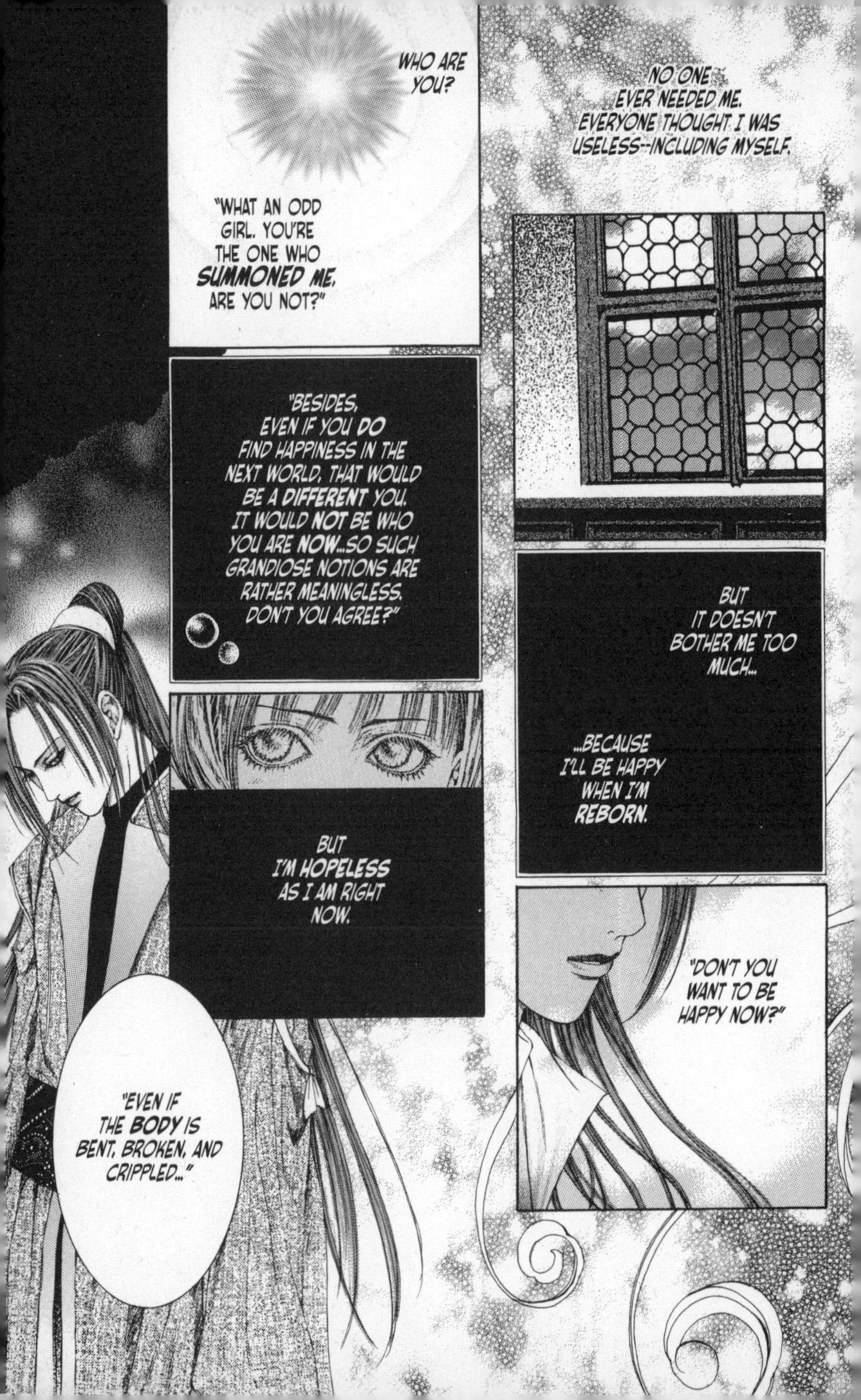
NO ONE EVER NEEDED ME. EVERYONE THOUGHT I WAS USELESS--INCLUDING MYSELF.
BUT IT DOESN'T BOTHER ME TOO MUCH...
...BECAUSE I'LL BE HAPPY WHEN I'M REBORN.
"DON'T YOU WANT TO BE HAPPY NOW?"
WHO ARE YOU?
"WHAT AN ODD GIRL. YOU'RE THE ONE WHO SUMMONED ME, ARE YOU NOT?"
"BESIDES, EVEN IF YOU DO FIND HAPPINESS IN THE NEXT WORLD, THAT WOULD BE A DIFFERENT YOU. IT WOULD NOT BE WHO YOU ARE NOW...SO SUCH GRANDIOSE NOTIONS ARE RATHER MEANINGLESS. DON'T YOU AGREE?"
BUT I'M HOPELESS AS I AM RIGHT NOW.
"EVEN IF THE BODY IS BENT, BROKEN, AND CRIPPLED..."

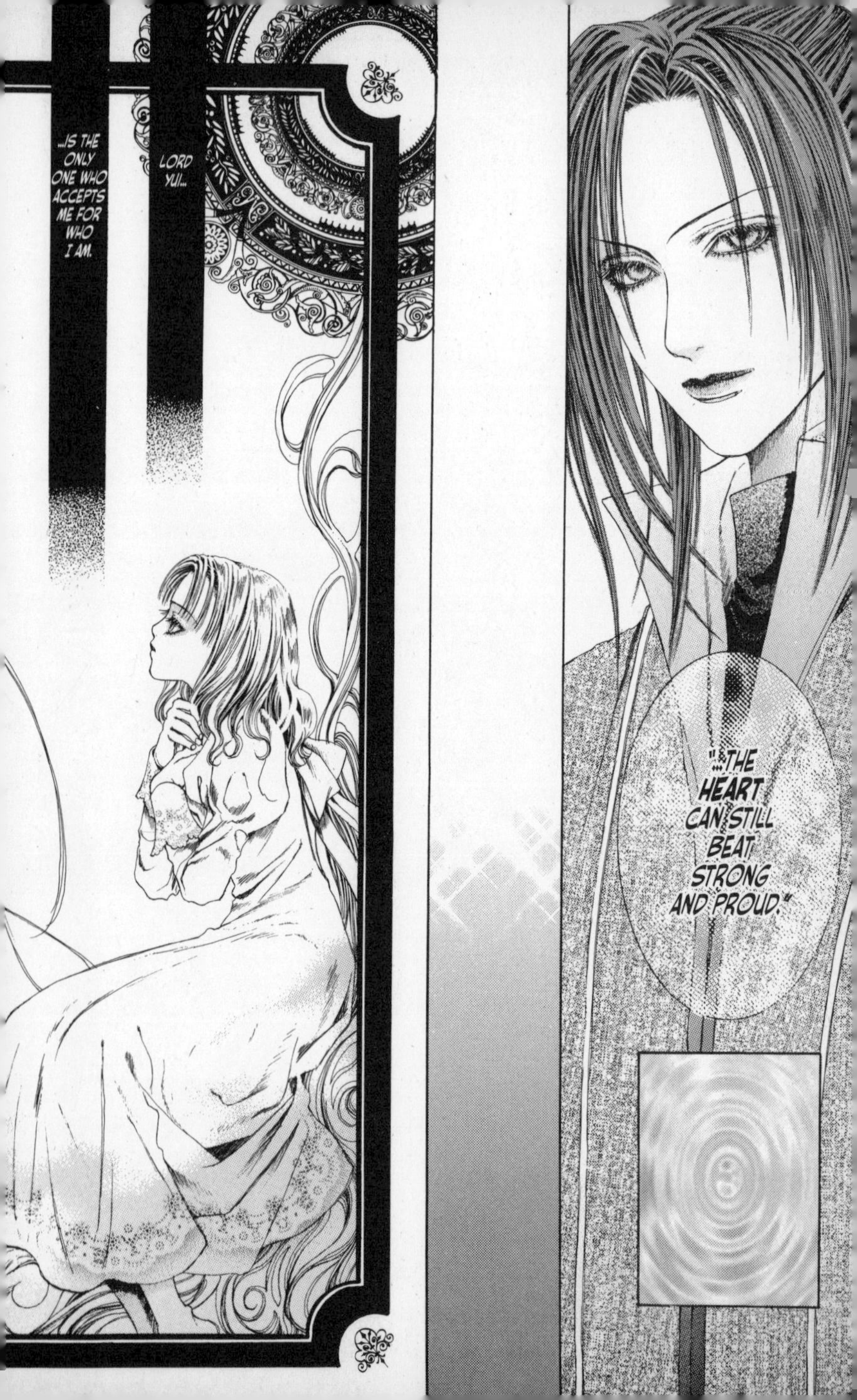
"...THE HEART CAN STILL BEAT STRONG AND PROUD."
LORD YUI...
...IS THE ONLY ONE WHO ACCEPTS ME FOR WHO I AM.

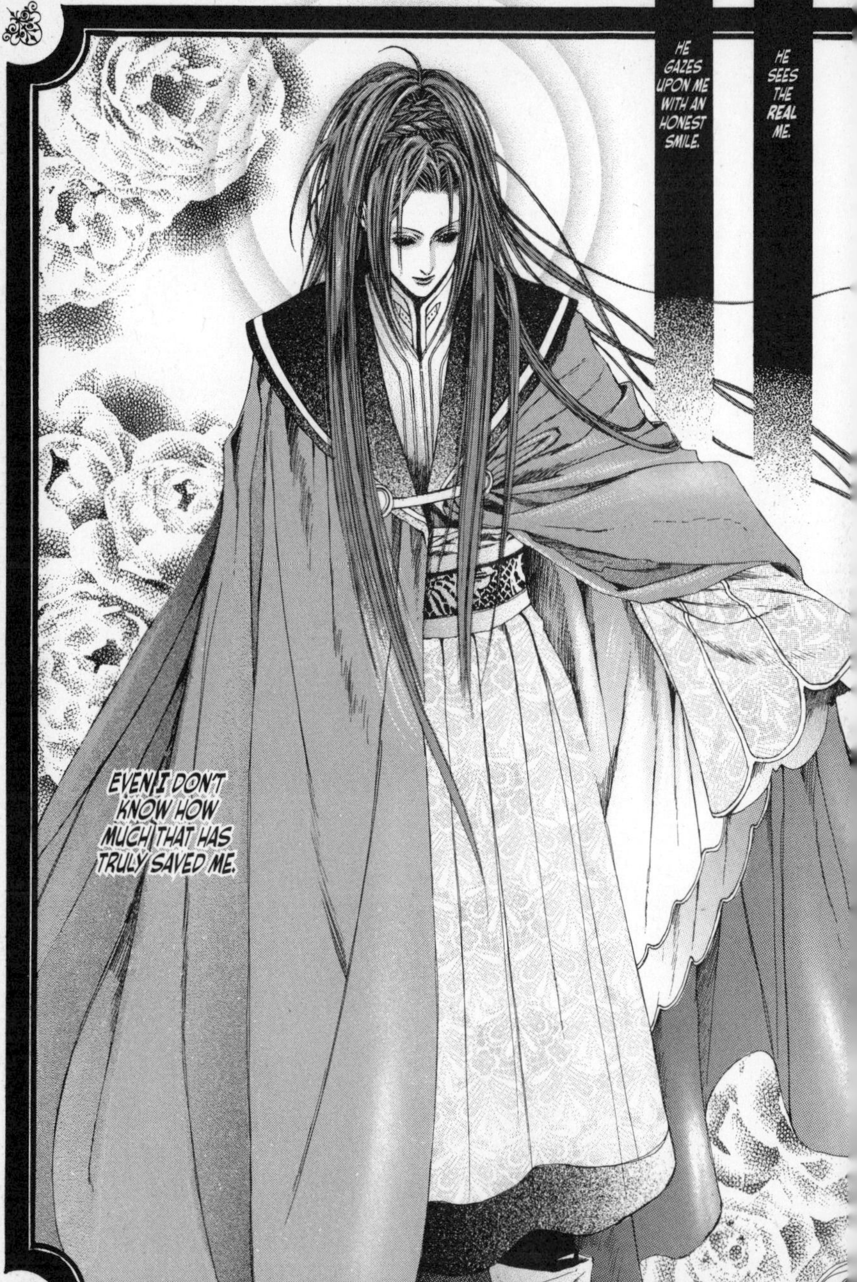
HE SEES THE REAL ME.
HE GAZES UPON ME WITH AN HONEST SMILE.
EVEN I DON'T KNOW HOW MUCH THAT HAS TRULY SAVED ME.

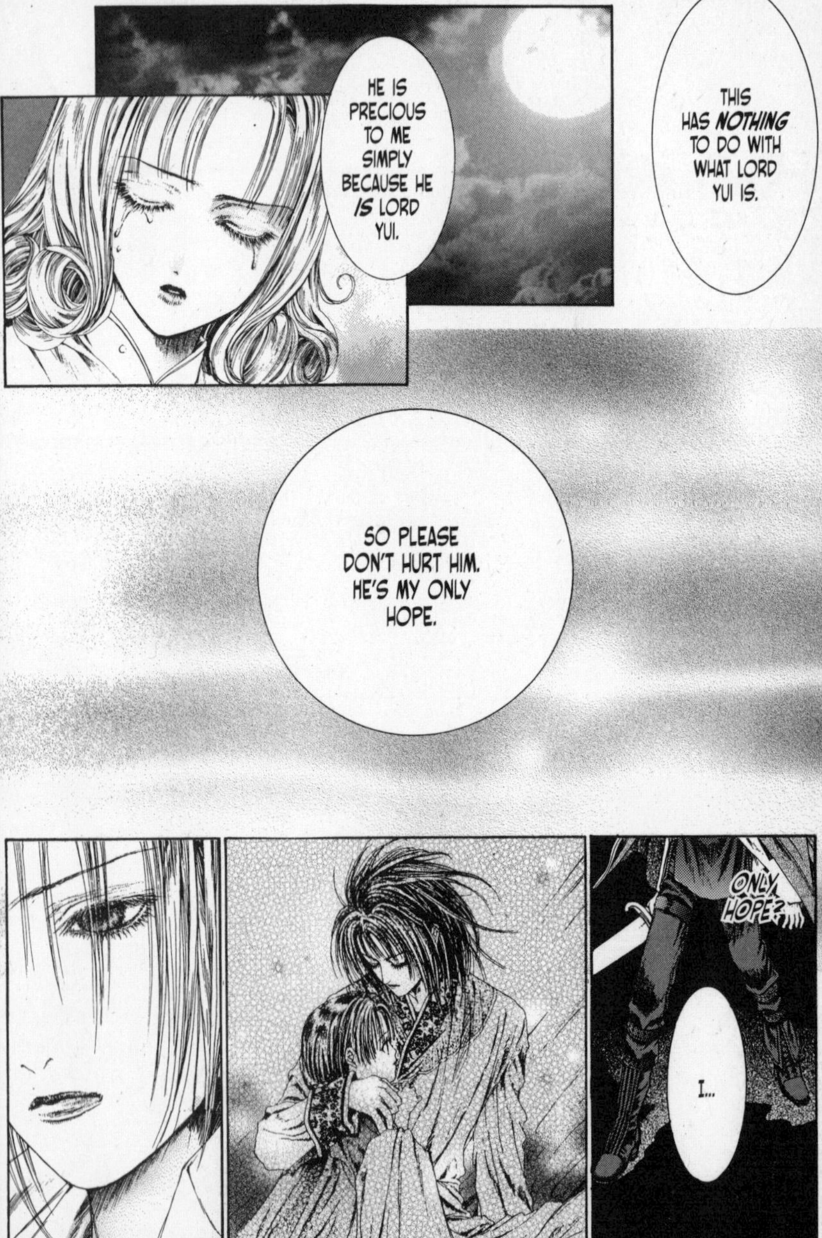
THIS HAS NOTHING TO DO WITH WHAT LORD YUI IS.
HE IS PRECIOUS TO ME SIMPLY BECAUSE HE IS LORD YUI.
SO PLEASE DON'T HURT HIM. HE'S MY ONLY HOPE.
ONLY HOPE?
I...

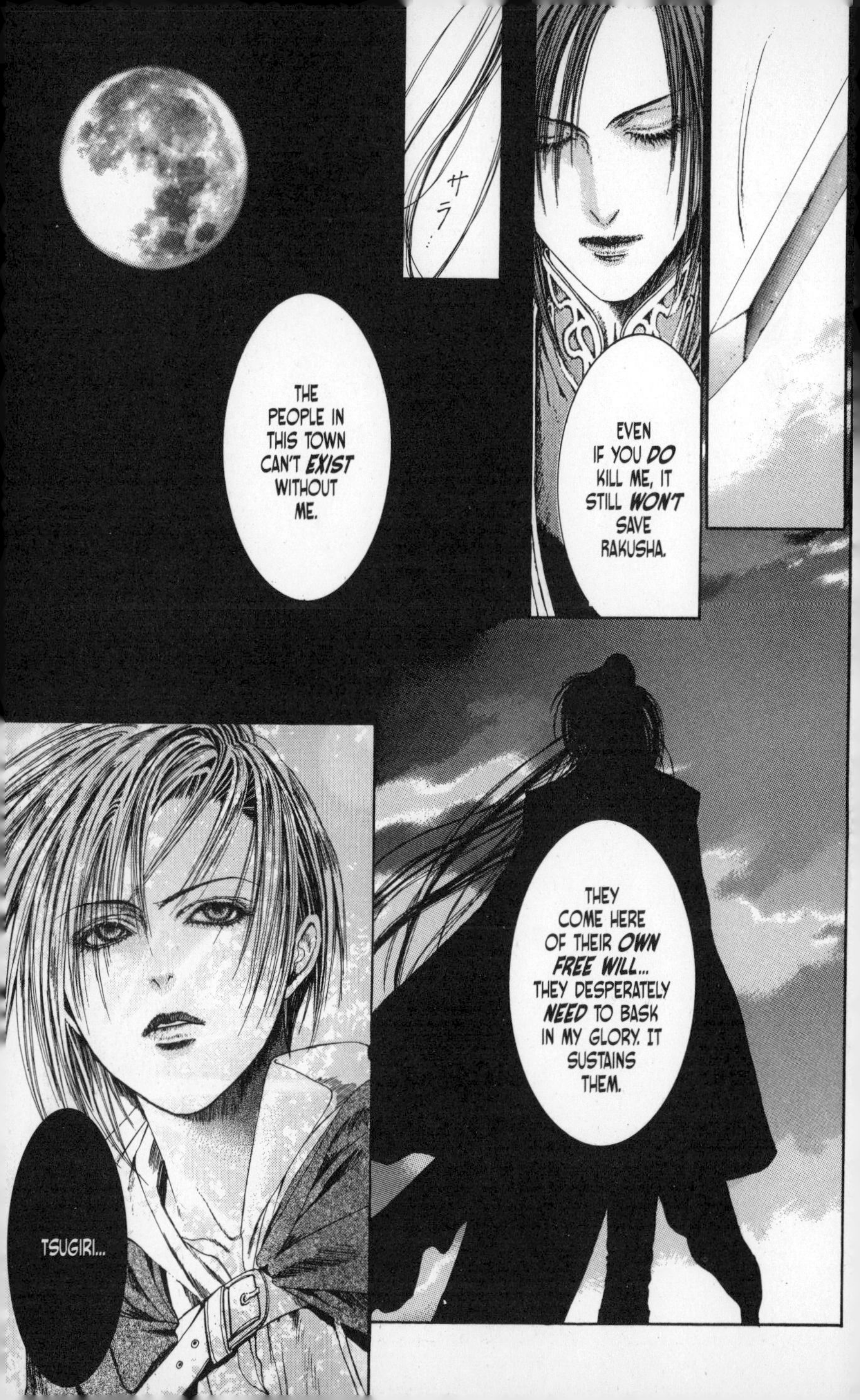
EVEN IF YOU *DO* KILL ME, IT STILL *WON'T* SAVE RAKUSHA.
サラ…
THE PEOPLE IN THIS TOWN CAN'T *EXIST* WITHOUT ME.
THEY COME HERE OF THEIR *OWN FREE WILL*... THEY DESPERATELY *NEED* TO BASK IN MY GLORY. IT SUSTAINS THEM.
TSUGIRI...

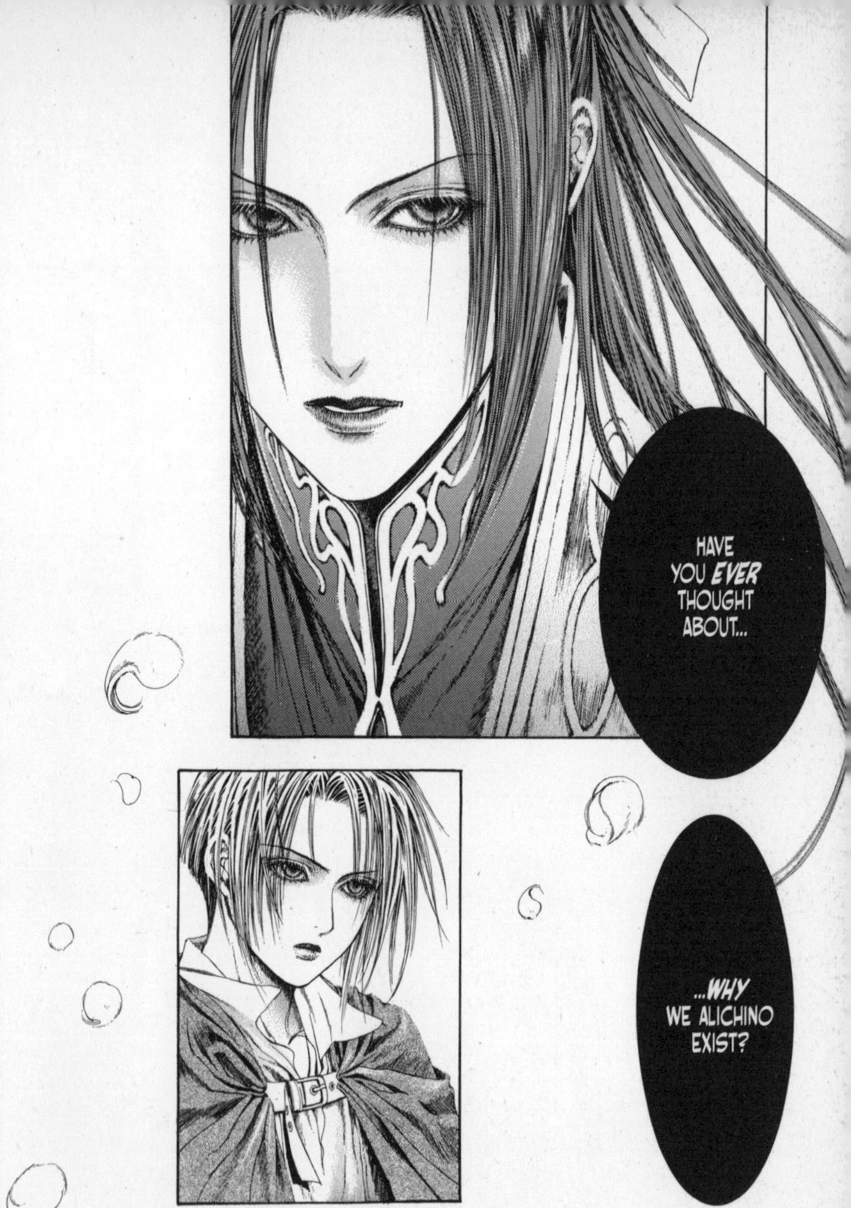
HAVE YOU EVER THOUGHT ABOUT...
...WHY WE ALICHINO EXIST?

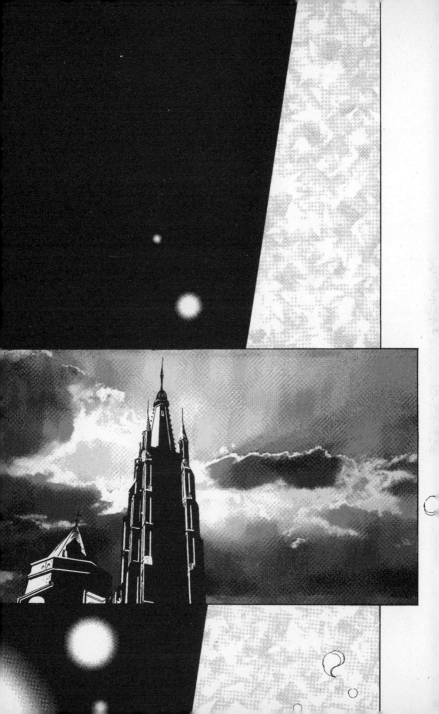

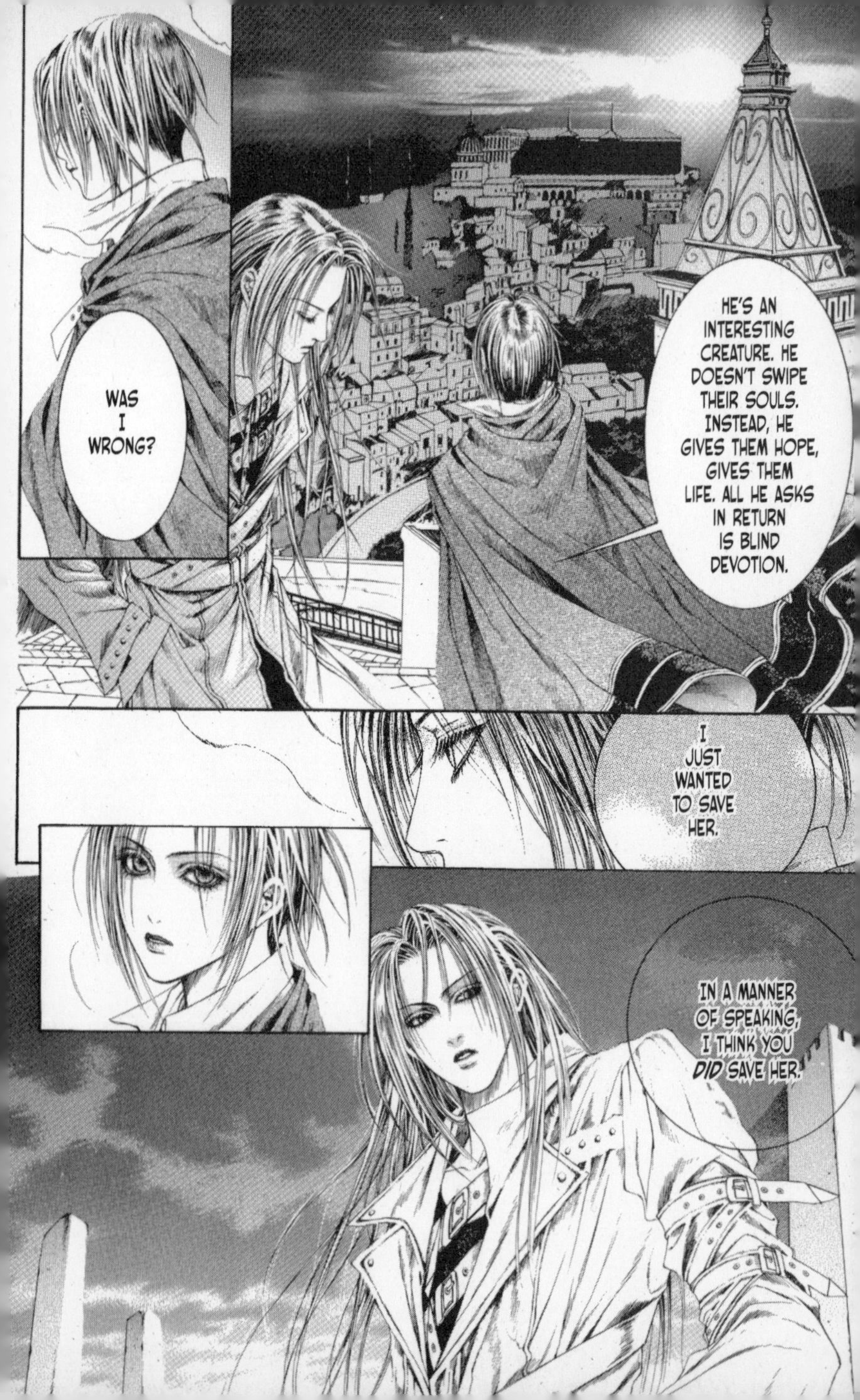
HE'S AN INTERESTING CREATURE. HE DOESN'T SWIPE THEIR SOULS. INSTEAD, HE GIVES THEM HOPE, GIVES THEM LIFE. ALL HE ASKS IN RETURN IS BLIND DEVOTION.
WAS I WRONG?
I JUST WANTED TO SAVE HER.
IN A MANNER OF SPEAKING, I THINK YOU *DID* SAVE HER.

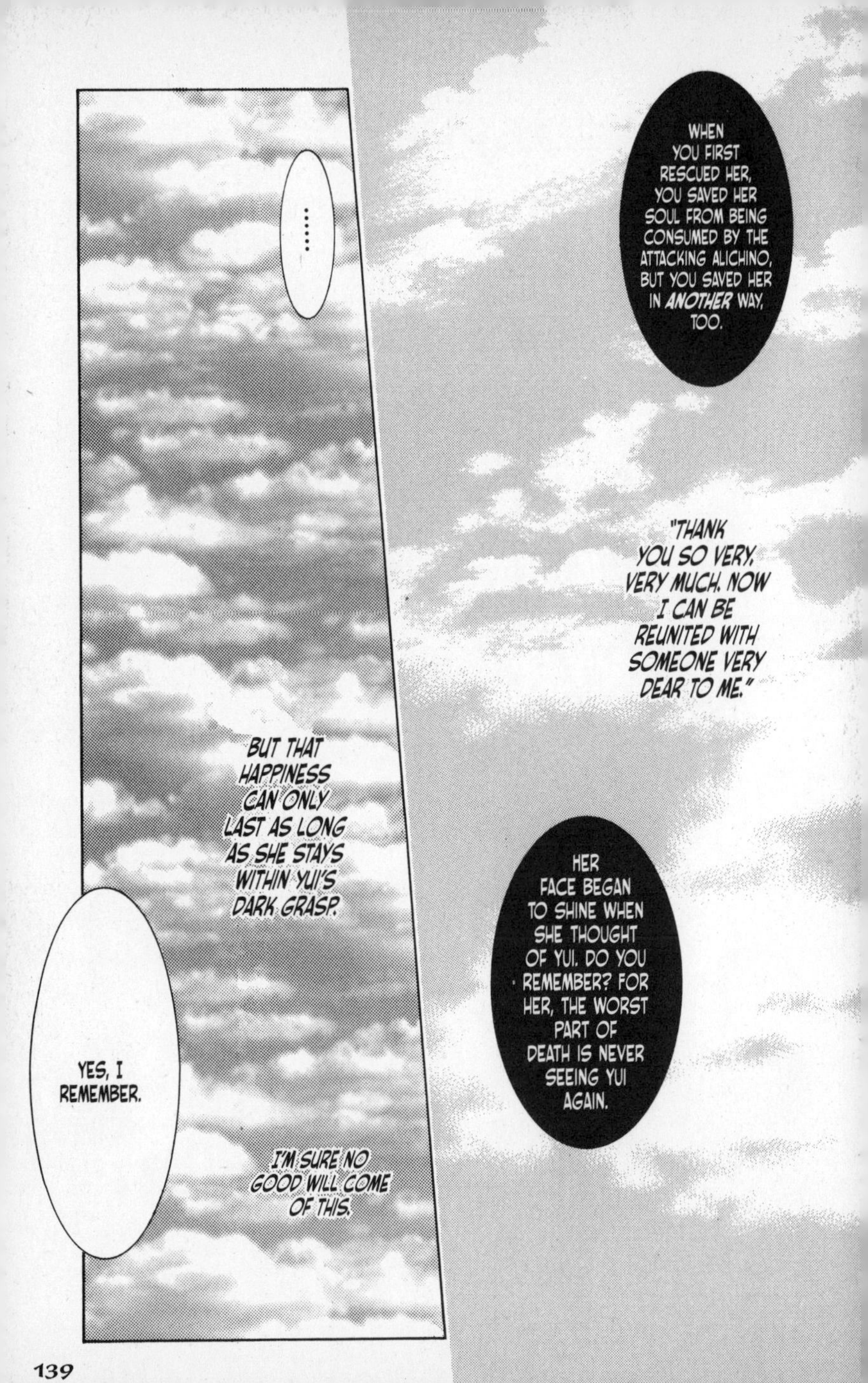

WHEN YOU FIRST RESCUED HER, YOU SAVED HER SOUL FROM BEING CONSUMED BY THE ATTACKING ALICHINO, BUT YOU SAVED HER IN *ANOTHER* WAY, TOO.
"THANK YOU SO VERY, VERY MUCH. NOW I CAN BE REUNITED WITH SOMEONE VERY DEAR TO ME."
HER FACE BEGAN TO SHINE WHEN SHE THOUGHT OF YUI. DO YOU REMEMBER? FOR HER, THE WORST PART OF DEATH IS NEVER SEEING YUI AGAIN.
......
BUT THAT HAPPINESS CAN ONLY LAST AS LONG AS SHE STAYS WITHIN YUI'S DARK GRASP.
YES, I REMEMBER.
I'M SURE NO GOOD WILL COME OF THIS.

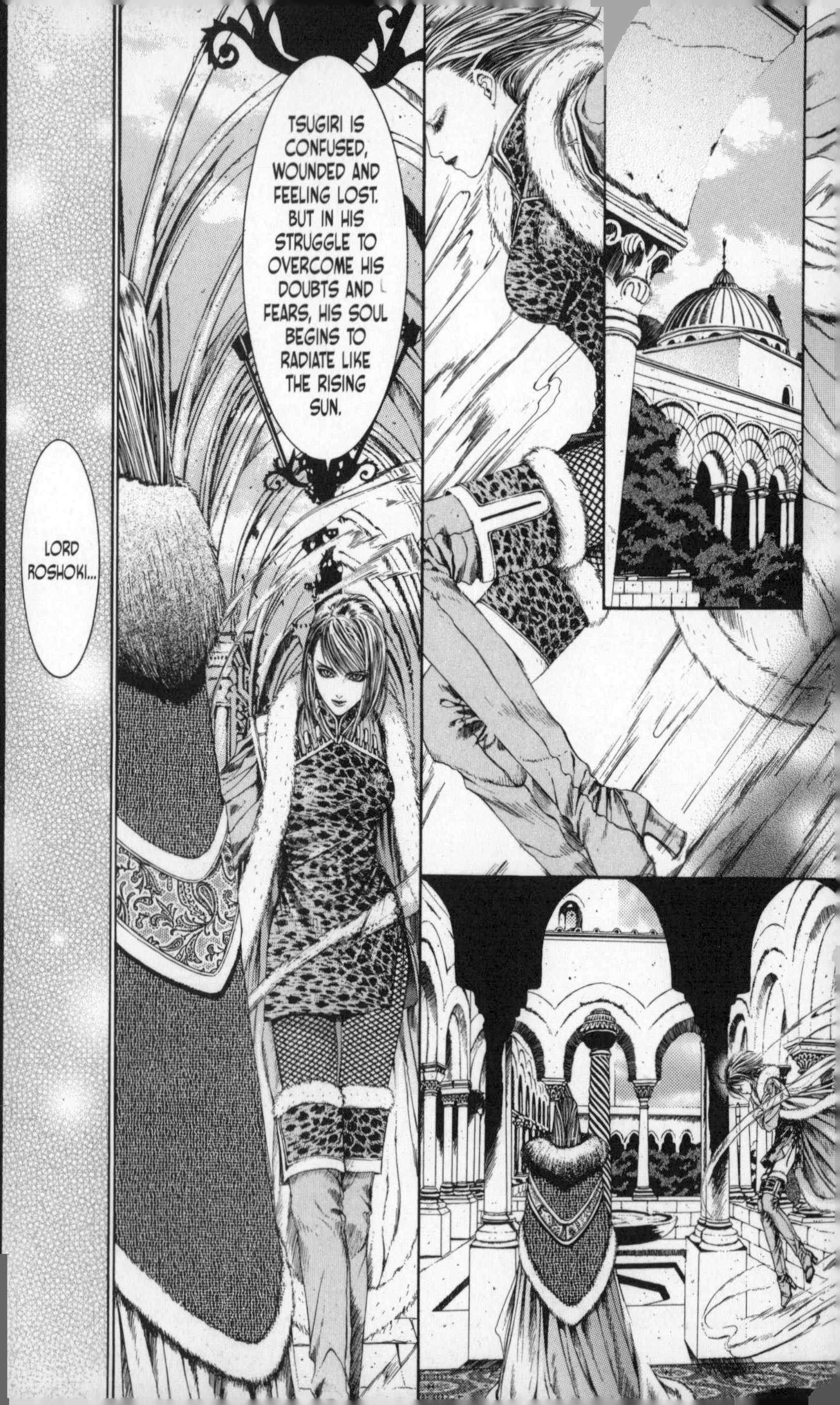
TSUGIRI IS CONFUSED, WOUNDED AND FEELING LOST. BUT IN HIS STRUGGLE TO OVERCOME HIS DOUBTS AND FEARS, HIS SOUL BEGINS TO RADIATE LIKE THE RISING SUN.
LORD ROSHOKI...

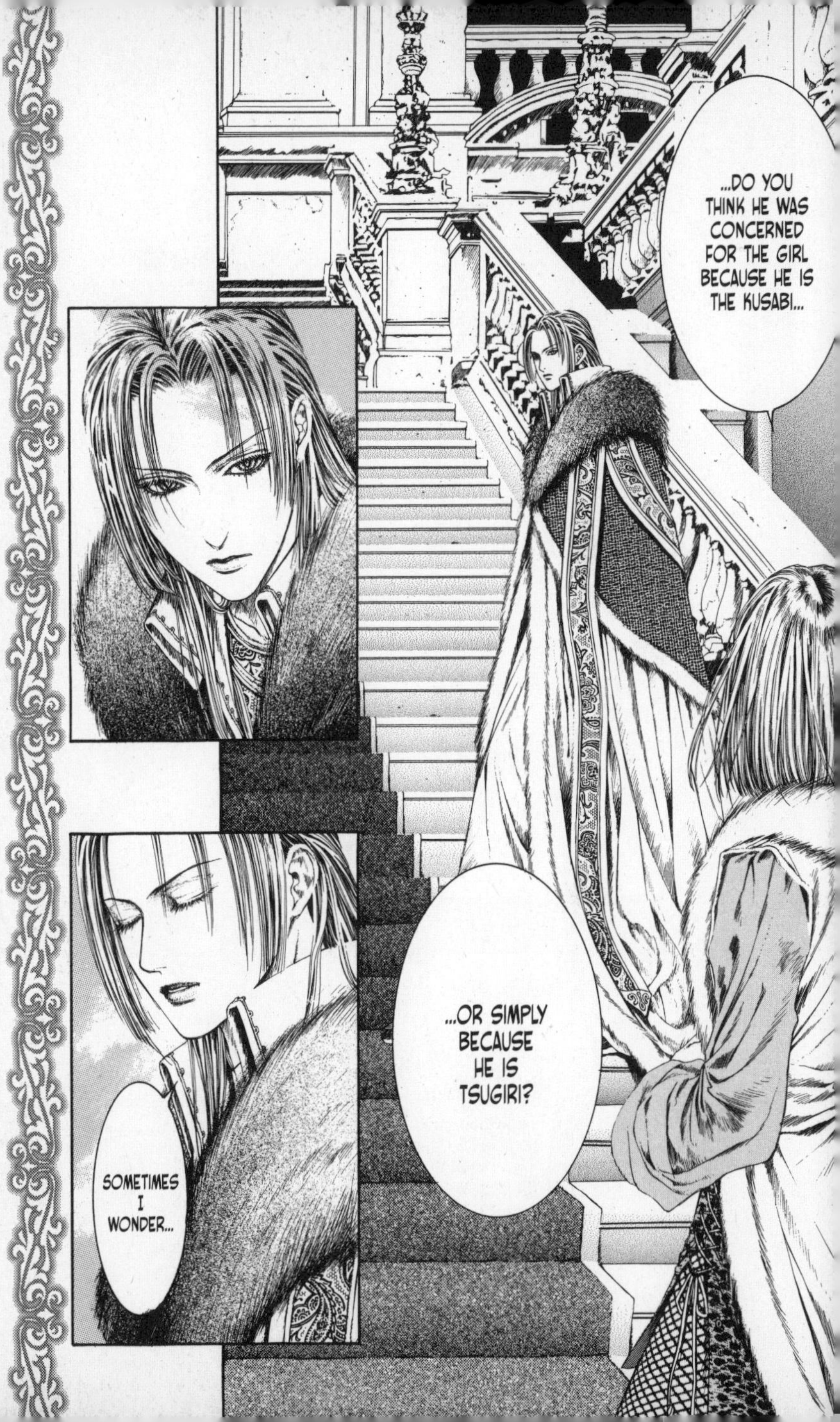
...DO YOU THINK HE WAS CONCERNED FOR THE GIRL BECAUSE HE IS THE KUSABI...
...OR SIMPLY BECAUSE HE IS TSUGIRI?
SOMETIMES I WONDER...

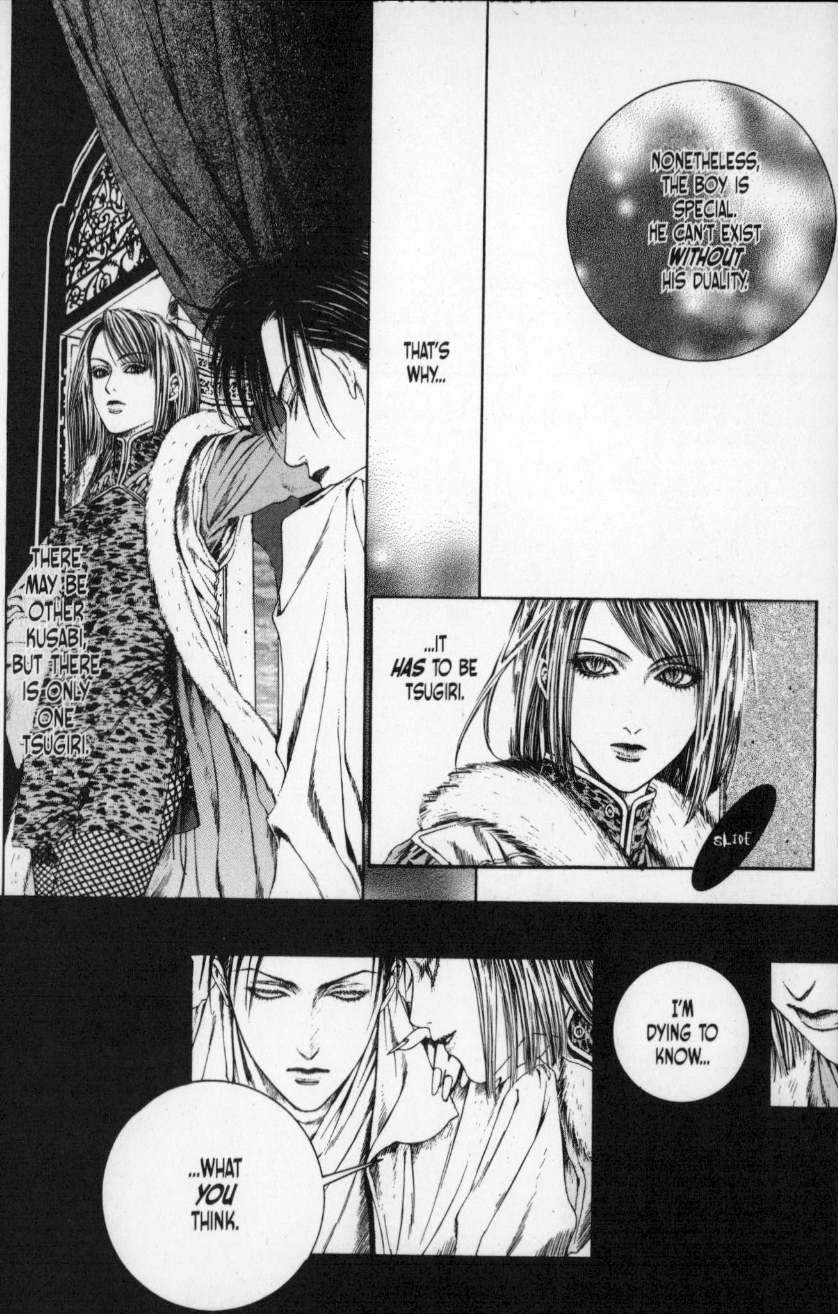
NONETHELESS, THE BOY IS SPECIAL. HE CAN'T EXIST WITHOUT HIS DUALITY.
THAT'S WHY...
...IT HAS TO BE TSUGIRI.
SLIDE
THERE MAY BE OTHER KUSABI, BUT THERE IS ONLY ONE TSUGIRI.
I'M DYING TO KNOW...
...WHAT YOU THINK.

Alichino 2 - End

◆Bonus Manga◆

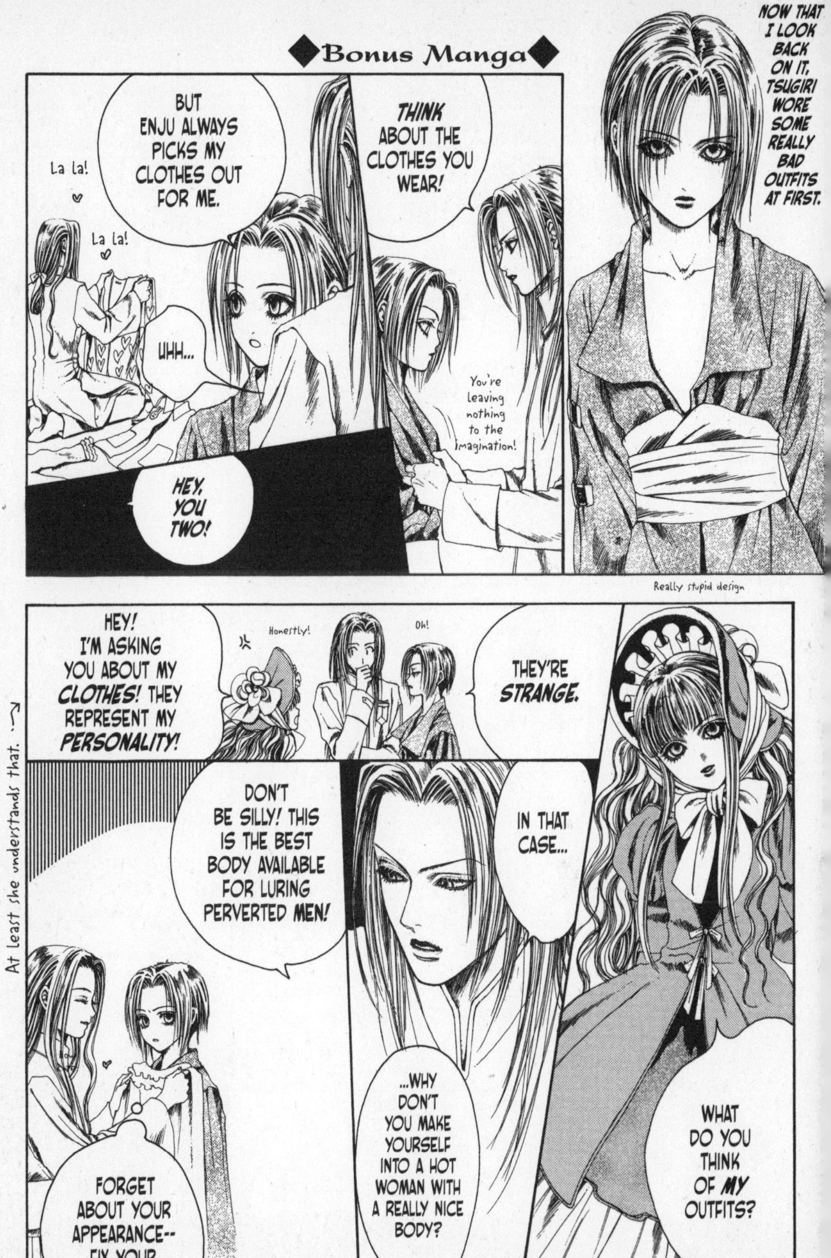
NOW THAT I LOOK BACK ON IT, TSUGIRI WORE SOME REALLY BAD OUTFITS AT FIRST.
Really stupid design
THINK ABOUT THE CLOTHES YOU WEAR!
You're leaving nothing to the imagination!
BUT ENJU ALWAYS PICKS MY CLOTHES OUT FOR ME.
La la!
La la!
UHH...
HEY, YOU TWO!
WHAT DO YOU THINK OF MY OUTFITS?
THEY'RE STRANGE.
Oh!
Honestly!
HEY! I'M ASKING YOU ABOUT MY CLOTHES! THEY REPRESENT MY PERSONALITY!
At least she understands that.
IN THAT CASE...
...WHY DON'T YOU MAKE YOURSELF INTO A HOT WOMAN WITH A REALLY NICE BODY?
DON'T BE SILLY! THIS IS THE BEST BODY AVAILABLE FOR LURING PERVERTED MEN!
FORGET ABOUT YOUR APPEARANCE--FIX YOUR PERSONALITY!

Thank you very much for buying this book. I can finally take a breath now that the second volume is done. When I think about it, this volume was harder than the first. I tried to make it smoother, but it didn't turn out that way. (grin)

This time, I made a lot of corrections. Other people seem to think I have ridiculous taste in art. That's so strange, because I wanted to make the art normal! There are some parts that are a little different from when it was originally published in the magazine, so it might be fun to compare the two.

Oh yeah, a lot of people ask me, "Is Enju a girl?" He's a boy! He is feminine looking, but maybe I just haven't done enough to make it obvious? (His age is hard to tell, too.) Different people have different opinions on the characters, so I'd love to hear what you think of them! I'll keep working hard, but it's difficult taking such loving care of them.

Someday I hope I can draw Tsugiri in 3-D, or have Myobi become a fabulous debutante! Well then, see you in the next volume!

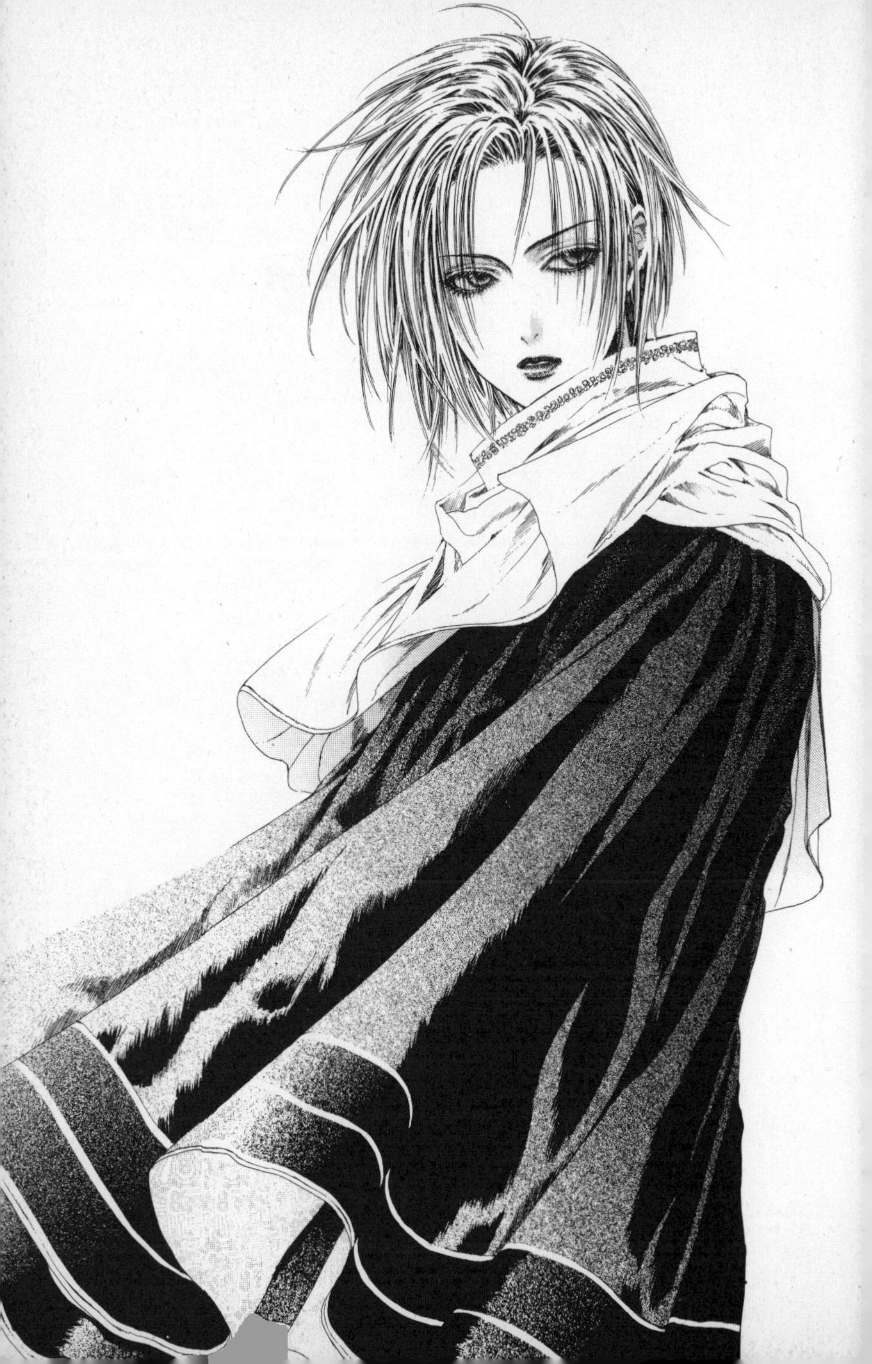

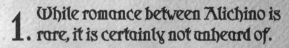

1. While romance between Alichino is rare, it is certainly not unheard of.

2. The master and servant contract popular among Alichino is usually a benevolent one, with both sides benefiting from the agreement...but not always.

3. Alichino possess great skill in battle. Skirmishes between them are often violent and bloody.

I have observed the relationship between Myobi and Ryoko and have determined that it is hard to categorize. There is an unmistakable subservience in the way that Myobi addresses Ryoko, but it is not consistent. In fact, it occasionally seems as if Myobi is the dominant of the two, with Ryoko enthusiastically obeying her orders. It feels very much like a human marriage at times, and indeed we have all seen glimpses of romantic longing between the two, or moments where they have torn down the façade of propriety and given in to their passion for each other. However, commenting farther on such matters would be inappropriate and insensitive.

I do not know Ryoko as I know Myobi, but I am aware that he is no stranger to romance. It is said that before accepting the contract with Myobi, Ryoko once loved Matsurika, the beautiful Alichino that now swears liegance to Roshoki. Little more than rumors, to be sure, but with Roshoki's recent interest in Tsugiri, we should not be so quick to brush them off. If we do, we do so at our own peril...

Alichino

TOKYOPOP

Kougyu Shusei   VOL 3

In Our Next Volume...

Right about now, you probably hunger for Volume 3 in much the same way as an Alichino hungers for the soul of a Kusabi. It's true that the next volume of Alichino won't be available until October 2005, but we thought we'd give you a little preview. Feast your eyes on the following pages. Once again, they're being reproduced here in the original Japanese, but don't worry. We'll have them translated for you by October.

Enjoy!

-Editor

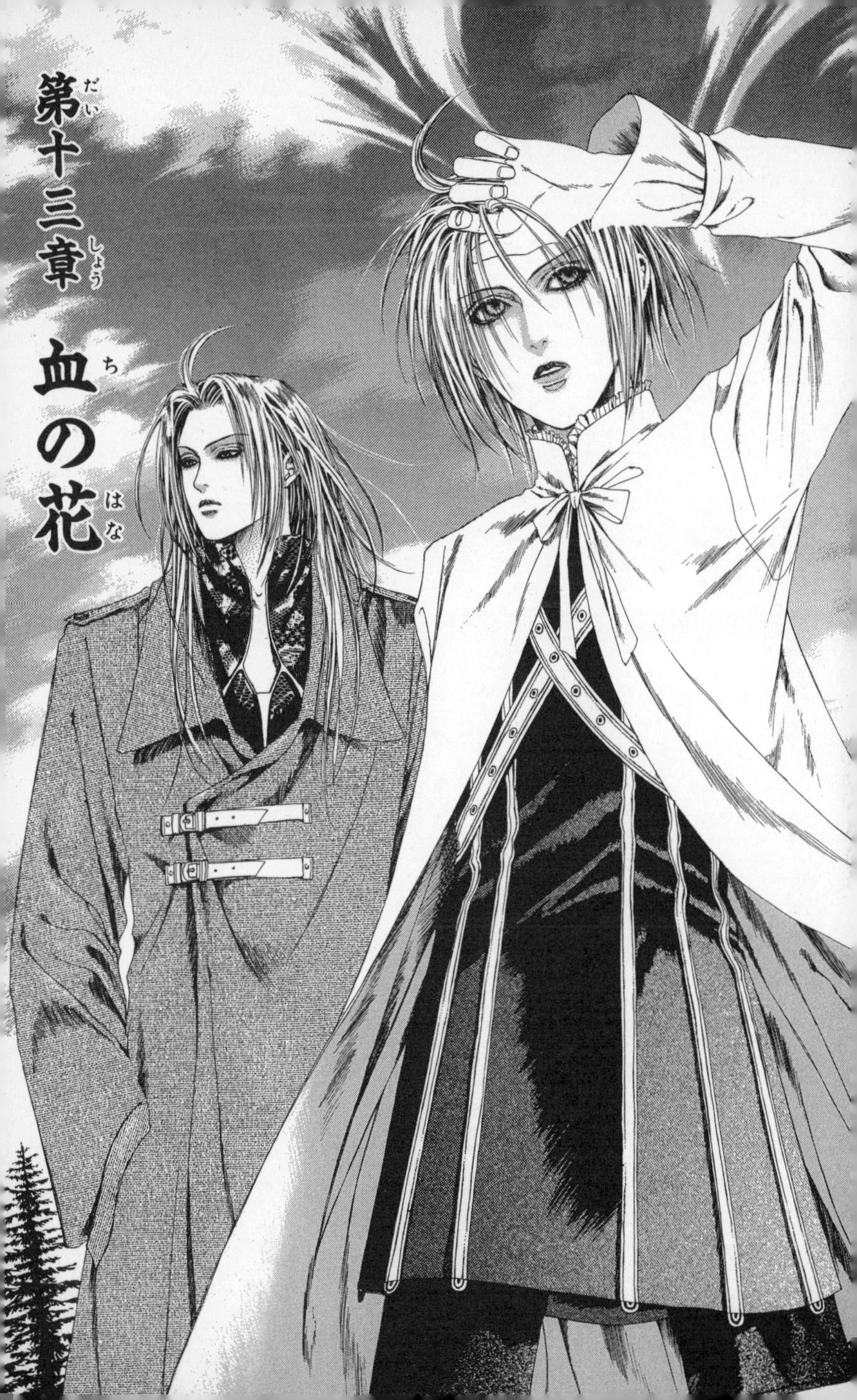
第十三章
血の花

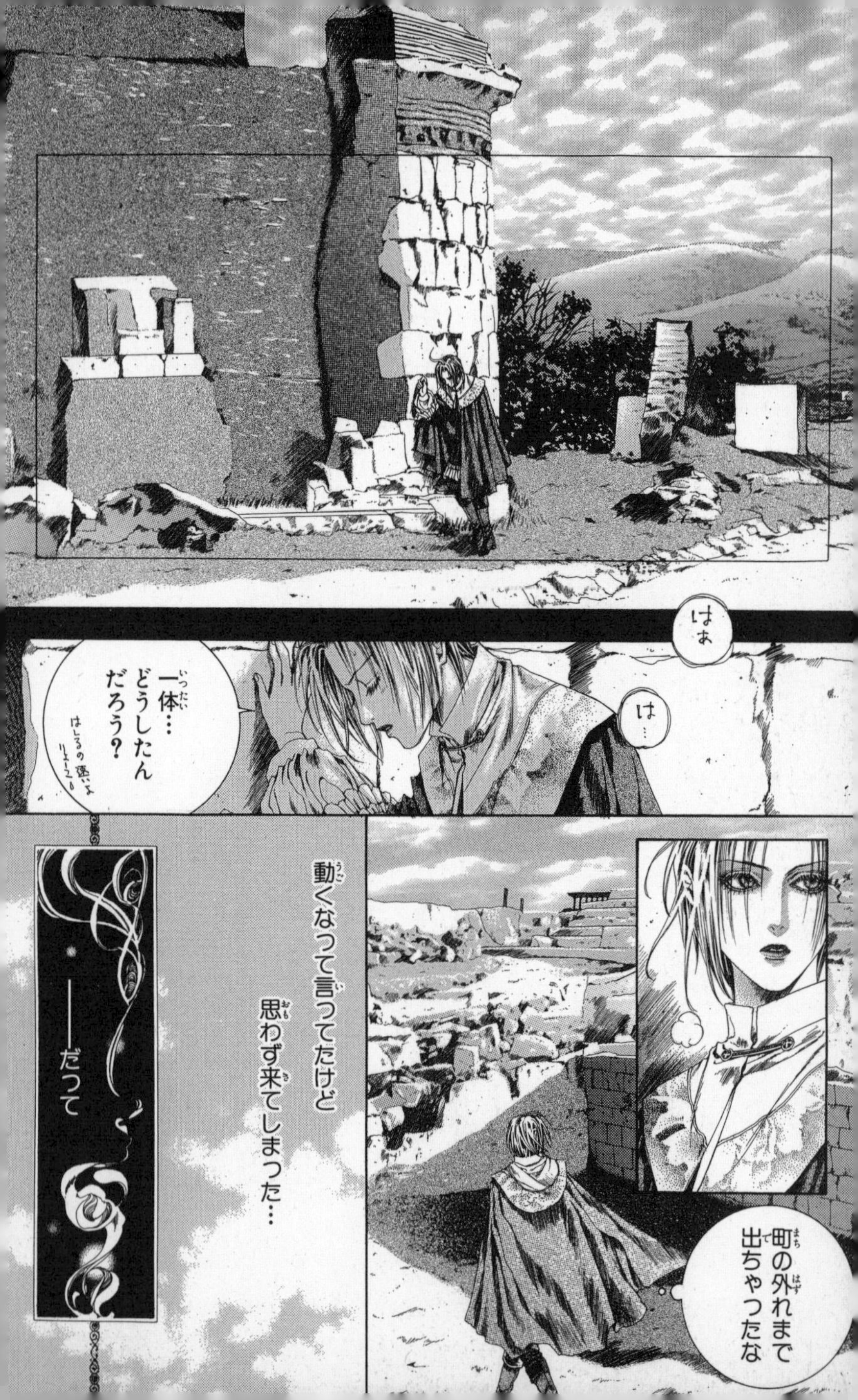
はぁ
は…
一体…どうしたんだろう？
はしるの遅いよリューマ。
町の外れまで出ちゃったな
動くなって言ってたけど
思わず来てしまった…
——だって

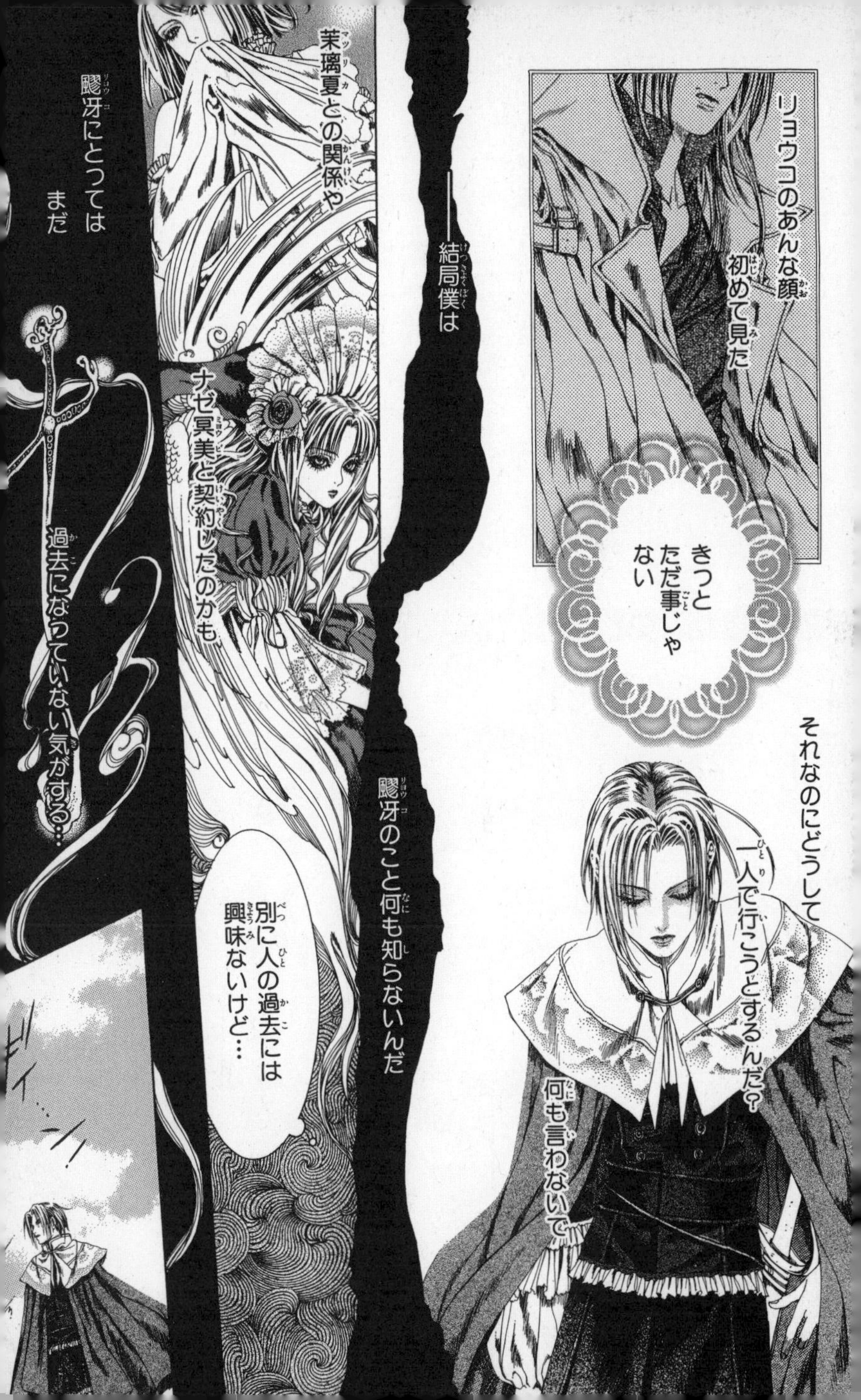
リョウコのあんな顔
初めて見た
きっと ただ事じゃ ない
それなのにどうして一人で行こうとするんだ？
何も言わないで
——結局僕は
茉璃夏との関係や
ナゼ冥美と契約したのかも
颶牙のこと何も知らないんだ
別に人の過去には興味ないけど…
颶牙にとっては まだ
過去になっていない気がする…
…ー!!

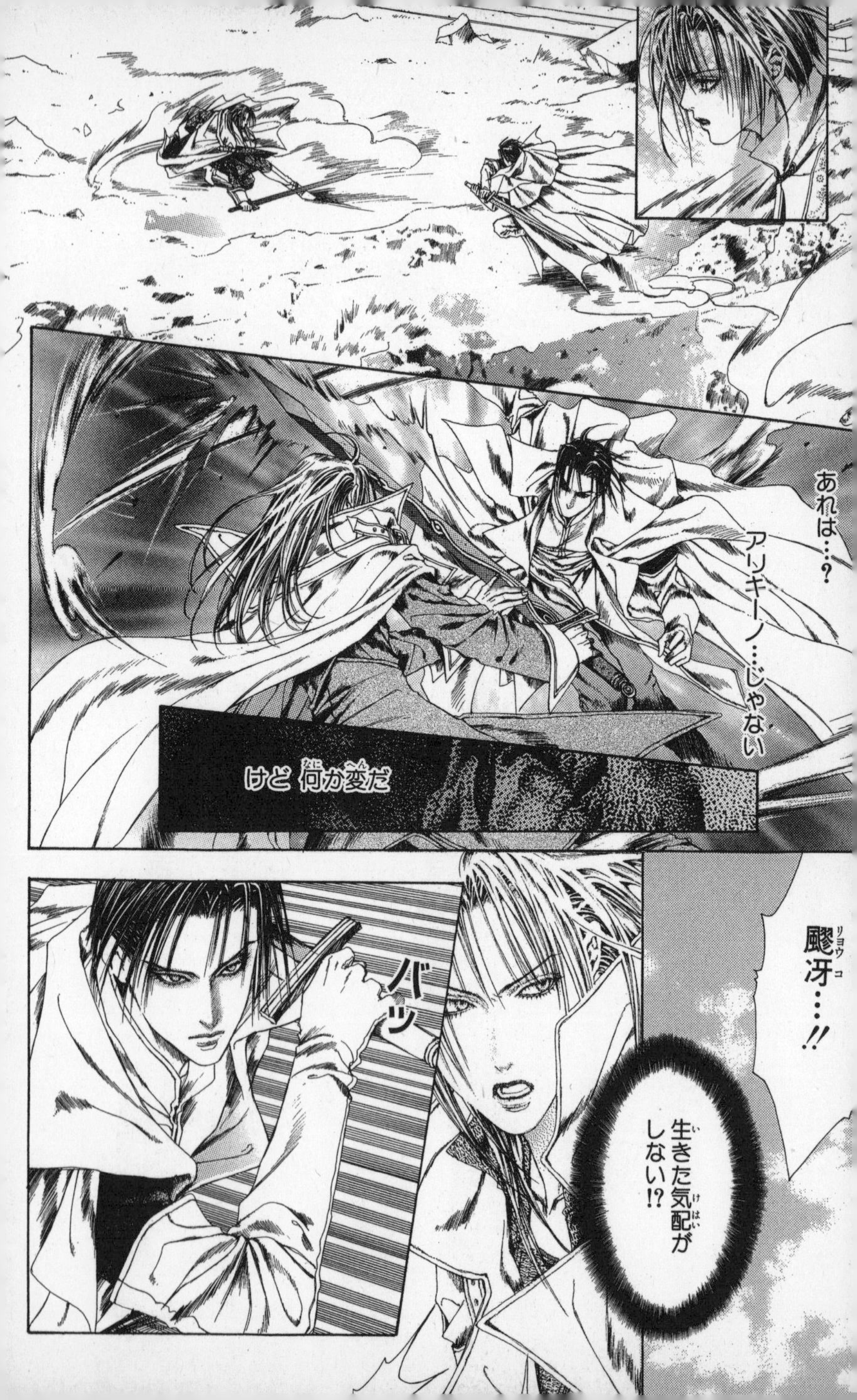
あれは…？
アリキーノ…じゃない
けど 何か変だ
飂冴…!!
生きた気配がしない!?
バッ

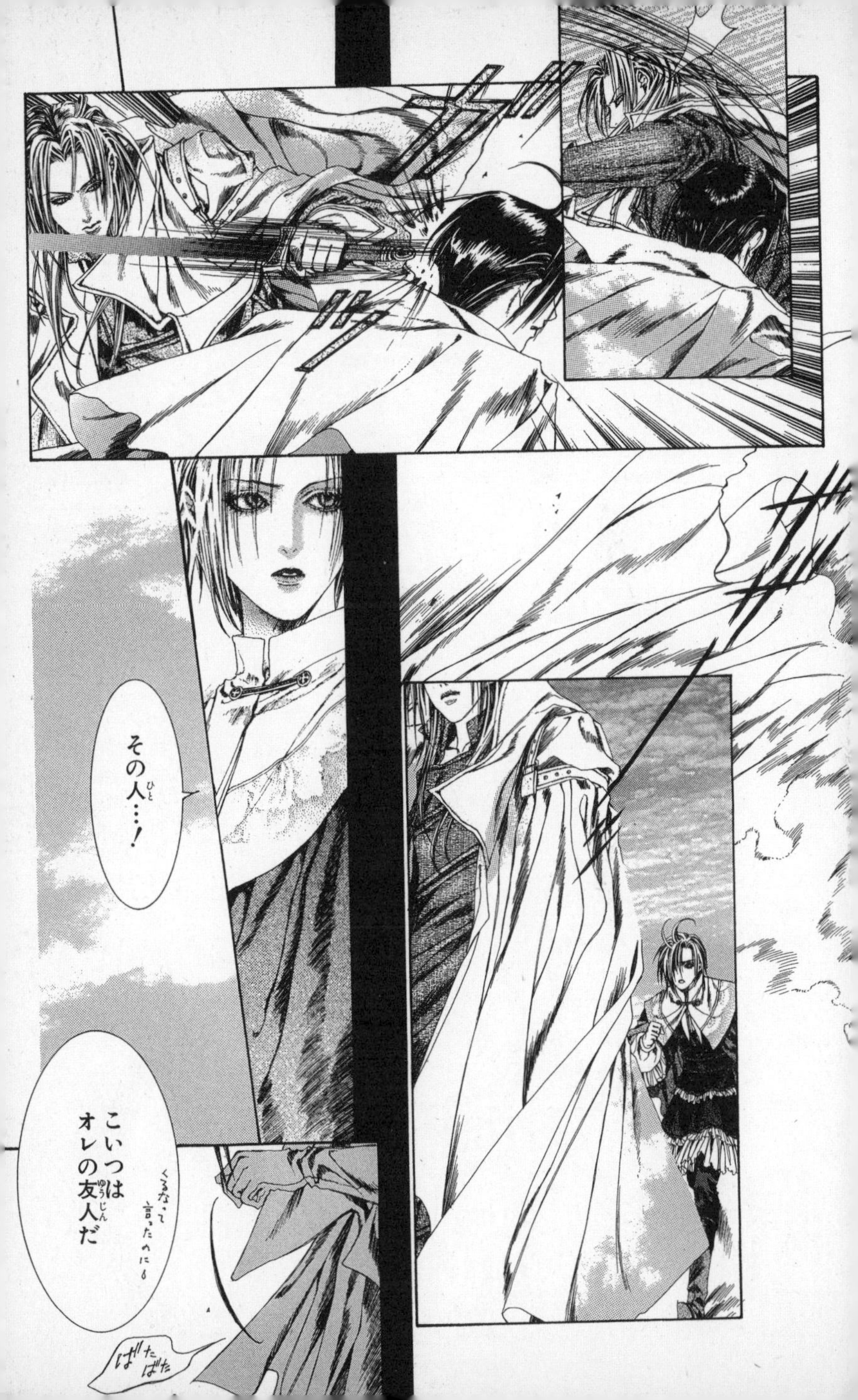
その人…！
こいつはオレの友人だ
くるなって言ったのに
ばたばた

TOKYOPOP SHOP

WWW.TOKYOPOP.COM/SHOP

HOT NEWS!
Check out the
TOKYOPOP SHOP!
The world's best
collection of manga in
English is now available
online in one place!

ARCANA

TOKYO MEW MEW A LA MODE

MBQ and other
hot titles are
available at
the store that
never closes!

MBQ

- LOOK FOR SPECIAL OFFERS
- PRE-ORDER UPCOMING RELEASES!
- COMPLETE YOUR COLLECTIONS

SPOTLIGHT
TOKYOPOP MANGA SUPPLEMENT

BECK: MONGOLIAN CHOP SQUAD

OT
OLDER TEEN
AGE 16+

ROCK IN MANGA!

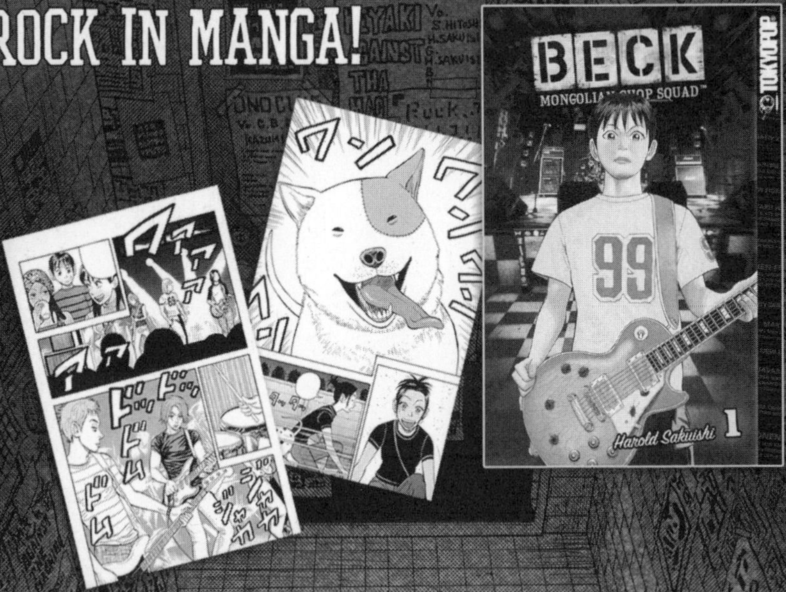

BECK
MONGOLIAN CHOP SQUAD™
TOKYOPOP
99
Harold Sakuishi
1

Yukio Tanaka is one boring guy with no hobbies, a weak taste in music and only a small vestige of a personality. But his life is forever changed when he meets Ryusuke Minami, an unpredictable rocker with a cool dog named Beck. Recently returned to Japan from America, Ryusuke inspires Yukio to get into music, and the two begin a journey through the world of rock 'n' roll dreams! With cameos of music's greatest stars—from John Lennon to David Bowie—and homages to supergroups such as Led Zeppelin and Nirvana, anyone who's anyone can make an appearance in *Beck*...even Beck himself! With action, music and gobs of comedy, *Beck* puts the rock in manga!

HAROLD SAKUISHI'S HIGHLY ADDICTIVE MANGA SERIES THAT SPAWNED A HIT ANIME HAS FINALLY REACHED THE STATES!

FOR MORE INFORMATION VISIT: WWW.TOKYOPOP.COM

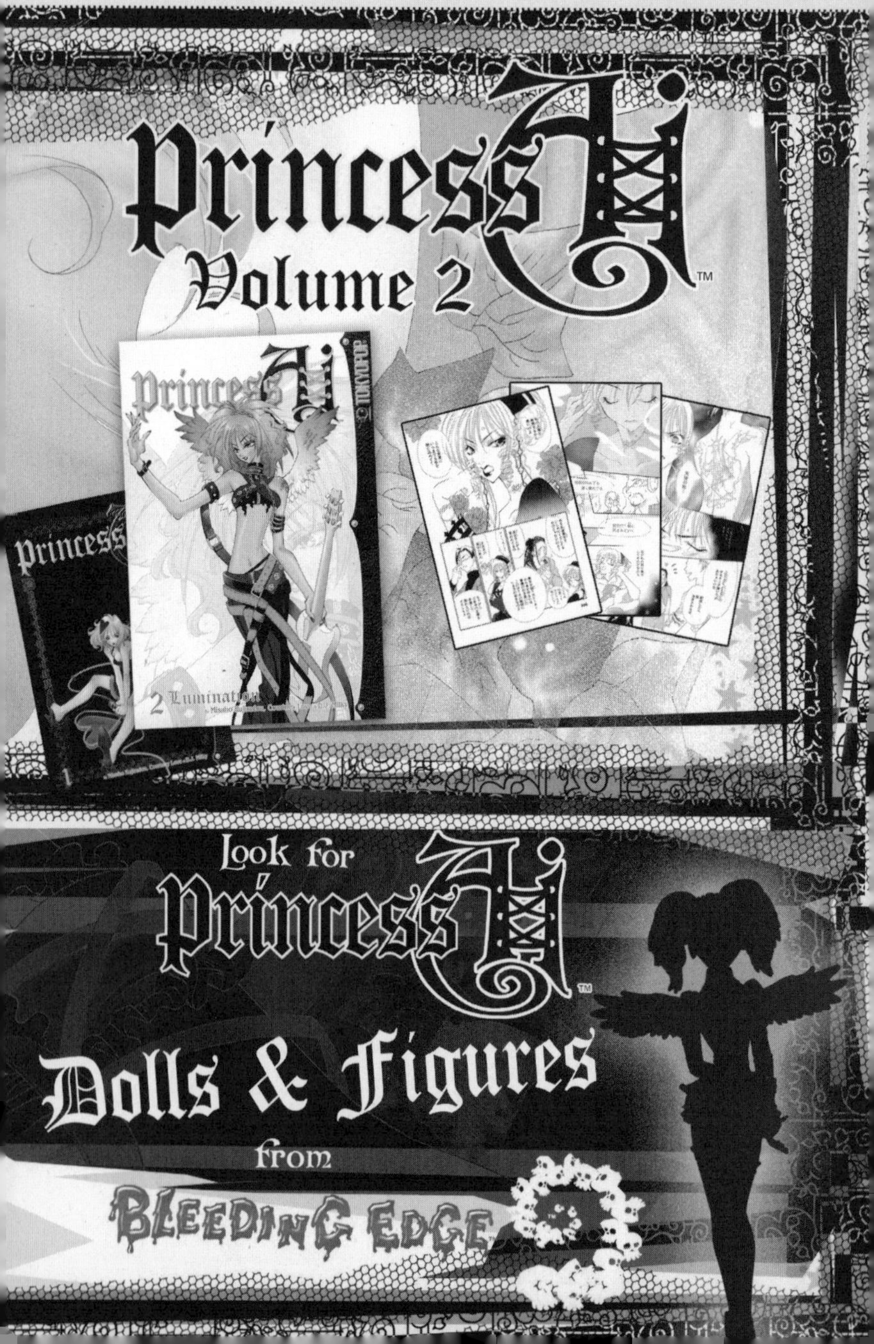

Princess Ai™
Volume 2
Look for
Princess Ai™
Dolls & Figures
from
BLEEDING EDGE

A Diva Torn from Chaos
A Savior Doomed to Love

Volume 2
Lumination

Ai continues to search for her place in our world on the streets of Tokyo. Using her talent to support herself, Ai signs a contract with a top record label and begins her rise to stardom. But fame is unpredictable—as her talent blooms, all eyes are on Ai. When scandal surfaces, will she burn out in the spotlight of celebrity?

Preview the manga at:
www.TOKYOPOP.com/princessai

T
TEEN
AGE 13+

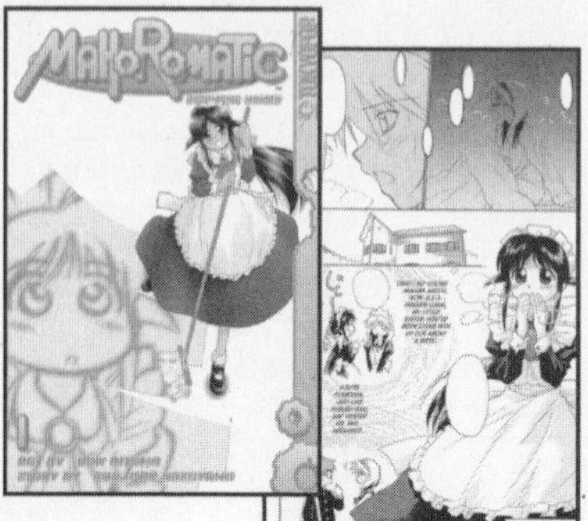
MAHOROMATIC

BY BUNJURO NAKAYAMA AND BOW DITAMA

MAHOROMATIC: AUTOMATIC MAIDEN

Mahoro is a sweet, cute, female battle android who decides to go from mopping up alien invaders to mopping up after Suguru Misato, a teenaged orphan boy... and hilarity most definitely ensues. This series has great art and a slick story that easily switches from truly funny to downright heartwarming...but always with a large shadow looming over it. You see, only Mahoro knows that her days are quite literally numbered, and the end of each chapter lets you know exactly how much—or how little—time she has left!

~Rob Tokar, Sr. Editor

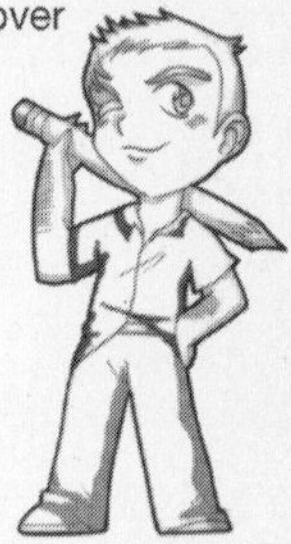

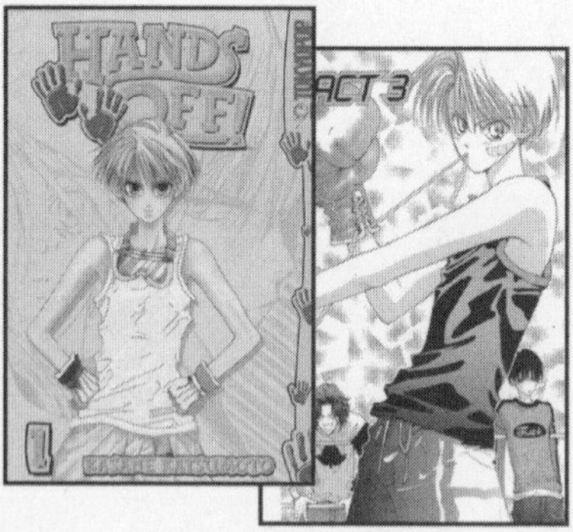
HANDS OFF!
ACT 3

BY KASANE KATSUMOTO

HANDS OFF!

Cute boys with ESP who share a special bond... If you think this is familiar (e.g. *Legal Drug*), well, you're wrong. *Hands Off!* totally stands alone as a unique and thoroughly enjoyable series. Kotarou and Tatsuki's (platonic!) relationship is complex, fascinating and heart-wrenching. Throw in Yuuto, the playboy who can read auras, and you've got a fantastic setup for drama and comedy, with incredible themes of friendship running throughout. Don't be put off by Kotarou's danger-magnet status, either. The episodic stuff gradually changes, and the full arc of the characters' development is well worth waiting for.

~Lillian Diaz-Przybyl, Jr. Editor

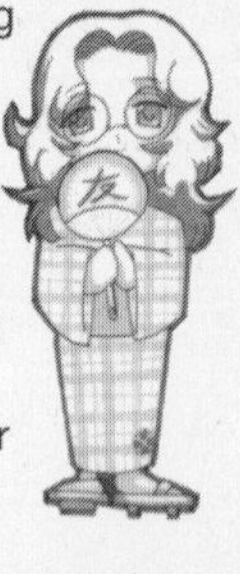

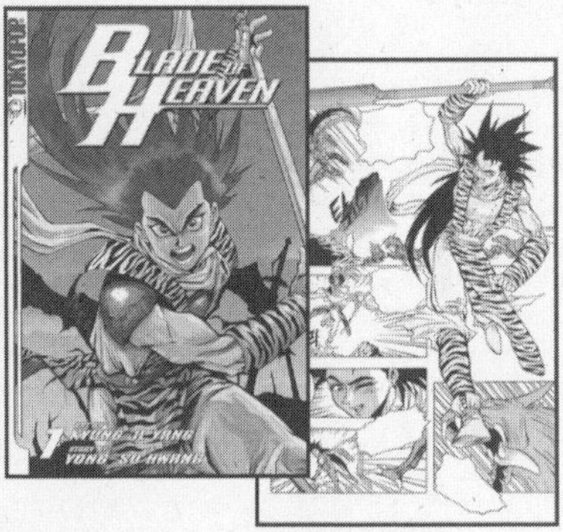

BY YONG-SU HWANG AND KYUNG-IL YANG

BLADE OF HEAVEN

Wildly popular in its homeland of Korea, *Blade of Heaven* enjoys the rare distinction of not only being a hit in its own country, but in Japan and several other countries, as well. On the surface, Yong-Su Hwang and Kyung-Il Yang's fantasy-adventure may look like yet another "Heaven vs. Demons" sword opera, but the story of the mischievous Soma, a pawn caught in a struggle of mythic proportions, is filled with so much humor, pathos, imagination—and yes, action, that it's easy to see why *Blade of Heaven* has been so popular worldwide.

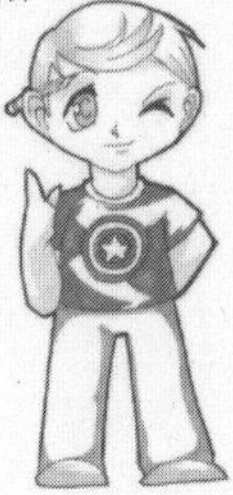

~Bryce P. Coleman, Editor

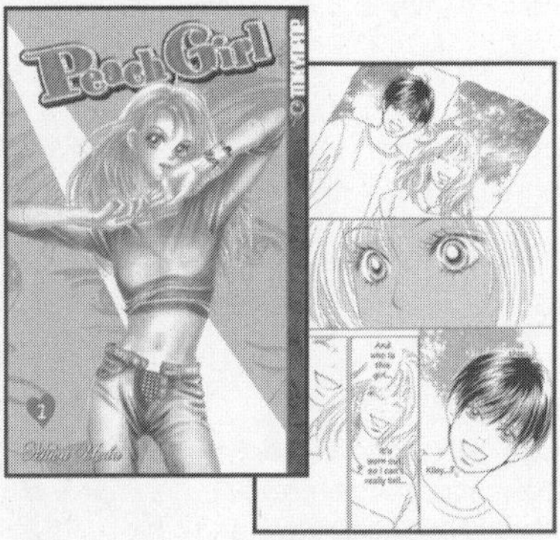
Peach Girl

BY MIWA UEDA

PEACH GIRL

Am I the only person who thinks that *Peach Girl* is just like *The O.C.*? Just imagine Ryan as Toji, Seth as Kiley, Marissa as Momo and Summer as Sae. (The similarities are almost spooky!) Plus, Seth is way into comics and manga—and I'm sure he'd love *Peach Girl*. It has everything that my favorite TV show has and then some—drama, intrigue, romance and lots of will-they-or-won't-they suspense. I love it! *Peach Girl* rules, seriously. If you haven't read it, do so. Now.

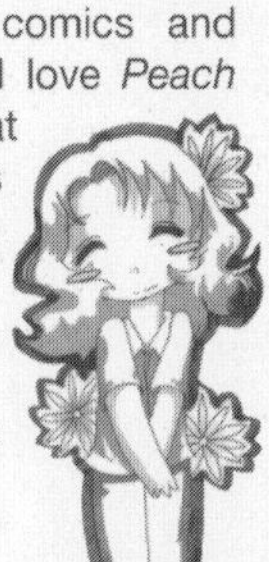

~Julie Taylor, Sr. Editor

ARCANA
BY SO-YOUNG LEE

Inez is a young orphan girl with the ability to communicate with living creatures of all kinds. She is the chosen one, and a great destiny awaits her! Inez must bring back the guardian dragon to protect her country's fragile peace from the onslaught of a destructive demon race.

From the creator of TOKYOPOP's *Model* comes an epic fantasy quest filled with wizards, dragons, deception and adventure beyond your wildest imagination.

T TEEN AGE 13+

© SO-YOUNG LEE, DAIWON C.I. Inc.

DEAD END
BY SHOHEI MANABE

When Shirou's memory is suddenly erased and his friends are brutally murdered, he is forced to piece together clues to solve a shocking and spectacular puzzle. As we follow Shirou's journey, paranoia assumes an air of calm rationality and the line between tormenter and prey is often blurred.

OT OLDER TEEN AGE 16+

© Shohei Manabe

TOKYO MEW MEW A LA MODE
BY MIA IKUMI AND REIKO TOSHIDA

The cats are back, and a new Mew emerges— the first Mew Mew with *two* sets of animal genes. Half cat, half rabbit, Berry joins the Mew Mew team just in time: a new gang is about to appear, and its leader loves wild game like rabbit—well done and served for dinner!

The highly anticipated sequel to *Tokyo Mew Mew* (*Mew Mew Power* as seen on TV)!

Y YOUTH AGE 10+

© Mia Ikumi and Kodansha

LAMENT of the LAMB™

SHE CAN PROTECT HER BROTHER FROM THE WORLD.
CAN SHE PROTECT THE WORLD FROM HER BROTHER?

www.TOKYOPOP.co

Dear Diary,
I'm starting to feel

STOP!

This is the back of the book.
You wouldn't want to spoil a great ending!

This book is printed "manga-style," in the authentic Japanese right-to-left format. Since none of the artwork has been flipped or altered, readers get to experience the story just as the creator intended. You've been asking for it, so TOKYOPOP® delivered: authentic, hot-off-the-press, and far more fun!

DIRECTIONS

If this is your first time reading manga-style, here's a quick guide to help you understand how it works.

It's easy... just start in the top right panel and follow the numbers. Have fun, and look for more 100% authentic manga from TOKYOPOP®!